Misery

STEPHEN KING

Level 6

Retold by Robin Waterfield
Series Editors: Andy Hopkins and Jocelyn Potter

Pearson Education Limited
Edinburgh Gate, Harlow,
Essex CM20 2JE, England
and Associated Companies throughout the world.

ISBN: 978-1-4058-7665-0

Typeset by Graphicraft Ltd, Hong Kong
Set in 11/14pt Bembo
Printed in China
SWTC/01

Published by Pearson Education Ltd in association with
Penguin Books Ltd, both companies being subsidiaries of Pearson Plc

For a complete … able in the P… … your local
Pearson Long… …ducation,

Contents

Introduction

He pushed the knife under the mattress. When Annie came back, he was going to ask her for a drink of water. She would bend over to give it to him, and then he would stab her in the throat. Nothing complicated.

Paul closed his eyes and went to sleep. When Annie's car came whispering into the farm at four o'clock in the morning, with its engine and its lights switched off, he did not move. It was only when he felt the sting of the syringe in his arm and woke to see her face close to his that he knew she was back.

Paul Sheldon is a world-famous writer. On his way to deliver the typewritten pages of his latest book, he has an accident on a snow-covered road. Paul is seriously injured and when he wakes up, he's in bed . . .

But it's not a hospital bed. And though the woman who saved him is one of his greatest admirers, she's also mad and very dangerous. On her lonely farm, she has Paul, his legs badly broken and in extreme pain, completely at her mercy. When she learns what he has just done to Misery Chastain, her favourite character from his books, Paul knows he's in trouble – *deep* trouble. Unable to escape or to contact the outside world, Paul must find a way to survive.

He learns about Annie Wilkes very quickly, and none of it is pleasant. The one thing you don't do with Annie is make her angry. She knows how to cause pain. The only question is, how much pain can a man bear?

Stephen King has been called the master of horror – and with good reason. Not all his stories are of this type, but many of them are very frightening. They also have another essential quality for success – they are horribly believable. *Misery* is typical of this combination

– everything that happens to Paul Sheldon and everything that Annie Wilkes does has a logic and reason to it. We can't quite believe it's happening, but we can explain and understand it. It may be unlikely, but it's all possible. It could happen to you, and that's the horror of it.

Like *Misery*'s fictional writer, Paul Sheldon, Stephen King does not plot his stories right through. He lets the story grow itself, and he often begins a story with no idea how it will end. Also like Sheldon, King suffered a serious accident (1991), although he was hit by a car whilst walking and was not actually driving. He was in hospital for three weeks and for some time after that he was unable to write for long periods at a time because he was in extreme pain. Curiously, car accidents had featured in many of his stories before this, including *Misery*. He also used his experiences of this accident in later writing.

King is known for his great eye for detail and his informal style of telling a story. This contrasts with the content of his horror stories. He likes to leave each chapter with a desperate situation at the end, which makes the reader want to keep turning the pages of his books. Many of them are set in the state of Maine, although the actual towns are often fictional.

Born in 1947 in Portland, Maine in the USA, King started his writing career when he was a student. He wrote a weekly column for the *Maine Campus*, the newspaper for the University of Maine. He studied to become an English teacher but was unable to find a teaching job immediately. Instead, he worked at a laundry and occasionally earned a little more money by selling short stories to magazines.

In 1971 King began teaching high school English classes and continued writing in the evenings and at weekends. When his first novel, *Carrie*, was published in 1974, he was able to leave teaching and write full-time. Other successful novels followed, and many have been made into films. *Carrie* was filmed in 1976, and other screen successes include *Salem's Lot*, *The Shining*, *The Shawshank Redemption* and *The Green Mile*.

The screen version of *Misery* was one of the most popular films of 1990. Kathy Bates won an Oscar for playing Annie Wilkes. James Caan played Paul Sheldon.

Stephen King has appeared in several of the films of his books, taking the parts of minor characters. He also directed the film *Maximum Overdrive* in 1985. This was adapted from his short story *Trucks*.

With the enormous success of books such as *The Shining*, *Salem's Lot* and *Misery*, Stephen King is one of the world's highest-earning writers. There are over 150 million copies of his novels in print, and he makes $2 million a month from his books and the films made of his books.

Since becoming successful, King and his wife Tabitha have given a lot of money to various charities and good causes around their home state of Maine. Much of this has gone to high school and college students from poor families so that they can continue their education.

In 2002, Stephen King announced that he would stop writing. This was partly because of the injuries from his accident, which had made sitting uncomfortable. However, he has continued to write, but he says, at a much slower speed. 'I'm 55 years old and I have grandchildren, two new dogs to house-train and I have a lot of things to do besides writing,' he said, 'and that in and of itself is a wonderful thing, but writing is still a big, important part of my life and of everyday.'

You can also read Stephen King's *The Breathing Method* and *The Body* in Penguin Readers.

Chapter 1   Kiss of Life

Memory was slow to return. At first there was only pain. The pain was total, everywhere, so that there was no room for memory.

Then he remembered that before the pain there was a cloud. He could let himself go into that cloud and there would be no pain. He needed only to stop breathing. It was so easy. Breathing only brought pain, anyway.

But the peace of the cloud was spoiled by the voice. The voice – which was a woman's voice – said, 'Breathe! You must breathe, Paul!' Something hit his chest hard, and then foul breath was forced into his mouth by unseen lips. The lips were dry and the breath smelled of the stale wind in the tunnel of an underground railway; it smelled of old dust and dirt. He began to breathe again so that the lips would not return with their foul breath.

Along with the pain, there were sounds. When the pain covered the shore of his mind, like a high tide, the sounds had no meaning: *'Bree! Ooo mus bree Pul!'* When the tide went out, the sounds became words. He already knew that something bad had happened to him; now he began to remember.

He was Paul Sheldon. He smoked too much. He had married twice, but both marriages had ended in divorce. He was a famous writer. He was also a good writer. But he was not famous as a good writer; he was famous as the creator of Misery Chastain, a beautiful woman from nineteenth-century England, whose adventures and love life now filled eight volumes and had sold many millions of copies.

He felt trapped by Misery Chastain, so he wrote *Misery's Child.* In the final pages of this book Misery died while giving birth to a daughter. Her death made Paul free, and he immediately started to write a serious novel, about the life of a young car-thief in New York.

He finished the novel late in January 1987. As usual he finished it in a hotel in the mountains of Colorado; he finished all his books in the same room, in the same hotel. Now he could drive to the airport and fly to New York for the publication of *Misery's Child*, and at the same time he could deliver the typescript of the new novel, which was called *Fast Cars*.

The weatherman on the radio said that the storm would pass to the south of Colorado. The weatherman was wrong. Paul was driving along a mountain road, surrounded by pine forest, when the storm struck. Within minutes a thick layer of snow covered the road. The car's wipers were unable to keep the windows clear and the tyres couldn't grip the surface of the road. Paul had to fight to keep the car on the slippery road ... then on a particularly steep corner he couldn't control it. He had time to notice that the sky and the ground changed places in an unbelievable way. Then the dark cloud descended over his mind.

He remembered all this before he opened his eyes. He was aware of the woman sitting next to his bed. When he opened his eyes he looked in her direction. At first he couldn't speak: his lips were too dry. Then he managed to ask, 'Where am I?'

'Near Sidewinder, Colorado,' she said. 'My name is Annie Wilkes.' She smiled. 'You know, you're my favourite author.'

Chapter 2   Tide of Pain

There was a question Paul wanted to ask. The question was, 'Why am I not in a hospital?' But by the time his mind was clear enough to form the question, he already knew better than to ask it.

For two weeks Paul drifted on the tide of pain. When the tide was out he was aware of the woman sitting beside his bed. More often than not she had one of his books – his Misery books – open on her lap. She told him she had read them all many times and could hardly wait for the publication of *Misery's Child*.

He soon learned that it was Annie Wilkes who controlled the tides. She was giving him regular doses of a pain-killing drug called Novril. When Paul was conscious more than he was unconscious or asleep, he knew that Novril was a powerful drug: he knew because he could no longer live without it. She was giving him two tablets every four hours and, by the time three or three-and-a-half hours had passed, his body was screaming for the relief which only the drug could bring.

The most important thing he learned, however, during these first few weeks when the tide of pain rolled in and out was that Annie Wilkes was insane. Some part of his mind knew this even before he opened his eyes.

Everybody in the world has a centre. Whatever mood a person is in, whatever clothes he or she is wearing, we recognize that person because he or she has a solid basis. Even if we haven't seen someone for many years, we can still recognize him: something inside him is permanent and the same as it always was and always will be. All a person's other qualities turn round this centre.

Annie Wilkes occasionally lost her centre. For periods of time which could last only a few seconds or longer, there was nothing solid in her. Everything about her was in motion, with no basis on which to rest. It was as if a hole opened up inside her and swallowed every human quality she possessed. She seemed to have no memory of these times. In contrast, however, her body was very solid and strong, especially for a middle-aged woman.

At first Paul was only aware that something was wrong with her, without knowing exactly what. His first direct experience of the hole came during a seemingly ordinary conversation.

Annie was, as usual, going on about how proud she was to have Paul Sheldon – *the* Paul Sheldon – in her own home. 'I knew your face,' she said, 'but it was only when I looked in your wallet that I was sure it was you.'

'Where is my wallet, by the way?' asked Paul.

'I kept it safe for you,' she answered. Her smile suddenly turned into a narrow suspiciousness which Paul didn't like: it was like discovering something rotten in a field of summer flowers. 'Why do you ask?' she went on. 'Do you think I'd *steal* something from it? Is that what you think, Mister Man?'

As she was speaking, the hole became wider and wider, blacker and blacker. In the space of a few seconds she was spitting words out viciously instead of politely. It was sudden, shocking, violent.

'No, no,' said Paul, disguising his shock. 'It's just a habit of mine to know the whereabouts of my wallet.'

Just as suddenly as it had opened, the hole in Annie closed up again and the smile returned to her face. But from then on Paul was careful about what he said or did. So he didn't ask about hospital, and he didn't ask to ring his daughter and his agent on the phone. In any case he wasn't worried. His car would be found soon. Even if his car was covered with snow for weeks or months, he was a world-famous writer and people would be looking for him.

But there were still plenty of questions which Paul could ask. So he gradually found out that he was in the guest-room on Annie's small farm. Annie kept two cows, some chickens – and a pig called Misery! Her nearest neighbours, the Roydmans, were 'some miles away', which meant that the town of Sidewinder was even further away. The Roydmans never visited, because – according to Annie – they didn't like her. As she said this Paul caught another quick flash of that darkness, that gap.

Day after day Paul listened for visitors, but no one came. Day after day he listened for the phone, but it never rang. He began to doubt that there was one in the house. He was completely helpless; he could not move his legs at all.

All information about her neighbours and the town had to be

squeezed out of Annie without making her suspicious. It was easier to get her to talk about the day of the storm.

'I was in town,' she smiled, 'talking to Tony at the shop. In fact I was asking him about the publication date of *Misery's Child*. He told me a big storm was going to strike, so I decided to make my way home, although my car can manage any amount of snow. I saw your car upside down in the stream bed. I dragged you out of the wreck and I could see straight away that your legs were a mess.'

She had pulled back the blankets the day before to show him his legs. They were broken and twisted, covered in strange lumps and bruises. His left knee was swollen up to twice its normal size. She told him that both legs were broken in about seven or eight places and that they would take months to heal. She had tied splints firmly and cleanly on to both legs. She seemed to know what she was doing and to have an endless supply of medicine.

Paul swam in and out of consciousness, riding on waves of drugged half-pain, as Annie continued with her story.

'It was a struggle getting you to the car, I can tell you. I'm strong, but the snow was waist deep. You were unconscious, which was a good thing. I got you home and put you on the bed. Then you screamed, and I knew you were going to live. Dying men don't scream. But twice over the next few days you nearly died – once when I was putting your splints on and once you just nearly slipped away. I had to take emergency steps.'

She blushed at the memory, and Paul too remembered. He remembered that her breath smelled foul, as if something had died inside her.

'Now you must rest, Paul,' she said, getting up off her bedside chair to leave the room. 'You must regain your strength.'

'The pain,' said Paul. 'My legs hurt.'

'Of course they do. Don't be a baby. You can have some medicine in an hour.'

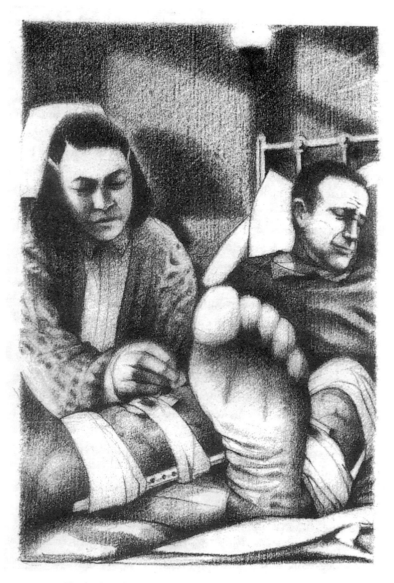

She had tied splints firmly and cleanly on to both legs.

'Now, please. I need it now.' He felt ashamed to beg, but his need for the drug made him do it.

'No,' she said firmly. 'In an hour.' Then, as she was leaving the room, she turned back towards him and said: 'You owe me your life, Paul. I hope you remember that. I hope you'll keep it in mind.'

Then she left.

Chapter 3 'Call Me Annie'

The hour passed slowly. He could hear her watching television. She reappeared as soon as it was eight o'clock, with two tablets and a glass of water. Paul eagerly lifted himself up on to his elbows when she sat down on his bed.

'At last I got your new book, two days ago,' she told him. '*Misery's Child*. I love it. It's as good as all the others. Better, in fact. It's the best.'

'Thank you,' Paul said. He could feel the sweat on his forehead. 'Please . . . my legs . . . very painful . . .'

'I *knew* she would marry Ian,' she said, smiling dreamily, 'and I believe Ian and Geoffrey will become friends again. Do they? No, no, don't tell me. I want to find out for myself.'

'Please, Miss Wilkes. The pain . . .'

'Call me Annie. All my friends do.'

She gave him the glass, but kept the tablets in her hand. Then she brought them towards his mouth, which he immediately opened . . . and then she took her hand away again.

'I hope you don't mind,' she said, 'but I looked in your bag.'

'No, of course I don't mind. The medicine −'

The sweat on his forehead felt first cold and then hot. Was he going to scream? He thought perhaps he was.

'I see there's a typescript in the bag,' she went on. She idly rolled the tablets from one hand to the other. Paul followed them with his eyes. 'It's called *Fast Cars*. It's not a Misery novel.' She looked at him with faint disapproval – but it was mixed with love. It was the kind of look a mother gives a child. 'Would you let me read it?'

'Yes, of course.' He tried to smile through the pain.

'I wouldn't do anything like that without your permission, Paul, you know,' she said. 'I respect you too much for that. In fact, Paul, I love you.' She blushed again, suddenly. One of the tablets dropped on to the blankets. Paul grabbed at it, but she was quicker. Then she went vacant and dreamy again. 'Your mind, I mean. It's your mind I love, Paul.'

'No, please read it,' Paul said in desperation. 'But . . .'

'You see,' Annie said, 'you're good. I knew you must be good. No one bad could create Misery Chastain and breathe life into her.'

Now she suddenly put her fingers in his mouth and he greedily sucked the tablets out of her hand, without waiting for the water.

'Just like a baby,' she said, laughing. 'Oh, Paul. We're going to be so happy here.'

And Paul thought: I am in so much trouble here.

Chapter 4   Bowl of Soup

The next morning she brought him a bowl of soup, which was his usual food these days. She told him she had read forty pages of his typescript. She told him she didn't think it was as good as his others.

'It's hard to follow,' she complained. 'It keeps jumping from one time to another.'

'Yes,' said Paul. 'That's because the boy is confused. So the changes in time reflect the confusion in his mind.' He thought she might be interested in a writer's ways.

'He's confused, all right,' replied Annie. She was feeding him soup automatically and wiping the corner of his mouth with the tip of a cloth, like a true professional; he realized that she must once have been a nurse. 'And he swears all the time. Nearly every word is a swear-word.'

'That's true to life, Annie, don't you think?' Paul asked. 'People do talk that way in real life.'

'No, they don't,' she said, giving him a hard look. 'What do you think I do when I go shopping in town? Do you think I say, "Now, give me some of that swear-word bread, and that swear-word butter"? And does the shopkeeper say, "All right, Annie. Here you swear-word are"?'

Her face was as dark as a thunderstorm now, and she was shouting. It wasn't at all amusing that she couldn't bring herself to say the real words; this made the situation all the more threatening. Paul lay back, frightened. The soup bowl was at an angle in her hands and soup was starting to spill out.

'And then do I go to the bank and say, "Here's one big swear-word cheque and you'd better give me fifty swear-word dollars"? Do you think that when I was in court in Denver –'

A stream of soup fell on to the blanket. She looked at it, then at him, and her face twisted. 'Now look what you've made me do!'

'I'm sorry.'

'I'm sure you are!' she screamed, and she threw the bowl into the corner. It broke into tiny pieces and soup splashed up the wall. Paul gasped in shock.

She turned off then. She just sat there for maybe thirty seconds. During that time Paul's heart seemed to stop. Gradually she came back.

'I have such a temper,' she confessed like a little girl.

'I'm sorry,' he said out of a dry throat.

'You should be. I think I'll finish *Misery's Child* and then return to the other book afterwards.'

'Don't do that if it makes you angry,' he said. 'I don't like it when you get angry. I . . . I do need you, you know.'

She did not return his smile. 'Yes, you do. You do, don't you, Paul?'

She came back into the room two hours later. 'I suppose you want your stupid medicine now,' she said.

'Yes,' said Paul, and then remembered. 'Yes, *please*.'

'Well, you're going to have to wait for me to clean up this mess,' she said. 'The mess *you* made.' She took a bucket of water and a cloth over to the corner and started to clean up the soup. 'You dirty bird,' she said. 'It's all dried now. This is going to take some time, I'm afraid, Paul.'

Paul didn't dare to say anything, although she was already late with his medicine and the pain was terrible. He watched in horror and fascination while she cleaned the wall. She did it slowly, deliberately. Paul watched the stain disappear. He couldn't see her face, but he was afraid that she had gone blank and would stay there for ever, wiping the wall with the cloth. At last, after half an hour of growing pain, she finished. She got up. *Now*, thought Paul. *Now give me the medicine.*

But to his amazement she left the room. He heard her pouring the water away and then refilling the bucket. She came back with the bucket and cloth.

'Now I must wash all that soap off the wall,' she said. 'I must do everything right. My mother taught me that.'

'No, please . . . the pain. I'm dying.'

'Don't be silly. You're not dying. It just hurts. In any case it's your fault that I have to clean up this mess.'

'I'll scream,' he said, starting to cry. Crying hurt his legs and hurt his heart.

'Go ahead, then,' she replied. 'Scream. No one will hear.'

He didn't scream. He watched her endlessly lift the cloth, wipe the wall and squeeze the cloth into the bucket. At last she got up again and came over to his bed.

'Here you are,' she said tenderly, holding out his two tablets. He

10

took them quickly into his mouth, and when he looked up he saw her lifting the yellow plastic bucket towards him.

'Use this to swallow them,' she said. Her voice was still tender.

He stared at her.

'I know you can swallow them without water,' she said, 'but if you do that I will make you bring them straight back out. Please believe me when I say that I can make you do that.'

He looked inside the bucket and saw the cloth in the grey water and soap floating on the surface. He drank quickly. His stomach started to move as if he was going to be sick.

'Don't be sick, Paul,' she said. 'There'll be no more tablets for four hours.' She looked at him for a moment with her flat, empty face, and then smiled. 'You won't make me angry again, will you?'

'No,' he whispered.

'I love you,' she said, and kissed him on the cheek.

Paul drifted into sleep. His last conscious thoughts were: *Why was she in court in Denver? And why would she want to take me prisoner?*

Chapter 5   Jug of Water

Two days later she came into his room early in the morning. Her face was grey. Paul was alarmed.

'Miss Wilkes? Annie? Are you all right?'

'No.'

She's had a heart attack, thought Paul, and the alarm was replaced by joy. *I hope it was a big one.*

She came and stood over his bed, looking down at him out of her paper-white face. Her neck was tense and she opened her hands and then closed them into tight fists, again and again.

'You ... you ... you *dirty bird*!' she stammered.

'What? I don't understand.' But suddenly he did understand. He remembered that yesterday she was three-quarters of the way

11

through *Misery's Child*. Now she knew it all. She knew that Ian and Misery could not have children; she knew that Misery gave birth to Geoffrey's child and died in the process.

'*She can't be dead!*' Annie Wilkes screamed at him. Her hands opened and closed faster and faster. '*Misery Chastain cannot be dead!*'

'Annie, please . . .'

She picked up a heavy jug of water from the table next to his bed. Cold water spilled on to him. She brought it down towards his head, but at the last second turned and threw it at the door instead of breaking his head open.

She looked at him and brushed her hair off her face. Two red marks had appeared on her cheeks. 'You dirty bird,' she said. 'Oh, you dirty bird, how could you do that? You killed her.'

'No, Annie, I didn't. It's just a book.'

She punched her fists down into the pillows next to his head. The whole bed shook and Paul cried out in pain. He knew that he was close to death.

'*I didn't kill her!*' he shouted.

She stopped and looked at him with that narrow black expression – that gap.

'Oh no, of course you didn't. Well, just tell me this, then, Mister Clever: if you didn't kill her, who did? Just tell me that. You tell lies. I thought you were good, but you're just dirty and bad like all the others.'

She went blank then. She stood up straight, with her hands hanging down by her sides, and looked at nothing. Paul realized that he could kill her. If there had been a piece of broken glass from the jug in his hand, he could have pushed it into her throat.

She came back a little at a time and the anger, at least, was gone. She looked down at him sadly. 'I think I have to go away for a while,' she said. 'I shouldn't be near you. If I stay here I'll do something stupid.'

'Where will you go? What about my medicine?' Paul called after her as she walked out of the room and locked the door. But the only reply was the sound of her car as she drove away.

He was alone in the house. Soon the pain came.

Chapter 6   A Job to Do

He was unconscious when she returned, fifty-one hours later. She made him sit up and she gave him some drops of water to heal his cracked lips and dry mouth. He woke up and tried to swallow a lot of water from the glass she was holding, but she only let him have a little at a time.

'Annie, the medicine, please . . . now,' he gasped.

'Soon, dear, soon,' she said gently. 'I'll give you your medicine, but first you have a job to do. I'll be back in a moment.'

'Annie, *no*!' he screamed as she got up and left the room.

When she came back he thought he was still dreaming. It seemed too strange to be real. She was pushing a barbecue stove into the room.

'Annie, please. I'm in terrible pain.' Tears were streaming down his face.

'I know, dear. Soon.'

She left and came back again with the typescript of *Fast Cars* and a box of matches.

'No,' he said, crying and shaking. 'No.' And the thought burned into his mind like acid: everyone had always said that he was crazy not to make copies of his typescripts.

'Yes,' she said, her face clear and calm. She held out the matches to him. 'It's foul, and it's no good. But you're good, Paul. I'm just helping you to be good.'

'No. I won't do it.' He shut his eyes.

When he opened them again she was holding a packet of Novril in front of them.

'I think I'll give you four,' she said, as if she was not talking to him but to herself. 'Yes, four. Then you'll feel peaceful and the pain will go. I bet you're hungry, too. I bet you'd like some toast.'

'You're bad,' said Paul.

'Yes, that's what children always say to their mothers. But mother knows best. I'm waiting, Paul. You're being a very stubborn little boy.'

'No, I won't do it.'

'I'm not sure that you'll ever wake up if you lose consciousness again,' she remarked. 'I think you're close to unconsciousness now.'

One hundred and ninety thousand words. Two years' work. But more importantly, it was what he saw as the truth. 'No.'

The bed moved as she got up. 'I can't stay here all day. I hurried back to see you, and now you behave like a spoiled little boy. Oh well,' she sighed. 'I'll come back later.'

'*You* burn it,' he shouted.

'No, it must be you.'

When she came back an hour later he took the matches. He remembered the joy of writing something good, something real. 'Annie, please don't make me do this,' he said.

'It's your choice,' she answered.

So he burned his book – a few pages, enough to please her, to show her that he was good. Then she pushed the barbecue out again, to finish the job herself. When she came back she gave him four tablets of Novril and he thought: *I'm going to kill her.*

Chapter 7   No Letter 'N'

When he woke up from his drugged sleep he found himself in a wheelchair. He realized that she was very strong: she had lifted him up and put him in the wheelchair so gently that he had not woken up. It hurt to sit in the wheelchair, but it was nice to be able to see

So he burned his book – a few pages, enough to please her, to show her that he was good.

out of the window; he could only see a little when he was sitting up in bed. The wheelchair was in front of a table by the window of his room. He looked out on to a small snow-covered farm with a barn for the animals and equipment. The snow was still deep and there was no sign that it was going to melt yet. Beyond the farm was a narrow road and then the tree-covered mountains.

He heard the sound of a key in the lock. She came and fed him some soup.

'I think you're going to get better,' she said. 'Yes, if we don't have any more of those arguments, I think you'll get healthy and strong.'

But Paul knew she was lying. One day his car would be found. One day someone – a policeman perhaps – would come and ask her questions. One day something would happen which would make Annie Wilkes frightened and angry. She was going to understand that you can't kidnap people and escape. She was going to have to go to court again, and this time she might not leave the court a free woman. She was going to realize all this and be afraid – and so she was going to have to kill Paul. How long was it before the snow melted? How long before his car was found? How long did he have to live?

'I bought you another present, as well as the wheelchair,' she was saying. 'I'll go and get it for you.' She came back with an old black typewriter. 'Well?' she said. 'What do you think?'

'It's great,' he said. 'A real antique.'

Her face clouded over. 'I didn't get it as an antique,' she said. 'I got it second-hand. It was a bargain, too. She wanted forty-five dollars for it, but I got it for forty because it has no "n".'

She looked pleased with herself. Paul could hardly believe it: she was pleased at buying a broken old typewriter!

'You did really well,' he said, discovering that flattery was easy.

Her smile became even wider. 'I told her that "n" was one of the letters in my favourite writer's name.'

'It's *two* of the letters in my favourite nurse's name,' replied Paul,

16

hating himself. 'But what will I write on this typewriter, do you think?'

'Oh, Paul! I don't think – I know! You're going to write a new novel. It'll be the best yet. *Misery's Return!*'

Paul felt nothing, said nothing; he was too surprised. But her face was shining with great joy and she was saying: 'It'll be a book just for me. It'll be my payment for nursing you back to health. The only copy in the whole world of the newest Misery book!'

'But Annie, Misery's dead.'

'No, she's not. Even when I was angry at you I knew she wasn't really dead. I knew you couldn't really kill her, because you're good.'

'Annie, will you tell me one thing?'

'Of course, dear.'

'If I write this book for you, will you let me go when I've finished?'

For a moment she seemed uncomfortable, and then she looked at him carefully. 'You talk as if I was keeping you prisoner, Paul.'

He didn't reply.

'I think,' she said, 'that when you've finished you should be ready to meet other people again.'

But she was lying. She knew that she was lying, and Paul knew she was lying too. The day he finished this new novel would be the day of his death. She started locking the door of his room whenever she left it.

Two mornings later she helped him into his wheelchair and fed him a bigger breakfast than usual. 'You'll need your strength now, Paul. I'm so excited about the new novel.'

He rolled over to the table by the window – and to the waiting typewriter. Thick snow was falling and it was difficult to recognize objects outside. Even the barn was just a snow-covered lump.

She came into the room carrying several packets of typing-paper. He saw straight away that the paper was Corrasable Bond and his face fell.

'What's the matter?' she asked.

'Nothing,' he said quickly.

'Something is the matter,' she said. 'Tell me what it is.'

'I'd like some different paper if you could get it.'

'Different from this? But this is the most expensive paper there is. I *asked* for the most expensive paper.'

'Didn't your mother ever tell you that the most expensive things are not always the best?'

'No, she did *not*. What she told me, Mister Clever, is that when you buy cheap things you get cheap things.' She was defensive now and Paul guessed that she would get angry next.

Paul was frightened, but he knew that he had to try to control her a little. If she always won, without any resistance from him, she would get the habit of being angry with him, and that would be worse. But his need for her and for the drug made him want to keep her happy; it took away all his courage to attack her.

Annie was beginning to breathe more rapidly now, and her hands were pumping faster and faster, opening and closing.

'And you'd better stop that too,' he said. 'Getting angry won't change a thing.'

She froze as if he had slapped her, and looked at him, wounded. 'This is a trick,' she said. 'You don't want to write my book and so you're finding excuses not to start. I knew you would.'

'That's silly,' he replied. 'Did I say that I was not going to start?'

'No, but . . .'

'I *am* going to start. Come here and I'll show you the problem.'

'What?'

'Watch.'

He put a piece of the paper into the typewriter and wrote: '*Misery's Retur* by Paul Sheldo '. He took the paper out and rubbed his finger over the words. The words immediately became indistinct and faint.

'Do you see?'

'Were you going to rub every page of your typescript with your finger?'

'The pages rubbing against one another would be enough.'

'All right, Mister Man,' she said in a complaining voice. 'I'll get your stupid paper. Just tell me what to get and I'll get it.'

'But you must understand that we're on the same side.'

'Don't make me laugh,' she said sarcastically. 'No one has been on my side since my mother died twenty years ago.'

'You can think what you like,' he said. 'At any rate you must believe that I'm on the book's side. If I type it on Corrasable Bond, in ten years' time there'll be nothing left for you to read.'

'All right, all right,' she said. 'I'll go *now*.'

Paul suddenly remembered that it was time for his medicine soon and he began to get nervous. Had he gone too far? Would she disappear for hours and hours? He needed his medicine.

'Tell me what kind of paper to get,' she said. Her face had turned to stone. He told her the names of some good kinds of paper.

She smiled then – a horrible smile. 'I'll go and get your paper,' she said. 'I know you want to start as soon as you can, since you're *on my side* –' These last words were spoken with terrible sarcasm. 'So I'm not even going to put you back into your bed. Of course it will hurt you to sit in the wheelchair for so long at first. Perhaps the pain will be so great that you have to delay starting to write. But that's too bad. I have to go, because you want your precious, stupid, Mister-Clever special paper.'

Suddenly her stony face seemed to break into pieces. She was standing at the door on her way out, and she rushed across the room at him. She screamed and punched her fist down on to the swollen lump which was Paul's left knee. He threw his head back and screamed too; the pain streamed out from his knee to every part of his body.

'So you just sit there,' she said, her lips still pulled back in that horrible grin, 'and think about who is in charge here, and all the things I can do to hurt you if you behave badly or try to trick me. You seem to think I'm stupid, but I'm not. And you can cry and shout all you want while I'm away, because no one will hear you. No one comes here because they all think Annie Wilkes is crazy. They all know what I did, although the court did say that I was innocent. There wasn't enough evidence, you see.'

She walked back to the door and turned again. He screamed again because he expected another rush and more pain. That made her grin more widely.

She left the room, locking the door behind her. A few minutes later he heard the roar of her car engine. He was left with his tears and his pain.

Chapter 8   Secret Supplies

His next actions might seem heroic, he imagined, if someone looked at just the actions without seeing inside his mind. In immense pain he rolled the wheelchair over to the door. He slid down in the chair so that his hands could touch the floor. This caused him so much pain that he fainted for a few minutes. When he woke up he remembered what he was trying to do. He looked at the floor and saw the hairpins which he had noticed earlier. They had fallen out of Annie's hair when she had rushed at him. Slowly, painfully, he managed to pick them up. There were three of them. Sitting up again in the chair brought fresh waves of pain.

While writing *Fast Cars* he had taught himself to open locks with things like hairpins. It had helped him write about a car-thief. It was surprisingly easy. Now he was going to open the door and go out into the house.

What made him overcome all his pain and do this? Was it because he was a hero? No, it was because he needed some Novril tablets and was afraid that Annie would not return for hours or would not give them to him when she did return. And he felt he needed an extra supply, to help him during those periods when she was too angry with him to give them to him.

It was an old, heavy lock. One pin sprang out of his hands, skated across the wooden floor and disappeared under the bed. The second one broke – but as it broke, the door opened.

'Thank you, God,' he whispered.

A bad moment followed – no, not a bad moment, an awful moment – when it seemed as if the wheelchair would not fit through the door. *She must have brought it into the room folded up*, he realized. In the end he had to hold on to the frame of the door and pull himself through it. The wheels rubbed against the frame and for one terrible moment he thought the chair was going to stick there. But then he was suddenly through the door.

After that he fainted again.

When he woke up, the light in the corridor was different. Quite some time had passed. How long did he have before she returned? Fifty hours, like the last time, or five minutes?

He could see the bathroom through an open door down the corridor. Surely she would keep the medicine there. He rolled down the corridor and stopped at the bathroom door. At least this door was a little wider. He turned himself round so that he could go into the bathroom backwards, ready for a quick escape if necessary.

Inside the bathroom there was a bath, an open cupboard for storing towels and blankets, a basin – and a medicine cupboard on the wall over the basin! But how could he reach it from his wheelchair? It was too high up the wall. And even if he could reach it with a stick or something, he would only make things fall out of it and break in the basin. And then what would he tell her? That Misery had done it while looking for some medicine to bring her back to life?

Tears of anger – and of shame at his need for the medicine – began to flow down his cheeks. He almost gave in and started to think about returning to his room. Then his eye saw something in the towel cupboard. Previously his eye had only quickly noticed the towels and blankets on the shelves. But there on the floor, underneath all the shelves, were two or three boxes. He rolled himself over to the cupboard. Now he could see some words printed on one of the boxes: MEDICAL SUPPLIES. His heart leapt.

He reached in and pulled one of the boxes out. There were many kinds of drugs inside the box – drugs for all sorts of diseases – but no Novril. He just managed to reach a second box. Again he was faced with an astonishing collection of medicines. She must have taken them from hospitals day after day. Most of the drugs were in small quantities. She had been careful: she hadn't taken a lot at once because they would have caught her.

He searched through the box. There at the bottom were a great many packets of Novril tablets; each packet contained eight tablets. He chewed three tablets straight away, hardly noticing the bitter taste.

How many packets could he take without her realizing that he had found the store? He took five packets and placed them down the front of his trousers, to leave his hands free for pushing the wheels. He looked at the drugs in the box. They had not been in any particular order before he searched the box and he hoped that Annie would not notice any difference.

Then, to his horror, he heard the noise of a car.

He straightened in the chair, eyes wide. If it was Annie he was dead. He couldn't get back to the bedroom and lock the door in time, and he had no doubt that she would be too angry to stop herself killing him immediately. She would forget that she didn't want to kill him before he had written *Misery's Return*. She would not be able to control herself.

The sound of the car grew... and then faded into the distance on the road outside.

OK, you've had your warning, he thought. *Now it's time to return to your room. The next car really could be hers.*

He rolled out of the bathroom, checking to make sure that he had left no tracks on the floor. How wide open had the bathroom door been? He closed it a little way. It looked right now.

The drug was beginning to take effect, so there was less pain now. His immediate need was satisfied. He was starting to turn the wheelchair, so that he could roll back to his room, when he realized that he was pointing towards the sitting-room. An idea burst into his mind like a light. He could almost see the telephone; he could imagine the conversation with the police station. Would they be surprised to learn that crazy Annie Wilkes had kidnapped him?

But he remembered that he had never heard the phone ring. He knew it was unlikely that there even was a phone in the house. But the picture of the phone in his mind drove him on; he could feel the cool plastic in his hand, hear the sound of the phone in the police station. He rolled himself into the sitting-room.

He looked around. The room smelled stale and was filled with ugly furniture. On a shelf was a large photograph, in a gold frame, of a woman who could only be Annie's mother.

He rolled further into the room. The left side of the wheelchair hit a table which had dozens of small figures on it. One of the figures — a flying bird of some kind — fell off the edge of the table. Without thinking, Paul put out his hand and caught it — and then realized what he had done. If he had thought about it he would not have been able to do it. It was pure instinct. If the figure had landed on the floor it would have broken. He put it back on the table.

On a small table on the other side of the room stood a phone.
⋆ Paul carefully made his way past the chairs and sofa. He picked up

the phone. Before he put it to his ear he had an odd feeling of failure. And yes – there was no sound. The phone was not working. Everything *looked* all right – it was important for Annie to have things looking all right – but she had disconnected the phone.

Why had she done it? He guessed that when she had arrived in Sidewinder she had been afraid. She thought that people would find out about whatever had happened in Denver and would ring her up. *You did it, Annie! We know you did. They let you go, but you're not innocent, are you, Annie Wilkes?* They were all against her – the Roydmans, everyone. No one liked her. The world was a dark place full of people looking at her with suspicion and hatred. So it was best to silence the phone for ever – just as she would silence him if she discovered that he had been in this room.

Fear suddenly overcame him and he turned the wheelchair around in order to leave the room. At that moment he heard the sound of another car, and he knew that this time it was Annie.

Chapter 9   Broken Hairpin

He was filled with the most extreme terror he had ever known, and he felt as guilty as a child who has been caught smoking a cigarette. He rolled the wheelchair out of the room as quickly as he could, pausing on the way only to look and make sure that nothing was out of place. He aimed himself straight at his bedroom door and tried to go through it at speed, but the right wheel crashed into the door-frame. *Did you scratch the paint?* his mind shouted at him. He looked down, but there was only a small mark – surely too small for her to notice.

He heard the noise of her car on the road and then turning in towards the house to park. He tried to move the wheelchair gently through the door without hurrying, but again he had to hold on to the frame and pull himself through it. At last he was in the room.

24

She has things to carry, he told himself. *It will take her time to get them out of the car and bring them to the house. You have a few minutes still.*

He turned himself round, grabbed the handle of the door and pulled it nearly shut. Outside, she switched off the car's engine.

Now he had only to push in the tongue of the lock with his finger. He heard a car door close.

The tongue began to move – and then stopped. It was stuck. Another car door shut: she must have got the groceries and paper out of the passenger seat.

He pushed again and again at the lock, and heard a noise inside the door. He knew what it was: the broken bit of the hairpin was making the lock stick. 'Come on,' he whispered in desperation and terror. 'Come on.' He heard her walking towards the house.

He moved the tongue in and out, in and out, but the broken pin stayed in the lock. He heard her walking up the outside steps.

He was crying now, sweat and tears pouring together down his face. 'Come on ... come on ... come on ... please.' This time the tongue moved further in, but still not far enough for the door to close. He heard the sound of the keys in her hand outside the front door.

She opened the door and shut it. At exactly the same time the lock on Paul's door suddenly cleared and he closed his door. *Did she hear that? She must have.* But the noise of the front door covered the noise of his door.

'Paul, I'm home,' she called cheerfully. 'I've got your paper.'

He rolled over to the table and turned to face the door, just as she fitted her key into the lock. He prayed that the broken pin would not cause any problems. It didn't. She opened the door.

'Paul, dear, you're covered in sweat. What have you been doing?' she asked suspiciously.

'I think you know, Annie. I've been in pain. Can I have my tablets now?'

'You see,' she said. 'You really shouldn't make me angry. I'm sure you'll learn, and then we'll be very happy together. I'll go and get your pills now.'

While she was out of the room Paul pushed the packets of Novril which he had taken as far as he could under the mattress of his bed. They would be safe there as long as she didn't turn the mattress.

She came back and gave him three tablets, and within a few minutes he was unconscious. He'd had six tablets now and he was exhausted. When he woke up, fourteen hours had passed and it was snowing again outside.

Chapter 10   'Can You?'

It was surprisingly easy to start writing about Misery again. It had been a long time and these were hardly ideal circumstances; but Misery's world was cheap, and returning to it felt like putting on an old, familiar glove.

Annie put down the first three pages of the new typescript.

'What do you think?' Paul asked.

'It's not right,' she said.

'What do you mean? Don't you like it?'

'Oh, yes, I love it. When Ian kissed her . . . And it was very sweet of you to name the baby after me.'

Clever, he thought. *Not sweet, but maybe clever.*

'Then why is it not right?'

'Because you cheated,' she explained. 'The doctor comes, when he couldn't have come. At the end of *Misery's Child* Geoffrey rode to fetch the doctor, but his horse fell and broke a leg, and Geoffrey broke his shoulder and lay in the rain all night until the morning, when that boy found him. And by then Misery was dead. Do you see?'

'Yes.' *How am I going to please her? How can I bring Misery back to life without cheating?*

'When I was a child,' Annie was saying, 'I used to go to the cinema every week. We lived in Bakersfield, California. They used to show short films and at the end the hero – Rocket Man or somebody – was always in trouble. Perhaps the criminals had tied him to a chair in a burning house, or he was unconscious in an aeroplane. The hero always escaped, but you had to wait until the next week to find out exactly what happened. I loved those films. If I was bored, or if I was looking after those horrible children downstairs, I used to try to guess what happened next. God, I hated those children. Anyway, sometimes I was right and sometimes I was wrong. That didn't matter, as long as the hero escaped in a fair way.'

Paul tried to stop himself laughing at the picture in his mind of young Annie Wilkes in the cinema.

'Are you all right, Paul? Are you going to sneeze? Anyway, what I'm saying is that the way the hero escaped was often unlikely, but always fair. Then one week Rocket Man was in a car. He was tied up and the car had no brakes. He didn't have any special equipment. We saw him in the film struggling to get free; we saw him still struggling while the car went off the edge of a mountain and burst into flames. I spent the whole week trying to guess what would happen, but I couldn't. How could he escape? It was really exciting. I was the first in the queue at the cinema the next week. And what do you think happened, Paul?'

Paul didn't know the answer to her question, but she was right, of course. He had cheated. And the writing had been wooden, too.

'The story always started by showing the ending from last week. So we saw Rocket Man in the car again, but this time, just before the car reached the edge, the side-door flew open and Rocket Man fell out on to the road. Then the car went over the edge. All the other children in the cinema were cheering because Rocket Man was safe, but I wasn't cheering. No! I stood up and shouted, "This is wrong! Are you all stupid? This isn't what happened last week! They cheated!" I went on and on, and then the manager of the cinema came and asked me to leave. "All right, I'll leave," I told him, "and I'm never coming back, because this is just a dirty *cheat*." '

She looked at Paul, and Paul saw clear murder in her eyes. Although she was being childish, the unfairness she felt was absolutely real for her.

'The car went over the edge and he was still in it. Do you understand that, Paul? *Do you understand?*'

She jumped up and Paul thought she was going to hurt him because he was another writer who had cheated in his story.

'*Do you?*' She seized the front of his shirt and pulled him forward so that their faces were almost touching.

'Yes, Annie, yes, I do.'

She stared at him with that angry, black stare. She must have seen in his eyes that he was telling the truth, because she let go of him, quietened down and sat back in her chair.

'Then you know what to do,' she said, and left the room.

How could he bring Misery back to life?

When he was a child he used to play a game called 'Can You?' with a group of other children. An adult would start a story about a man called Careless Corrigan. Within a few sentences Careless Corrigan would be in a hopeless situation – surrounded by hungry lions perhaps. Then the adult would pass the story on to one of the children. He would say, 'Daniel, can you?' And then Daniel – or one of the other children – had to start the story again within ten seconds or he had failed.

Once Daniel had told his story, explaining how Careless Corrigan escaped from the lions, the adult asked the other question:

'Did he?' And if most of the children put their hands in the air and agreed that Careless Corrigan *did* – that what Daniel had said was all right – then Daniel was allowed to stay in the game.

The rules of the game were exactly the same as Annie's rules. The story didn't have to be *likely*, but it did have to be *fair*. As a child, Paul had always been good at the game.

So can you, Paul? Yes, I can. I'm a writer. I live and earn money because I can. I have homes in New York and Los Angeles because I can. There are plenty of people who can write better than I can, but when the question is 'Did he?', sometimes only a few hands go up for those people. But the hands go up for me, or for Misery, which is the same thing I suppose. Can I? Yes, you bet I can. I can't mend cars or taps, I can't be an electrician; but if you want me to take you away, to frighten you, to make you cry or make you smile, then yes, I can.

Two hours later Annie came and stood at the entrance to his room. She stood for a long time, watching him work. He was typing fast and he didn't even notice her standing there. He was too busy dreaming Misery back to life. When he was working well a hole seemed to open in the paper in front of him; he would fall through the hole into the world of Misery Chastain and her lovers.

Chapter 11   Visitor

'Well?' he asked several days later, when she interrupted him. 'Is it fair?'

Annie sat on his bed, holding the first six chapters of the typescript. She looked a bit pale.

'Of course,' she said, as if they both already knew the answer – which he supposed they did. 'It's not only fair, it's also good. Exciting.'

'Shall I go on?' he asked.

'I'll kill you if you don't!' she replied, smiling a little. Paul didn't smile back. This common remark would once have seemed ordinary to him; when Annie Wilkes said it, it didn't seem ordinary at all.

'You won't have to kill me, Annie,' he said. 'I *want* to go on. So why don't you leave me to write?'

'All right,' she said. She stood up and quickly dropped the typescript on his table, and then moved away. It was as if she was afraid of being burned by him. She was thinking of him now as the famous author, the one who could capture her in the pages of his books and burn her with the heat which his words made.

'Would you like to read it as I write it?' he asked.

Annie smiled. 'Yes! It would be almost like those films when I was young.'

'I don't usually show my work before it's all finished,' he said, 'but this is a special situation, so I'd be glad to show it to you chapter by chapter.' *And so began the thousand and one nights of Paul Sheldon*, he thought. 'But will you do something for me?'

'What?'

'Fill in all those "n"s,' he said.

She smiled at him with real warmth. 'That would make me very proud,' she said. 'I'll leave you alone now.'

But it was too late: her interruption closed the hole in the paper for the rest of the day.

Early the next morning Paul was sitting up in bed with his pillows piled up behind him, drinking a cup of coffee and looking at those marks on the sides of the door. Suddenly Annie rushed into the room, her eyes wide with fear. In one hand she held a piece of cloth; in the other, some rope.

'What –?'

It was all he had time to say. She seized him with frightened strength and pulled him forward. Pain – the worst for days – ran through his legs, and he screamed. The coffee cup flew out of his hand and broke on the floor. His first thought was that she had seen the marks on the door and now she was going to punish him.

'Shut up, stupid!' she whispered urgently. She tied his hands behind him with the rope, and just then he heard the sound of a car turning off the road and towards her house.

He opened his mouth to say something and she pushed the cloth into it. It tasted foul.

'Keep completely quiet,' she said with her head close to his. 'I warn you, Paul. If whoever this is hears something – or even if *I* hear something and *think* he might have heard something – I will kill him, then you, then myself.'

She ran out of the room and Paul heard her putting on her coat and boots.

Through the window he saw an old Chevrolet stop and an elderly man get out. Paul guessed that he was here on town business, because he could think of no other reason for anyone to come. The man looked like a local official, too.

Paul had often imagined someone coming to the house. In his mind there were several versions of what happened, but one thing was the same in every version: the visit shortened Paul's life.

Annie hurried out of the house to meet the man. *Why not invite him inside, Annie?* thought Paul, trying not to choke on the cloth. *Why don't you show him what you keep inside the house?*

The man pulled a piece of paper out of his pocket and gave it to Annie. He seemed to be apologizing. She looked quickly at the paper and began to speak. Paul couldn't hear what she was saying, but he could see the clouds of mist which formed in the cold air in front of her mouth. She was talking fast and waving her finger in the man's face.

She led the man a little way from his car, so that Paul could no

31

longer see them, only their shadows. He realized that she had done it on purpose: if he couldn't see the man, then the man couldn't see him. The shadows stayed there for five minutes. Once Paul heard Annie's voice; she was shouting angrily, although he couldn't hear the actual words. They were five long minutes for Paul: the cloth in his mouth was making him feel sick.

Then the man was walking back to his car, with Annie behind him. She was still talking. He turned to say something before getting into the car, and Paul could see some emotion on his face. It wasn't quite anger: he was disgusted. It was obvious that he thought she was crazy. The whole town probably regarded her as crazy and he didn't like having the job of visiting her.

But you don't know the extent of her madness, do you? thought Paul. *If you did, you wouldn't turn your back on her.*

Now the man got into the car and started to reverse towards Annie's gate. Annie had to shout even louder so that he could hear her over the noise of the engine, and Paul heard her words too: 'You think you're so clever, don't you? You think you're such a big wheel, helping the world to turn round. Well, I'll tell you something, Mister Big Wheel. Little dogs go to the toilet all over big wheels. What do you think about that?'

When the man had driven away, Annie rushed back into the house. She shut the front door with a loud bang and Paul knew that she was extremely angry. He was frightened that her anger with the man would become anger with him.

She came into his room and began to walk around, waving the piece of paper in her hand. 'I owe them five hundred dollars' tax, he says. I haven't been paying the tax on my house, he says. Dirty tax! Dirty lawyers! I hate lawyers!'

Paul choked and tried to speak through the cloth, but she didn't seem to notice. She was in a world of her own.

'*Five hundred and six dollars!*' she shouted. 'And they send

32

someone out here to visit when they know I don't want anyone here. I told them. Now he says they'll take my house away from me if I don't pay soon.'

She absent-mindedly pulled the piece of cloth from his mouth and Paul swallowed great mouthfuls of air in relief, trying not to be sick. 'My hands . . .' he gasped.

'What? Oh, yes. Sometimes you're such a baby.' She pulled him forward again – which hurt again – and untied his hands. 'I pay my taxes,' she protested. 'I just . . . this time I just . . . You've been keeping me so busy.'

You forgot, didn't you, Annie? You try to make everything seem normal, but you forgot. This is the first time you've forgotten anything this big, isn't it? In fact, Annie, you're getting worse, aren't you? You're starting to get a little worse every day. Your blank periods are getting longer and happening more often. Mad people can usually manage their lives, and sometimes – as I think you know – they get away with some very nasty actions. But there's a border between manageable madness and unmanageable madness, and you're getting closer to it every day . . . and part of you knows it.

Paul had a brilliant idea. 'I owe you my life,' he said, 'and I'm just a nuisance to you. I've got about four hundred dollars in my wallet. I want you to have it.'

'Oh, Paul, I couldn't.' She was looking at him in confusion and pleasure.

Paul smiled and tried to look as sincere as possible. 'It's yours,' he said. 'You saved two lives, you know – Misery's as well as mine. And you showed me that I was going wrong, writing other kinds of books. Four hundred dollars is nothing for all that. If you don't take the money you'll make me feel bad.'

'Well, if you say so . . . All right,' she said, with a shy smile. 'They all hate me, you know. They're all against me, Paul.'

'So you must pay their dirty taxes today,' Paul said. 'That'll show them. I bet there are other people in the town – the Roydmans, for

33

example – who haven't paid their taxes for years. They're just trying to make you go, Annie.'

'Yes, I'll pay their stupid taxes,' she said. 'That'll teach them a lesson. I'll stay here and spit in their eyes!'

She went and fetched his wallet. The money was still in it, but everything which showed that it belonged to Paul Sheldon had gone. He remembered going to the bank and taking the money out. The man who had done that had felt good. He had just finished *Fast Cars* and was feeling younger than his age. His legs were not useless sticks.

He gave Annie the money and she bent over and kissed him on the lips. He smelled the foul smell which came from the rotten places inside her. 'I love you,' she said.

'Would you put me in the wheelchair?' he said. 'I want to write.'

'Of course, my dear,' she replied. Then she left to go to town.

While she was out Paul unlocked the door – he now had four hairpins under the mattress, next to the tablets – and tried to clean the marks on the door-frame.

Three weeks passed. Although there were times when he felt close to tears, Paul was on the whole curiously happy. He was enjoying writing the book. Usually the most he could write was two or three pages a day, but he was sometimes writing twelve pages of *Misery's Return* in a day! He was living such a regular and healthy life. Annie was cooking him three meals a day. He wasn't drinking any alcohol or smoking cigarettes; he suffered from none of his usual headaches. He woke up in the morning, ate breakfast, worked, had lunch, slept for a while, worked again, ate again and then slept like a baby all night long. There was nothing else for him to do – nothing to interrupt the routine. Ideas for the book were flooding into his mind. *Can you? Yes, I can.*

Then the rain came, and everything changed.

Chapter 12   Rat Trap

The beginning of April was fine. The sun shone from a clear blue sky and it was warm enough to melt some of the snow. Mud and grass began to appear in Annie's field. Annie sometimes took Paul in his wheelchair out of the house at the back, and let him sit in the sunshine and read a book. She sang while she worked around the house, and laughed at jokes she heard on the TV. She left his door unlocked and open while she was in the house. Paul tried not to think of the snow melting and uncovering his car.

The morning of the fifteenth, however, was windy and dull, and Annie changed. She didn't come into his room with his tablets until nine o'clock, and by then he needed them quite badly — so badly that he nearly got some from under the mattress. Then, when she came, she was still in her night-clothes and she brought him only the tablets, no breakfast. There were red marks on her arms and cheeks, and her clothes were messy with spilled food. She dragged her feet along the corridor. Her hair was untidy and her eyes were dull.

'Here.' She threw the pills at him and they fell into his lap. She turned to go, dragging her feet. arrasu...

'Annie?' She stopped without turning round. 'Annie, are you all right?'

'No,' she said carelessly, and turned to face him. She looked at him in that same dull way. She began to pinch her lower lip between her finger and thumb. She pulled it out and twisted it, while pinching it hard. Drops of blood began to fall down her chin. She turned and left without speaking another word, before his astonished mind could persuade itself that he had really seen her do that. She closed the door and locked it.

He heard her sit down in her favourite chair. There was silence. She didn't switch on the TV as usual. She was just sitting there — just sitting there being not all right.

Then there *was* a sound – a single, sharp sound which was unmistakable: she had hit herself, hard, in the face.

He remembered reading that when mad people start to become deeply, seriously depressed, they hurt themselves. This signals the start of a long period of depression. He was suddenly very frightened.

She hadn't returned by eleven that morning, so Paul decided to try to get into the wheelchair by himself; he wanted to try to work. He succeeded, although it hurt him a lot, and he rolled himself over to the table.

He heard the key in the lock. Annie was looking in at him and her eyes burned black holes in her face. Her right cheek was swelling up and she had been eating jam with her hands. She looked at him and Paul looked back at her. Neither of them said anything for a while. Outside, the first drops of rain hit the window.

'If you can get into that chair by yourself, Paul,' she said at last, 'then I think you can fill in your own stupid "n"s.'

She closed the door and locked it again. Paul sat looking at it for a long time, as if there was something to see. He was too surprised to do anything else.

He didn't see her again until late in the afternoon. After her visit work was impossible. At two in the afternoon the pain was bad enough for him to take two tablets from under the mattress. Then he slept on the bed.

When he woke up he thought at first that he was still dreaming; what he saw was too strange for real life. Annie was sitting on the side of his bed. In one hand she held a glass full of Novril tablets, which she placed on the table next to his bed. In her other hand was a rat-trap. There was a large grey rat in it. The trap had broken the rat's back. There was blood around its mouth, but it was still alive. It was struggling and squeaking.

*In her other hand was a rat-trap. There was a large grey rat in it.
The trap had broken the rat's back.*

This was no dream. He realized that now he was seeing the real Annie. She looked terrible. Whatever had been wrong with her this morning was much worse by now. The flesh on her face seemed to hang as loosely as the clothes on her body. Her eyes were blank. There were more red marks on her arms and hands, and more food spread here and there on her clothes.

She held up the trap. 'They come into the cellar when it rains,' she explained. 'I put down traps. I always catch eight or nine of them. Sometimes I find others –'

She went blank then. She just stopped and went blank for nearly three minutes, holding the rat in the air. The only sounds were the rat's squeaks. *You thought things couldn't get worse, didn't you? You were WRONG!*

'– drowned in the corners. Poor things!' She looked down at the rat and a tear fell on to its fur. 'Poor, poor things.'

She closed one of her strong hands around the rat and began to squeeze. The rat struggled and whipped its tail from side to side. Annie's eyes never lost that blank, distant look. Paul wanted to look away, but couldn't; it was disgusting, but fascinating. Annie's hand closed into a fist. Paul heard the rat's bones break and blood ran out of its mouth. Annie threw the crushed body into a corner of the room. Some of the rat's blood was on her hand.

'Now it's at peace,' she said, and laughed. 'Shall I get my gun, Paul? Maybe the next world is better for people as well as for rats – and people are almost the same as rats anyway.'

'Wait for me to finish,' he said. It was hard to speak; his mouth felt thick and heavy. *I'm closer to death than I've ever been in my life,* he thought, *because she means it. She's as insane as the husband who murders his whole family before killing himself – and who thinks he is being a good husband and father.*

'Misery?' she asked, and Paul thought – or hoped – that there was a tiny sign of life in her eyes.

'Yes.' *What should he say next? How could he stop her killing him?* 'I agree that the world's an awful place. I mean, I've been in so much pain these last few weeks, but –'

'Pain?' She interrupted him. 'You don't know what pain is, Paul. You haven't any idea at *all*.' She looked at him with contempt.

'No, I suppose not – not compared with you, anyway.'

'That's right.'

'But I want to finish this book. I want to see what happens to Misery. And I'd like you to be here too. Don't you want to find out what happens?'

There was a pause, a terrible silence for a few seconds, and then she sighed. 'Yes, I suppose I do want to know what happens. That's the *only* thing left in the world that I still want.'

Without realizing what she was doing she began to suck the rat's blood off her fingers.

'I can still do it, Paul. I can still go and get my gun. Why not now, both of us together? You're not stupid. You know I can never let you leave here. You've known that for some time, haven't you? I suppose you think of escape, like a rat in a trap. But you can't escape. You can't leave here...but I could go with you.'

Paul forced himself to keep his eyes looking straight into hers. 'We all go eventually, don't we, Annie? But I'd like to finish what I've started first.'

She sighed and stood up. 'All right. I must have known that's what you'd want, because I've brought you your pills. I don't remember bringing them, but here they are. I have to go away for a while. If I don't, what you or I want won't make any difference. I do things, you see...I go somewhere when I feel like this – a place in the hills. I call it my Laughing Place. Do you remember that I told you I was coming back from Sidewinder when I found you in the storm? I lied. I was coming back from my Laughing Place, in fact. Sometimes I do laugh when I'm there, but usually I just scream.'

'How long will you be away, Annie?'

'I don't know. I've brought you plenty of pills.'

But what about food? Am I supposed to eat that rat?

She left the room and he listened to her walking around the house, getting ready to go. He still half expected her to come back with her gun, and he didn't relax until he heard the car disappearing up the road outside.

Chapter 13   No Way Out

Two hours later Paul unlocked his door with a hairpin for the last time, he hoped. He was determined to escape. He had blankets and all his tablets in his lap. Sidewinder was downhill from here and, even if he had to slide all the way in the rain, he intended to try.

Why hadn't he tried to escape before? Writing the book had become an excuse. It was true that it kept him alive, because it gave Annie a reason to want him alive; he was her pet writer, producing a book just for her. But it was also true that he was enjoying writing the book and didn't want to leave it. But now he didn't care. Annie could destroy the book if she wanted.

He rolled himself into the sitting-room. It had been tidy before, but now it was a mess. There were dirty dishes piled up on all the surfaces. Empty containers of sweet things of all kinds – jam, ice-cream, cake, biscuits, Pepsi-Cola – were everywhere. There was no sign of any spoons or forks; Annie used her hands when she was in this condition. There were splashes of ice-cream on the floor and the sofa.

The figure of the flying bird was still on the table, but most of the other figures had been thrown into a corner, where they had broken into sharp little pieces. In the middle of the floor was an overturned vase of dead flowers. Underneath a small table lay a photograph album. *Don't you know it's a bad idea to think about the past when you're feeling depressed, Annie?*

He rolled across the room. Straight ahead was the kitchen; on the right was the hall leading to the front door. He knew there was a door in the kitchen and he hoped he might get out of the house that way. But first he wanted to check the front door; he might get a surprise.

He didn't. There were three locks on the door. Two of them were Kreigs – the best locks in the world. A thousand hairpins would be useless. And Annie of course had the keys with her.

He reversed down the hall and went into the kitchen. The room was not as much of a mess as the sitting-room, although there was the smell of rotten food. Here it was the same story: the door had the same system of locks. Roydmans, stay out; Paul, stay in. He imagined her laughing.

The windows were too high. Even if he did manage to break one and pull himself through he would probably break his back falling on to the ground. Then he'd have to pull himself through deep mud and crawl up to the road in the hope of being found. It was not a good idea.

Another door in the kitchen had no locks. Paul opened it and saw that it led down some steep stairs to the cellar. He heard the squeaking of rats and smelled the foul smell of rotten vegetables. He quickly closed the door.

Paul felt desperate. There was no way out. For a moment he thought about killing himself. He had found plenty of food in cans on the kitchen shelves, and also some boxes of matches. Perhaps he should just burn the whole house down in revenge, and kill himself at the same time?

Maybe I will have to kill myself eventually, but I'll kill her first. That is my promise. I will never give up.

Chapter 14   Dragon Lady

On his way back through the sitting-room he stopped to pick up the album. He was curious to see photographs of Annie's family and of Annie herself when she was younger. When he opened the album, however, he found that it was full of stories cut from newspapers.

The first two pages told of the wedding of Annie's parents and the birth of her elder brother, Paul – another Paul in her life – and of Annie herself. She was born on 1 April 1943. She must have hated being an April Fool.

The next page contained a report of a fire in a house in Bakersfield, California, in 1954. Five people had died in the fire. Three of them had been the children who lived in the ground-floor apartment, downstairs from the Wilkes family (who had been out of the house at the time). The fire had started because of a cigarette in the cellar.

Annie's voice echoed in Paul's mind: *God, I hated those children.*

Paul's blood began to run cold.

But she was only eleven years old.

That's old enough – old enough to let a candle burn down in the cellar so that the flame could light a pool of petrol. It's an old trick but hard to beat. Maybe she just wanted to frighten them and accidentally did more than that. But she did it, Paul. You know she did it.

He turned the page and found a story about the death of Annie's father. He had fallen over a pile of clothes at the top of the stairs in his house and broken his neck. The newspaper called it a 'curious accident'.

On the next page a newspaper from Los Angeles, hundreds of miles from Bakersfield, used exactly the same words – a 'curious accident'. This time it was a student nurse who had fallen over a dead cat at the top of the stairs and broken her neck. The name of the person who shared the student's apartment was Annie Wilkes. The year was 1959.

Paul felt pure terror rise up in him.

The 'accidents' had happened in different places and at different times, and no one had made the connection. Why should they? People were always falling down stairs.

Why had she killed them? He seemed to hear Annie's answers in his mind. The answers were absolutely mad, and Paul knew they were right.

I killed her because she played the radio late at night; I killed her because she let her boyfriend kiss her too much; I killed her because I caught her cheating; I killed her because she caught me cheating. I killed her to see whether I could. What does it matter? She was just a Miss Clever – so I killed her.

The next page of the album showed that Annie had graduated as a nurse and had got a job at St Joseph's Hospital in Pennsylvania. There followed several pages containing short newspaper reports of deaths at the hospital. There was nothing suspicious about any of these deaths. Most of the people were old and had been ill for a long time. Some were young – one was even a child – but they all had serious illnesses or injuries.

And what were these reports doing in Annie's album? She had killed them all. The reports were so short that several could fit on a single page of the album – and the album was thick.

Again Paul asked the question: *Why, Annie? Why kill these people?*

Again he heard Annie's voice echoing in his mind: *Because they were rats in a trap.* And he remembered Annie's tears falling on the rat she held in her hand, while she said: *'Poor, poor things.'*

Over the next few years she had moved from hospital to hospital around the country. The pattern in the album was always the same: first, the list of new hospital staff, with Annie's name among them; then pages of short reports of deaths.

In 1978, nine years ago, she had arrived at a hospital in Denver, Colorado. The usual pattern began again with a report of the death of an elderly woman. Then the pattern changed. Instead of reports of deaths there was a report of Annie's marriage to a man called Ralph Dugan, a doctor. There was a photograph of the house they had bought outside Sidewinder in 1979 – *this* house. Several months had passed without any killings. It was unbelievable, but Annie must have been happy!

Then there was a report, from August 1980, of their divorce. It was clear that *he* had divorced her rather than the other way round. He had understood something about her. Maybe he had seen the cat at the top of the stairs – the one he was supposed to fall over. Annie had torn into this report with a pen as she wrote vicious words across it, so that Paul had difficulty reading it.

Annie moved to a hospital in Boulder, Colorado. It was clear that she was very hurt and very angry, because the killings started again, and more often than before: the newspaper reports came every few days.

God, how many did she kill? Why did nobody guess?

At last, in 1982, Annie made a mistake. She moved to the childbirth department of the hospital. Annie had carefully kept a record of the whole story.

Killing new-born babies is different from killing badly injured or seriously ill adults. Babies don't often die and people notice if they do. Parents care as well. And Annie had started to kill even healthy babies. They must have all seemed to her to be 'poor, poor things' by now – now that she was even crazier than before.

Five babies died between January and March 1982. A hospital

investigation found nothing suspicious in their deaths – which was not surprising, thought Paul, since Annie was the chief nurse of the department and was probably doing the investigation herself.

Another baby had died in April. Two in May.

Then at the beginning of June there was a newspaper report with the heading: NURSE WILKES QUESTIONED ON BABY DEATHS. The police were reported as saying that she was not under arrest and they were not accusing her of anything: they were just questioning her. And the next day: NURSE WILKES RELEASED.

She had got away with it. How? Paul couldn't imagine, but she had got away with it. Now, he thought, she will move to another hospital in another town. But no: she was too insane for that now.

The *Boulder News*, 2 July: THE HORROR CONTINUES: THREE MORE BABIES DIE.

Pages and pages of the album contained reports of Annie's arrest and trial. Annie had also included a selection of letters from the citizens of Boulder that had been printed in the newspapers. It was clear that she had chosen the most vicious of the letters – those which reminded her that everyone was against her and that it was *their* fault. The newspapers began to call her 'the Dragon Lady'.

But there was not enough evidence. On 16 December the huge heading in the paper read: DRAGON LADY INNOCENT!

There were plenty more pages in the album, but few of them had been used. Annie had kept any further reports that she had seen about the baby deaths, but there were no more killings until 1984. The Sidewinder *Gazette* had reported in November of that year the discovery of the body of a young man called Andrew Pomeroy. What was left of his body – some bits had been cut off with an axe – had been found in a stream bed quite a few miles from the town. *How far from here?* Paul wondered.

He turned the page and looked at the last report in the album. For a moment his breath stopped: it was about him! The report was only two weeks old. It had been cut out from *Newsweek* and told how 'famous novelist Paul Sheldon, last seen seven weeks ago in Boulder, Colorado' was missing. The reporter had interviewed Paul's agent, but she had not been worried, probably because she thought Paul was staying with a woman he had met! Well, that was true, thought Paul.

He put the album down carefully so that Annie would not see that it had been moved. He felt sick and close to tears.

Outside, the wind suddenly blew heavy rain against the house and Paul jumped in fear.

An hour later, full of Novril, the wind seemed comforting rather than frightening. He was thinking: *So there's no way out. You can't escape, and Superman's too busy making films in Hollywood. But there's one thing you can do. Can you, Paul? Can you do it?* The only way out of this was to kill her. *Yes, I can.*

Chapter 15   Butcher's Knife

The storm continued throughout the next day. The following night the clouds blew away and the temperature dropped. All the world outside froze solid. The roads were pure ice. Annie couldn't come back that day even if she was ready to.

And that was too bad for the animals. He could hear the cows complaining in the barn: Annie hadn't milked them and they were in pain. As the days passed he heard no more noises from them.

Paul's routine was easy. During the daytime he ate food which Annie would not miss from the kitchen. She had stored hundreds of cans of food, and it was easy for Paul to take a few cans from here and a few from there so that Annie would not notice. So he had enough to eat, he took his tablets regularly, slept and wrote his novel; in the evenings he played 'Can You?' with ideas about killing Annie. A lot of ideas came to him, but most of them were impossible or too complicated. This was no game, this was his life. It would have to be something simple.

In the end he went to the kitchen and chose the longest, sharpest butcher's knife he could find. On the way back into his room he stopped to rub at the new marks he was making on the door-frame. The marks were clearer than before. *But it doesn't matter*, he thought, *because as soon as she returns, the first time she comes into my room . . .*

He pushed the knife under the mattress. When Annie came back he was going to ask her for a drink of water. She would bend over to give it to him and then he would stab her in the throat. Nothing complicated.

Paul closed his eyes and went to sleep. When Annie's car came whispering into the farm at four o'clock that morning, with its engine and its lights switched off, he did not move. It was only when he felt the sting of the syringe in his arm and woke to see her face close to his that he knew she was back.

Chapter 16   Good News, Bad News

In his dream he was stung by a bee, so at first he thought he was dreaming.

'Paul?'

In his dream the bee was dangerous and he wanted desperately to escape.

'Paul!'

That was no dream-voice: it was Annie's voice.

He saw the syringe in her hand and understood that it hadn't been a bee: she had given him an injection.

He forced his eyes open. She was standing there in the shadows as if she had never been away, wearing her ugly clothes. He saw the syringe in her hand and understood that it hadn't been a bee: she had given him an injection. But what had she –?

Fear came again, but his mind was too dull to feel it strongly. Whatever drug she had given him was making things unreal for him. He tried to lift his hands and it felt as if there were invisible weights hanging from them.

It's the end, he thought. *The end of the story of Paul Sheldon.* Curiously, the thought almost made him happy. *The end of the thousand and one nights.* Strange, half-formed ideas kept coming into his mind as the powerful drug crept into all the corners of his brain.

'There you are!' Annie said. 'I see you, Paul . . . those blue eyes. Did I ever tell you that I think your eyes are lovely? But I suppose plenty of women have told you that – and bolder women than me.'

She was sitting on the end of his bed. She bent down to check something on the floor and for a moment all he could see was her broad, strong back. He heard the sounds of something metal and something wooden – and the unmistakable sound of a box of matches.

She turned back towards him and smiled. Whatever else might have happened, she was no longer depressed. That must be good, mustn't it?

'What do you want first, Paul?' she asked. 'The good news or the bad news?'

'Good news first.' He managed a big, foolish grin. 'I suppose the bad news is that you don't really like the book. I tried. I thought it was going well.'

She looked at him sadly. 'I *love* the book, Paul. Why do you think I asked you to fill in all the "n"s yourself? Because I don't want to read any more until the end. I don't want to spoil it.'

Paul's drugged grin widened. If she loved the book she wasn't going to kill him – at least not yet.

Annie smiled back at him, 'The good news,' she said, 'is that your car has gone. I've been very worried about your car, Paul. I knew only a big storm would wash it away. When the snow melted in the spring the water from the mountains was enough to wash away the body of that dirty bird Pomeroy, but a car is much heavier than a man, isn't it? But the storm and the melting snow at the same time did it. Your car has gone. That's the *good* news.'

Alarm bells rang in Paul's mind. Who was Pomeroy? Then he remembered: the young man in Annie's album.

'Don't pretend, Paul,' she said. 'I know you know about Pomeroy. I know you've read my album. I suppose I wanted you to read it; otherwise, why would I have left it out? But I wanted to be sure – and when I came back the hair was broken.'

'Hair?' he said faintly.

'Yes, I read about it somewhere. If you think someone has been looking through your belongings you stick some hair over the drawers or the book or whatever. Then if the hair is broken or moved you know that someone has been there.'

Again she bent over the end of the bed. Again there were the sounds of something metal and something wooden.

'So I crept in this morning,' she said, 'as quiet as a mouse – and yes, all three hairs were broken, so I *knew* you'd been looking at my album.' She paused, and smiled again. 'I wasn't surprised. I knew you had been out of the room. *That's* the bad news, Paul. I've known for a long, long time.'

He should feel angry or disappointed or something, he supposed, but the drug made it impossible.

'Anyway, we were talking about your car,' she said. 'Early yesterday afternoon I felt a lot better. I spent most of the time up there on my knees, praying to God; and you know, Paul, when you pray sincerely to God he always answers your prayers. I knew what I had to do. I put the special tyres on the car, for driving on ice, and drove slowly down from the hills. It was very dangerous, Paul, but I felt safe in the arms of God.'

'That's very nice, Annie,' Paul tried to say, but the sounds were indistinct: *That'sh very nishe Annie.*

'I stopped on the way down to look for your car. I knew what I would have to do if I saw it. If it was there, visible, there would be questions, and I'd be the first one they'd question because they know about my past. Actually, one of the reasons I rescued you and brought you home was that you crashed there.'

'What do you mean?'

'I parked there, in exactly the same place, when I got rid of that Pomeroy.' She slapped her hand in contempt. 'He said he was an artist, but he was just another dirty bird. He was hitch-hiking and I picked him up. He said he was going to Sidewinder to do a job there. I let him stay here. We were lovers.'

She looked at Paul, challenging him to deny it. He didn't say anything, but he didn't believe her at all.

'Then I found out that he didn't have a job in Sidewinder. I looked at some of his drawings and they were terrible. *I* could have drawn better pictures. He came in while I was looking at them and we had an argument. He laughed at me, so I . . .'

'You killed him,' Paul said.

She seemed uncomfortable. 'I guess it was something like that. I don't remember very well. I only remember him being dead. I remember giving him a bath.'

He looked at her and felt sick, soupy horror. He could see in his mind Pomeroy's body in the bath with no clothes on, eyes open and staring up at the ceiling . . .

'I *had* to,' she said. 'You probably don't know what the police can do with just one hair or a piece of dirt from someone's finger. You don't know, but I do, because I worked in hospitals for ten years. I *know. I know.*' She was making herself angry with that special mad Annie anger which he knew so well by now. 'They're all out to get

51

me, *all* of them! Do you think they would have listened if I'd tried to tell them about him? They'd probably say that I'd tried to kiss him and he laughed at me and then I killed him.'

And you know what, Annie? I think that just might be closer to the truth.

'The dirty birds around here would say *anything* to make trouble for me.' She paused, breathing hard, and again seemed to challenge him to deny what she was saying. 'I washed him . . . what was left of him . . . and drove up into the hills. I parked and carried him about a mile into the woods. I didn't hide him or anything. No, I knew the snow would cover him and I thought the spring floods would take his body and clothes away. It worked even better than I'd imagined. They didn't find his body for a whole year! And twenty-seven miles away! But your car won't go so far, Paul. It's too heavy. It'll just be stuck somewhere in the thick forest. Maybe someone will find its rusty body in two years' time or in five years' time, when wild animals have made their home on the back seat and plants are growing through the windows. And by then the book will be finished and you'll be back in New York or somewhere and I'll be living my quiet life here. Maybe we'll write to each other sometimes.' She smiled at her imagination. 'Anyway, I was thinking, you see. Your car had gone, so I knew you *could* stay and finish the book, and that made me happy because I love you so much.'

'Thank you, Annie,' he said.

'But would you *want* to stay?' she went on. 'That was the question I had to ask myself. And I knew the answer. I knew the answer even before I saw that you were getting stronger, and noticed those marks on the door over there and realized you had been out of the room. Then I started to look carefully and I saw that one of the figures on my table was in a different position. That bird *always* flies south, Paul. The first time you went out was after we had that silly fight about the paper, wasn't it, Paul?'

'Yes.' What was the point in denying it?

'You wanted your pills, of course. I should have guessed, but when I'm angry, I get . . . you know . . .'

I certainly do know, Annie.

'Then two days later, one afternoon when you were asleep, I tried to come into your room to give you your medicine and the door handle wouldn't turn at first. There was a noise inside it as if something was loose. So I gave you some stronger medicine to make sure that you wouldn't wake up, and I took the whole lock and handle off the door, and look! Look what I found!'

She put her hand in her pocket, pulled out a broken bit of hairpin and showed it to Paul.

'Then, of course, I realized what was happening, and found the marks on the door-frame, too.'

Paul couldn't help himself; he began to laugh. He had been so stupid.

Chapter 17   A Little Operation

When he quietened down she asked: 'How many times did you leave the room?'

The knife. Oh, no, the knife.

'Twice. No, three times. I had to get some water yesterday. But I wasn't trying to escape, Annie. I'm writing a book.'

'You didn't try the telephone, I suppose, or investigate the locks. No, you were such a good little boy.'

'Of course I did.' He was beginning to wish she would go away. The drug was making him partly tell the truth, but he also badly wanted to sleep.

'How many times did you go out?'

'I *told* you. Three times.'

'How many times?' Her voice was rising. *'Tell the truth.'*

'I *am* telling the truth. Three times!'

'You're treating me like a fool.'

'Annie, I swear –' jurar   idiota, engañar

'Oh, yes, you swear. People who tell lies love to swear. Let me tell you, Mister Clever. I stretched hairs all over the place – upstairs, downstairs, out in the barn – and a lot of them have gone.'

Annie, how could I have gone upstairs? How could I have gone outside to the barn? But she didn't give him time to protest; she went straight on.

'So you tell me that you left the room only three times, Mister Clever, and I'll tell you that you're the fool, not me. *How many times?*'

'Three.'

'Once for medicine.'

'Yes.'

'Once for food.'

'Yes.'

'And once for water.'

'Yes. Yes, I told you.'

She reached into her pocket again and brought out the butcher's knife.

'I looked under your mattress just before I gave you the injection for your operation, and see what I found.'

What did she mean by 'operation'? He was suddenly sure that she intended to use the knife on him.

'But you didn't get it out of the kitchen, did you? You only went for medicine, food and water. The knife must have flown here all by itself. What kind of fool do you think I am, Paul? *How many times?*'

'All right, all right. I got the knife when I went for water. But, Annie, what did you mean by "operation"?'

'I think you went seven times,' she said.

'Yes, if that's what you want to hear, I left the room seven times,' Paul said. He was angry now, because he was frightened.

54

Then she started to speak softly and he began to drift, almost into sleep.

'Do you know what the British used to do to workers in their diamond mines who tried to escape, Paul?'

'They killed them, I suppose,' he said, still with his eyes closed.

'Oh, no,' she replied. 'That would be like throwing away a whole car just because some little thing went wrong. No, they still needed them for the mines, so they just made sure that they couldn't run away again. They performed a little operation, Paul, and that's what I'm going to do to you. It's for your own good. Please try to remember that.'

The ice-cold wind of fear blew over Paul's body and his eyes flew open. She got up from the bed and pulled back the blankets so that his legs and feet were uncovered.

'No,' he said. 'No...Annie...whatever it is you're planning, we can talk about it, can't we? Please ...you don't have to...'

She bent over and picked up some things from the floor. When she straightened up she was holding an axe in one hand and a blowlamp in the other. The blade of the axe shone dully. She bent down again and picked up the box of matches and a bottle of dark liquid.

'Annie, no!' he screamed. *'Annie, I'll stay here, I promise. I won't even get out of bed. I'll do whatever you say!'*

'It's all right,' she said, and her face now had that blank look. Some part of his mind which was not filled with fear knew that when this was over she would remember hardly anything at all about it. This was the woman who graduated in 1966 and now, in 1987, told him that she had been a nurse for only ten years. She probably hardly remembered killing all those babies. He suddenly knew that this was the axe she had used on Pomeroy.

He continued to scream. He tried to turn over, as if he could get away from her, but his broken legs and drugged body refused to obey.

Annie poured some of the liquid on to his left ankle and some more on to the blade of the axe. The smell reminded Paul of doctors' offices in his childhood.

'There won't be much pain, Paul. It won't be bad.'

'Annie Annie oh Annie please no please don't Annie I swear to you I'll be good I swear to God I'll be good please give me a chance to be good ANNIE PLEASE LET ME BE GOOD –'

'Just a little pain, Paul, and then this unpleasant matter will be behind us.'

She threw the empty bottle over her shoulder, her face completely blank now. She seized the axe in both hands and moved her feet so that she was standing firmly on the floor.

'ANNIE OH PLEASE PLEASE DON'T HURT ME!'

'Don't worry,' she said, and her eyes were gentle. 'I'm a nurse.'

The axe whistled through the air and buried itself in Paul Sheldon's left leg just above the ankle. Pain exploded in his body. Blood splashed her face and the wall. He heard the blade rub against the bone as she pulled it free. He looked down and saw his toes moving. Then he saw her raising the axe again; drops of blood were falling off it. Her hair was hanging loosely around her blank, calm face.

He tried to pull back in spite of the pain, but he realized that, although his leg was moving, his foot wasn't. All he was doing was widening the cut, making it open like a mouth. He realized that his foot was joined to his leg by only a little flesh – and then the axe whistled down again. It cut through his leg and sank deep into the mattress.

Annie pulled the axe out of the mattress and threw it on to the ground. She picked up the blowlamp and lit it with a match.

'There isn't time to sew all this up,' she explained. 'You're losing blood too fast.' She turned the flame on to the stump of his leg. Fresh pain seized Paul's body. Sweet-smelling smoke drifted up to his nose.

She seized the axe in both hands and moved her feet so that she was standing firmly on the floor.

'Nearly finished,' she said. The blankets were burning now. Annie bent down again and picked up the yellow bucket. She poured water over the flames. Paul screamed again.

Annie stood and looked at him. 'You'll be all right,' she said. Her eyes seemed to move round the room aimlessly. It was a relief for her to notice something on the floor. 'I'll just get rid of the rubbish,' she said.

She picked up Paul's foot. The toes were still moving. She started to walk out of the room and then turned and said, 'Don't blame me for this. It was your own fault.'

Paul dived into the cloud, hoping that it would bring death this time, not just unconsciousness. He dimly heard himself screaming and smelled his burned flesh. As his thoughts faded, he thought: *Dragon Lady! Kill you! Dragon Lady! Kill you!*

Then there was nothing except nothing.

Chapter 18   Happy Birthday

Some weeks later, on the first day of summer, the old typewriter lost its 't' as well. Paul thought: *I am going to complain. I am not just going to* ask *for a new typewriter, I am going to* demand *one. I know she can afford it.*

Of course he would ask Annie for nothing and certainly would not demand. Once there had been a man who would at least have *asked*. That man had been in much more pain, but he still would have asked.

He had been that man and he supposed he ought to be ashamed, but *that* man had two big advantages over this one: *that* man had two feet . . . and two thumbs.

Paul sat quietly for a moment, staring at the typewriter, and then simply continued to type. It was better that way – better not to ask, better not to protest. Annie had become too strange. He had known

58

for a long time what she was *capable* of doing; but these days he couldn't guess what would make her do it.

So he continued to work, but after five or six pages the typewriter lost the letter 'e', the most common letter in the English language. Paul could hardly believe it. *What shall I do now?* he thought, but of course the answer was obvious. He would write by hand.

But not now. The hole in the paper – the hole through which Misery and Ian and Geoffrey lived – had closed with a crash.

He listened to the sound of the lawnmower outside. Annie had a lawnmower which was like a small tractor. As soon as he thought of Annie he remembered the axe rising and falling, her calm face splashed with his blood. He remembered every word she had spoken, every word he had screamed, every sound and movement.

Why couldn't he forget? You're supposed to forget, aren't you? People who have car crashes forget what happened and are surprised when they wake up in hospital. So why couldn't *he* forget?

Because writers remember everything, Paul, especially the things that hurt. If you point to a writer's scars, he will tell you the story of every small one. From the big ones you get novels.

Perhaps memory would heal him. But why should he bother to remember? She had done it, and all the time between then and now had been painful and boring, except when he had worked on his silly book in order to escape feeling pain and being bored. There was no point in remembering, no point in anything.

But there was. The point was Misery, because Misery kept him alive. As long as he was writing the book Annie let him live. But he wasn't writing the book for Annie; he wasn't writing the book to please Annie, but to escape from her. And then he realized that as long as he was writing the book he let *himself* live too. He could have died that day, the day of the axe, but he didn't – and he didn't because he wanted to finish the book! It wasn't just Annie: *he* wanted to know what happened too.

He was a writer, and writers remember everything, so he let himself remember.

This time the cloud had been darker, thicker, smoother. There was a feeling not of floating but of sinking. Sometimes thoughts came and sometimes, dimly, he heard Annie's voice. She sounded afraid: 'Drink this, Paul . . . you've *got* to!'

How close had he come to sinking on the day of the axe? He didn't know, but he felt almost no pain during the week after the 'operation', which seemed to show that he was close to death. So did the fear in Annie's voice.

He had lain there, hardly breathing. And what brought him out of it, out of the cloud, was Misery. The book was unfinished. Paul didn't know what the ending was going to be and he didn't know how some of the details fitted together. He never knew everything about the novels he wrote; he always waited to find out as eagerly as any reader. And this meant that there were unfinished questions in his mind. Those questions worried him – and so he came out of the cloud to find out what would happen to Misery. He chose to live.

She didn't want to let him return to work – not at first. He could see in her eyes that she had been frightened and was still uncertain. She had come closer to killing him than she had intended. She was taking extraordinary care of him – changing the bandages on his stump every eight hours, washing him down.

While he was unconscious she also filled in all the 'n's in the typescript. It was as if she was saying to him: *You can't think that I'm cruel to you, Paul, when I look after you so well and even write all those 'n's.*

He was finally able to persuade her that returning to work would help him, not harm him. And she too wanted urgently to know what was going to happen in the book. This was the one thing the two of them in that house shared: this crazy interest in Misery's adventures.

He had always known he could write *good* books – books like *Fast Cars* – and that the Misery books were just a way of making money. But why had he written so many Misery books? He had plenty of money. It was – and he almost hated to admit it to himself – because they gave him something his other books did not: the Misery books gave him the excitement of needing to know what would happen in the adventure. He shared this with his millions of readers, who eagerly turned the pages; he shared this with Annie. It was crazy. He was going to die anyway; she was going to kill him. But he still had to write. It was more than just a way of escaping the cruel reality of his situation: he had to find out how the story would end. And it *was* the best Misery novel he had ever written, just as Annie had said it would be.

At first, sitting and typing were extremely painful and he could work only for short periods of time. The pain in his stump would burst into flame and it would flash through his body. But gradually he was able to work more, and he was right: he did regain some strength. He would never be the man he had been in the past, but he did recover some health.

One day Annie had come in with some ice-cream. Although he didn't like it, he forced himself to eat it for fear of angering her. There was something about her that day which worried him. It was as if she was pretending to be cheerful. And then she came out with it – the reason for the gift of the ice-cream. She put her spoon down, wiped her chin with the back of her hand and said pleasantly: 'Tell me the rest.'

Paul put his own spoon down. 'I beg your pardon?'

'Tell me the rest of the story. I can't wait.'

He ought to have guessed that this would happen. 'I can't do that,' he said.

Her face had darkened immediately. 'Why not?'

'Because I'm a bad storyteller.'

She ate the rest of her ice-cream in five huge mouthfuls. Paul's teeth ached just from watching her. Then she put her dish down and looked at him angrily, not as if he was the great Paul Sheldon, her hero, but as if he was someone who had dared to *criticize* the great Paul Sheldon.

'If you're a bad storyteller, how have you written so many books – books which have sold millions and millions of copies?'

'I didn't say I was a bad story-*writer*. I think I'm good at that, in fact. But I'm a useless story-*teller*.'

'You're just making up a stupid excuse.' Now her hands were closed into fists, tight against the sides of her skirt. He found that he didn't really care that she was angry. He was frightened of being hurt again, but part of him didn't care what happened.

'It's not an excuse,' he said. 'The two things are quite different. People who tell stories usually can't write stories. If you think writers are any good at talking you ought to watch some poor fool of a novelist being interviewed on TV. Apart from that, I never quite know what the ending of one of my stories is going to be. I only really know when I've written it.'

'Well, I don't want to wait,' she said like a spoiled child. 'I brought you some nice ice-cream, and at least you could tell me a *few* things. All right, you needn't tell me the whole story, but . . .'

Annie fired some questions at Paul about the book, but Paul shook his head to show that he wouldn't tell.

She became even blacker, but her voice was soft. 'You're making me very angry. You know that, don't you, Paul?'

'Of course I know it, but I can't help it.'

'I could *make* you tell,' she said, but she knew she couldn't. She could hurt him so that he said a lot of things, but she couldn't make him tell a story whose ending he didn't know. The blackness was beginning to disappear from her face. She was fighting an impossible fight.

'Annie, I'm not being selfish. I'm not telling you because I really want you to like the story. If I try to tell you it'll come out wrong, and then you won't like it and you won't want the book any more.'
And then what will happen to me?

'But does Hezekiah really know about Misery's father? You could at least tell me that.'

'Do you want the novel or do you want a bedtime story?' he asked.

'Don't you dare be so sarcastic with me!' she shouted.

'Then don't pretend that you don't understand what I'm saying,' he shouted back.

She pulled back from him in surprise and the last of the blackness disappeared from her face.

He had skated on thin ice that time. He had expected her to get angry or depressed, but instead they had returned to the old routine: Paul wrote and Annie read what he wrote each day and filled in the missing letters. But in fact he *had* made her angry. Her anger stayed just below the surface, however, so he was never aware of it – at least not until a week later, when he had complained about the typewriter, about the missing 'n'.

'Well, if it bothers you so much I'll have to give you something to stop you thinking about that stupid "n",' Annie said. She left the room and he heard her in the kitchen, looking for something in the drawers. She was cursing in her peculiar way about 'stupid' this and 'dirty' that.

Ten minutes later she came in with the syringe, the bottle of dark liquid and an electric knife. Paul immediately began to scream. Anne tested the knife and Paul again begged and promised to be good. He twisted and turned in his wheelchair.

'Stay still,' she ordered, 'or I'll use this knife on your throat.' He stayed still while she poured the liquid on his thumb and on the blade of the knife. She switched the knife on and bent over him, concentrating on her work. As the blade hit into the flesh between his thumb and finger she told him – in a voice which suggested that this was going to hurt her more than it was going to hurt him – that she loved him.

She had cut his thumb off in the morning, and then that night she had hurried into his room, carrying a cake and singing 'Happy Birthday to You'. It wasn't his birthday. There were candles all over the cake, in no order. There, in the exact centre of the cake, like an extra big candle, had been his thumb – his now-grey thumb – with the nail a little rough because he sometimes chewed it when he was thinking. *If you promise to be good*, she had told him, *you can have a piece of cake, but you won't have to eat any of the special candle.* So he had promised to be good – and so he wasn't going to complain that the typewriter had now lost its 't' and its 'e' as well.

Paul was nearly asleep, sitting in his wheelchair by the window, listening to the steady sound of the lawnmower's engine and remembering. He jumped and wondered what had woken him up. At first he didn't believe what he saw out of the window coming into Annie's farm; he thought he must really be asleep.

It was a police car.

Chapter 19   Another Visitor

I won't scream!

He sat at the window, totally awake now, totally aware that the police car he was seeing was as real as his left foot had once been.

Scream, you fool, scream!

He wanted to, but he could hear Annie's voice saying, *Don't you dare scream.* When he tried to scream his voice dried up and his mind was filled with pictures of the axe and the electric knife. He remembered the sounds: he remembered screaming *then*, but not to gain attention from anyone.

64

He tried again to open his mouth – and failed; he tried to raise his hands – and failed. A faint, low sound broke out from between his lips, and his hands moved lightly on the sides of the typewriter, but that was all he could do. Nothing which had happened in the past – except perhaps for the moment when he had realized that, although his left leg was moving, his foot stayed still – was as terrible as the hell of not being able to move. In real time it didn't last long – perhaps five seconds – but inside Paul Sheldon's head it seemed to go on for years.

He could escape! All he had to do was break the window and scream: *Help me! Help me! Save me from Annie! Save me from the Dragon Lady!* But at the same time another voice was screaming: *I'll be good, Annie! I won't scream! I promise! Don't cut off any more of me!* He knew he was frightened of her, but he hadn't realized until now the extent of his fear.

His mind told him that he was going to die anyway. As soon as he had finished the book she was going to kill him. So if he screamed, and if the policeman saw him, and if that made Annie kill him now, what was the difference? Perhaps two weeks of life. *There's not much to lose, then, and a lot to win. So scream, Paul, scream! What's the matter with you? Are you already dead?*

The policeman got out of the car. He was young – about twenty-three years old – and was wearing very dark glasses, which completely hid his eyes and reflected the light like a mirror. He paused, just twenty metres away from Paul's window, and adjusted his jacket.

Scream! Don't scream. *Scream and you're dead.* I'm not dead yet. I'M NOT DEAD YET! *Scream, you coward!*

Paul forced his lips open, sucked air into his lungs and closed his eyes. He had no idea what was going to come out of his mouth. Was anything going to come out?

'*DRAGON!*' Paul screamed. '*DRAGON LADY!*'

Now his eyes opened wide. The policeman was looking towards

the house. Paul could not see his eyes, but he seemed to have heard something.

Paul looked down at the table. Next to the typewriter was a heavy glass vase, which had been empty for weeks. He seized it and threw it at the window. The glass broke and fell on to the ground outside. Paul thought it was the best sound he had ever heard. It made his tongue free.

'I'm here! Help me! Watch out for the woman! She's crazy!'

The policeman looked straight at Paul. His mouth dropped open. He reached into his pocket and brought out something which could only be a picture. He looked at it and then walked a few steps closer. Then he spoke the only four words Paul ever heard him say, the last four words *anyone* ever heard him say. After that he would make a few sounds, but no real words.

'Oh, God!' the policeman exclaimed. 'It's you!'

Paul had been staring at the policeman, so he didn't see Annie until it was too late. She was still riding the lawnmower, so that she seemed to be half human, half something else. For a moment Paul's mind saw her as an actual dragon. Her face was pulled into an expression of extreme hatred and anger. In one hand she was carrying a wooden cross.

The cross had marked the grave of one of the cows that had died while Annie was away in her Laughing Place. When the ground had become soft in the spring, Paul had watched Annie burying the rotten cows. It had taken her most of the day to dig the holes in the ground. Then she dragged the bodies out of the barn with her car and dropped them into the holes. After she had filled the holes in again she solemnly planted crosses on the piles of earth and said some prayers.

Now she was riding towards the policeman with the sharp end of the cross pointing towards his back.

'Behind you! Look out!' Paul shouted. He knew that it was too late, but he shouted anyway.

With a thin cry Annie stabbed the cross into the policeman's back.

'AG!' said the policeman, and took a few steps forward. He bent his back and reached both hands over his shoulder. He looked to Paul like a man who was trying to scratch his back.

In the meantime Annie got off the lawnmower and stood watching the policeman. Now she rushed forward and pulled the cross out of his back. He turned towards her, reaching for his gun, and she drove the cross into his stomach.

'OG!' said the policeman this time, and fell on to his knees, holding his stomach.

Annie pulled the cross free again and drove it into the policeman's back, between his shoulders. The first two blows had perhaps not gone deep enough to kill him, but this time the wooden post went at least five centimetres into the kneeling policeman's back. He fell face down on to the ground.

'THERE!' Annie cried, standing over the man and pulling the cross out again. 'HOW DO YOU LIKE THAT, YOU DIRTY BIRD!'

'Annie, stop it!' Paul shouted.

She looked at him. Her dark eyes shone like coins and she was grinning the grin of the madman who has stopped controlling himself at all. Then she looked down at the policeman again.

'THERE!' she cried, and stabbed the cross into his back again – and then into his neck, and then into his thigh and his hand and into his back again. She screamed 'THERE!' every time she brought the cross down. At last the cross broke.

Annie threw the bloody and broken cross away as if it no longer interested her and walked away from the policeman's body.

Paul was sure that she would come and kill him next. At least, if she did intend to hurt him, he hoped that she would kill him rather than cut any more pieces off his body.

Then he saw the policeman move. *He was still alive!*

The policeman raised his head off the ground. His glasses had fallen off and Paul could see his eyes. He was very young – young and hurt and frightened. He managed to get up on to his hands and knees, but then he fell forward. He got up again and began to crawl towards his car. He got about half of the way when he fell over. He struggled up again. Paul could see the bloody marks spreading on his uniform.

Suddenly the sound of the lawnmower was louder.

'Look out!' Paul screamed. *'She's coming back!'*

The policeman turned his head with a look of alarm on his face. He reached for his gun. *That's right!* thought Paul. He got his gun out.

'SHOOT HER!' Paul screamed.

But instead of shooting her the policeman's wounded hand dropped the gun. He reached out his hand for it. Annie pulled the wheel of the lawnmower-tractor around and ran over the reaching hand and arm. The young man in the policeman's uniform screamed in pain. Blood stained the grass.

Annie pulled the lawnmower around again and her eyes fell for a moment on Paul. Paul was sure it was his turn next. First the policeman, then him.

When the policeman saw the lawnmower coming for him again, he tried to crawl under the car. But he was too far away and he didn't even get close. Annie drove the tractor as fast as she could over his head.

Paul turned away and was violently sick on the floor.

Chapter 20   Rats in the Cellar

He opened his eyes again only when he heard the sound of Annie's key in the lock of the outside door. The door to his room was open and he watched her coming down the hall in her boots and her man's shirt, which was splashed with blood. He wanted to say something, to tell her not to cut anything else off his body because he would die – he would *make* himself die; but no real sounds came out of his mouth.

'I'll come to you later,' she said. She closed his door and locked it; she had fitted a new Kreig lock on it.

He turned his head and looked dully out of the window. He could see only the lower half of the policeman's body, since his head was still under the lawnmower. The lawnmower was nearly on its side, up against the police car. It was supposed to cut grass, not people's heads, so it had fallen over – but the accident had unfortunately not hurt Annie.

Paul felt terribly sorry for the young man, but was surprised to find another feeling mixed in with the sorrow. He recognized the feeling as envy. The policeman would never go home to his wife and children if he had them, but he had escaped Annie Wilkes.

Annie came round the corner of the house. She grabbed the policeman's bloody hand and pulled him down to the barn. She drove the police car into the barn and then she drove the lawnmower closer to the barn. There was blood all over the lawnmower.

She fetched a large plastic bag and began to tidy up. She whistled while she picked up pieces of uniform, the gun and the broken cross, and her face was calm and clear. She took the bag to the barn doors and threw it inside.

She came back to the front of the house and stopped outside Paul's window. She picked up the vase and passed it to him politely through the broken window.

'Here you are, Paul,' she said. 'I'll clean up the little pieces of glass later.'

For a second he thought of bringing the heavy vase down on to the back of her head as she bent over. But then he thought what she would do to him if he failed to kill her – and the vase was not heavy enough for him to be sure that he would kill her with it.

She looked up at him through the hole in the window. 'I didn't kill him, you know,' she said. '*You* killed him. If you had kept your mouth shut he would have left here safely. He'd be alive now and there would be none of this horrible mess to clean up.'

'Yes,' said Paul. 'And what about me?'

'I don't know what you mean.'

'He had my picture,' Paul said. 'You picked it up just now and put it in your pocket. You know what that means. If a policeman had my picture, then my car has been found. They're looking for me, Annie, and you know it. Why do you think the policeman was here?'

'I don't know what you're talking about,' said Annie. But Paul could see from her face that she did. The usual madness was there, but something else – pure evil was there too. 'And I don't have time to talk about it now,' she went on. 'Can't you see I'm busy?'

By the evening she had finished cleaning up. There was no sign of blood anywhere outside. She had washed down the lawnmower too – but Paul noticed that she forgot to clean underneath it. She often seemed to forget things if they were not directly in front of her face. Annie's mind was like the lawnmower, Paul thought – clean on the outside but disgusting underneath.

After she had finished outside she came into the house, and Paul heard her taking some things down to the basement. When her key turned in the lock on his door he thought: *This is it. She's got the axe and she's coming to get me.*

The door opened and Annie stood there. She had changed into clean clothes, too. When she came in he was surprised to find that he could talk to her quite calmly. He said, 'Go on, then. Kill me, Annie, if that's what you've come to do. But please don't cut anything else off me.'

'I'm not going to kill you, Paul,' she replied. 'I *should* kill you, but with a little luck I won't have to.'

She pushed him in his wheelchair across the room and down the hall. She opened the kitchen door and rolled him into there. The door to the cellar was open and he could smell the damp. She pushed the wheelchair to the edge of the stairs down to the cellar.

Spiders down there, he thought. *Mice down there. Rats down there!*

'No, Annie,' he said. 'I'm not going down there.'

'Yes, you are,' she said. 'The only question is: are you going down there on my back or shall I just let you fall out of the wheelchair down those stairs? I'll give you five seconds to decide.'

'On your back,' he said straight away.

'Very sensible,' she said. She stood on the stairs in front of him so that he could put his arms round her neck. 'Don't do anything stupid, Paul. Don't try to choke me. I'm very strong, as you know. I'll throw you to the ground and you'll break your back.'

She lifted him easily out of his chair. His twisted, ugly legs hung down at her sides. She had taken the splints off some weeks ago. The left leg was now shorter than the right one by about ten centimetres. He had tried standing on the right leg by itself and he could do so, but only for a few minutes before the pain became too great.

She carried him down the stairs. She had put a thin mattress on the floor, some food and water and some medicine. She let him get off her back and on to the mattress.

When she turned round she was holding a syringe.

'No,' he said as soon as he saw it. 'No, no!'

Chapter 21   Annie's Plan

'You must think I'm in a really bad mood,' Annie said. 'I wish you'd relax, Paul. I'm not going to give you an injection. I'm leaving the syringe here with you, because it's damp down here and your legs might ache quite badly before I get back. Now, we have to talk.'

She settled down and told him her plan. She was drinking constantly from plastic bottles of Pepsi-Cola. She explained that she needed a lot of sugar at the moment.

'Listen to me. We're going to be all right if it gets dark before anyone comes to check on that policeman. It'll be dark in about an hour and a half. If someone comes sooner, there's this,' she said. She reached into her bag and pulled out the policeman's gun. 'First I kill whoever comes, then you, then me.'

Once it was dark, she said, she was going to drive the police car up to her Laughing Place, with her husband's old motor bike in the back. She could hide the car up there and it wouldn't be found for months.

'I'd take you with me, because you've shown that you can be a real nuisance,' she said, 'but I couldn't bring you back on the bike. It'll be hard enough driving on those mountain paths by myself. I might fall off and break my neck!'

She laughed at her joke, but Paul said, 'And then what would happen to me?'

'Don't worry so much, Paul, you'd be fine,' she replied, but he knew he wouldn't. He would die like a dog down here in the damp basement and make a meal for the rats. There was a Kreig lock on the cellar door by now and the stairs were steep anyway. There were tiny windows, high up one wall, but they were covered in dirt.

'So I'm going to put him in his car and take him up to my Laughing Place and bury him there – him and his . . . you know . . . his *bits* – in the woods.'

Paul said nothing. He just remembered the cows complaining from the barn and then becoming silent. Annie had left them to die and he hoped she wasn't going to forget him too.

'I just hope nobody comes to the house while I'm away. I don't *think* they'd hear you down here even if they came right up to the house. But I'm going to put a chain across the gate from the road and hang a note on the chain saying that I've gone away for a few days. That might stop them coming up to the house.'

Annie was not taking any chances, Paul realized. She was playing 'Can You?' in real life, while he could only play it when he was writing books.

'I should be back by midday tomorrow,' she continued. 'I don't expect the police will come before then. They *will* come, of course; I know that. But I don't think they'll come asking questions before then. They'll just drive along the roads, looking for his car. So if I'm back by midday I'll have you back in your room before they come. I'll even let you watch me talk to them, if you promise to be good. I say "them" because I think two of them will come, don't you?'

Paul agreed.

'But I can handle two, if I need to.' She patted the handbag which held the policeman's gun. 'I want you to remember that young man's gun while you watch me talk to them, Paul. I want you to remember that it's going to be in here all the time I'm talking to them, whenever they come – tomorrow or the day after or whenever. You can see them, but if they see you – either by accident or because you do something stupid like you did today – if that happens I'm going to take the gun out of the bag and start shooting. And remember: you're already responsible for one policeman's death.'

'Nonsense,' said Paul, knowing that she would hurt him for saying it.

But she didn't. She just smiled her calm, mother-knows-best smile.

'Maybe you don't care for them, Paul. Maybe you don't care if you kill two more people. But if I have to kill those two policeman, I'll have to kill you and me as well, and I think you still care for yourself.'

'Not really, Annie,' Paul said. 'I don't really mind leaving this life any more.'

'Oh, yes, I've heard that before,' she said. 'But as soon as you switch off their medical equipment or pick up the pillow to put it on their faces, then they struggle and try to cry out.'

But you never let that stop you, did you, Annie?

'Anyway, I just wanted to tell you,' she said. 'If you really don't care, then when they come you can shout to them. When they come I'll meet them and they'll ask me about the young policeman. "Yes," I'll say, "he was here yesterday. He showed me a picture of Paul Sheldon. I told him I hadn't seen him and then he went away." They'll be surprised. "How can you be sure that you've never seen Paul Sheldon?" they'll ask. "He disappeared last winter." I'll tell them that Paul Sheldon is my favourite author, so I'd remember seeing him. I have to say that, Paul. Do you remember?'

He remembered. He remembered a photograph in her album. In the picture Annie was sitting in prison while she was waiting for the jury to return to court and pronounce her guilty or innocent. Under the picture was written: *Miserable? Not the Dragon Lady. Annie sits quietly and reads while she waits for the jury.* And in the picture Annie was holding up her book so that everyone could see she was reading the latest Misery novel.

'So,' Annie went on, 'I'll say that the young policeman wrote all this down in his book and said thank you. I'll say that I invited him in for a cup of coffee. He refused, but he accepted a bottle of cold Pepsi, because the day was so hot.' She held up an empty bottle of Pepsi. 'I'm going to stop and throw this in a ditch three or four kilometres up the road,' she said. 'But first I'll put his fingers all over it, of course.'

She smiled at him – a dry smile, with no humour in it.

'They'll find the bottle, and then they'll know that he went past my house – or they'll *think* they know, which is just as good, isn't it? They'll search for him for a while, but then they'll come back. Oh, yes, they'll come back, because I'm the Dragon Lady. I'm the only crazy one in the area, so they'll come back, and they'll come into the house this time. But they'll believe me at first – that's the point. So we'll have some time, Paul. Maybe as much as a week.' She looked at him coolly. 'You're going to have to write faster, Paul.'

Chapter 22   A Sudden Idea

Darkness fell and no police came. Annie spent the time putting new glass in Paul's window and picking up the broken pieces, so that when they came they would see nothing suspicious. *Unless they look under the lawnmower*, thought Paul. But why would they do that?

Before she left, Paul asked her to bring him some paper so that he could continue writing the book while she was away. He needed the drug of writing. She shook her head regretfully.

'I can't do that, Paul. I'd have to leave the light on down here and someone might see the light through the windows. And if I give you a torch or a candle you might try to shine it through the windows.'

He thought of being left alone down here in the cellar in the dark, and his skin felt cold. He thought of the rats hiding in their holes in the walls, waiting for darkness so that they could come out. He wondered whether they could smell his fear.

'Don't leave me in the dark, Annie. The *rats*.'

'I have to. Don't be such a baby. I've got to go now. If you need an injection, push the syringe into your leg. Don't worry about the rats, Paul. They'll probably recognize that you're a rat too.' She laughed at her joke and continued laughing all the way up the stairs.

When she closed the door to the kitchen it became totally black. He could hear her drive away. He imagined that she was still laughing. In the darkness his imagination soon began to play games with his mind. He imagined that the young policeman came to life in the

Suddenly an idea burst into his mind like a bright light. He looked at the idea from all directions and it still seemed sweet.

barn and crawled up to the house; he imagined that he came through the wall into the cellar. He felt one of the policeman's cold, dead fingers touch his cheek – but it was only a large spider and Paul realized that he had been dreaming.

His legs were painful now and he gave himself an injection. Then he fell properly asleep, and, when he woke up, the dull light of early morning was filling the cellar. He saw a huge rat sitting in the plate of food which Annie had left, eating cheese. He screamed and the rat ran away.

He took some Novril and looked round the cellar. He saw the barbecue stove with all its tools and equipment, and remembered burning *Fast Cars* . . . and suddenly an idea burst into his mind like a bright light. He looked at the idea from all directions and it still seemed sweet. At last he had a plan which might be successful. He fell asleep again with a smile on his face, dreaming about the next pages he would write.

Annie came back in the middle of the afternoon. She was silent, but seemed tired rather than depressed. Paul asked her if everything had gone all right and she nodded.

'Do you want another injection, Paul?' she asked. 'Your legs must be hurting a lot by now.'

It was true. The damp had made his legs hurt terribly, but he wanted her out of the cellar as quickly as possible, so he told her he was OK. When he got on to her back for the ride up the stairs he had to bite his lips to stop himself shouting in pain. At the bottom of the stairs she paused, and he hoped . . . prayed . . . that she would not notice the missing can of barbecue fuel; he had pushed it down the back of his trousers.

She didn't seem to notice anything. When he was back in his room he said, 'I think I would like that injection now, Annie.'

She looked at his face, which was covered in sweat from the pain, and then nodded.

As soon as she left the room to fetch the medicine he pushed the small, flat fuel can under the mattress. He hadn't hidden anything there since the knife, so he didn't expect her suddenly to look there. Anyway, he wasn't planning to leave it there for long.

After she had given him the injection she said she was going to sleep. 'If a car comes I'll hear it,' she said. 'I'll leave your wheelchair next to your bed so that you can get up and work if you want to.'

'I probably will, later,' he said. 'There isn't much time now, is there, Annie?'

'No, there isn't, Paul. I'm glad you understand that.'

'Annie,' he said innocently. 'Since I'm getting to the end of the book, I wonder if you'd do something for me.'

'What?'

'Please don't read any more. When I've finished it all, then you can read all the last chapters. Will you do that? It'll make it more exciting for you.'

'Yes, thank you, Paul. Yes. I'll do that.'

Four hours later she was still asleep. He had heard her go to bed upstairs at four o'clock and had heard nothing since then. He felt safe. He got into his wheelchair as quietly as possible and rolled himself over to his table by the window. Not long ago he had discovered a loose board in the floor. Under the board was a narrow space. The space was just big enough for the can of fuel. Paul sighed in relief when the board was back in position. He gently blew the dust back over the board so that it looked the same as all the surrounding boards. He wrote some pages of the book and then went back to bed and slept peacefully.

Chapter 23   More Visitors

Next day the police came. Paul heard the car and then heard Annie running down the corridor to his room. He put the pencil carefully down on the paper he was covering in his untidy handwriting.

Annie ran into the room. 'Get out of sight.' Her face was tight. She already had the bag with the gun around her shoulder. 'Get out of s–' She paused and saw that he had already rolled the wheelchair away from the window. 'Are you going to be good, Paul?'

'Yes,' he said.

Her eyes searched his face. 'I'm going to trust you,' she said.

She left the room and went outside to meet the policemen. Paul moved so that he could see out of the window without being seen himself.

The policeman who had come three days ago had been hardly more than a child; these two were completely different. One was in uniform and one was a detective. Both were old and experienced. The detective looked tired, but his eyes were watching everything. The other policeman was large and obviously extremely strong.

They got out of the car and stood close to Annie while they asked her some questions which Paul could not hear. He thought about breaking the window again, but two things stopped him. First, the detective had his coat buttoned, so he would not be able to get his gun quickly. If he had noticed that, then Annie certainly had too. She would shoot the other policeman first and then the detective. The second thing that stopped him was his desire for revenge. The police would only put Annie in prison. He himself could hurt her, and he wanted to do that.

The big policeman pointed towards the house and Annie led them in through the kitchen door. Paul could now hear the conversation. The policemen were asking her about Officer Kushner, which was the young man's name, and Annie was telling them her story. She sounded very calm, but Paul thought he noticed some signs of suspicion in the policemen's voices.

They left and Annie came into Paul's room. She stared at him for a full minute.

'Why didn't you shout?' she asked. She couldn't understand it. In her world everyone was against her, so why hadn't he shouted?

'Because I want to finish the book,' he said. 'Because I want to finish it for you, Annie.'

She looked at him uncertainly, wanting to believe. Finally she did believe him. It was the truth, anyway.

Three days later the local TV news programme sent a crew to Annie's farm. Annie refused to let them on to her land and fired a shot into the air to warn them off. Afterwards she said, 'You know what they want, Paul? This is what they want.' She scratched her forehead viciously with her fingernails, so that blood flowed down her face.

'Annie, stop it!'

'This is what they want too.' She hit herself on the cheek. 'And this.' She hit her other cheek, hard.

'STOP IT!' he screamed.

'It's what they want!' she screamed back. She pressed her hands against the wounds on her forehead and then held her hands out to him so that he could see the blood. Then she left the room and he took up his pencil and fell through the hole in the paper again.

The next clay two different policemen came, to take a statement from her. She told them the story about Kushner and the Pepsi-Cola bottle. They asked her about the scratches on her forehead. 'How did you get those?'

'I had a bad dream last night.'

'What?'

'I dreamed that people remembered me after all this time and started coming out here again,' Annie said.

When they had gone Annie came into his room. Her face was distant and she looked ill. 'How much longer, Paul? When will you finish the book?'

'Tomorrow,' he said.

'Next time they'll have permission to search the house,' she said, and left before he could reply. It didn't take him long to get back to work. His swollen fingers were still locked tightly on to the pencil. Now more than ever he needed to finish the book.

Chapter 24   A Final Cigarette

She woke him up the next morning with his breakfast. 'It's a very special day, Paul, isn't it?'

'Yes.'

She bent over and kissed him. 'I love you, Paul. Can I start reading it now?'

'No, Annie, you must wait. It's important that you wait.'

But she had gone blank again. He waited patiently for her to return and then repeated his answer, so that this time she would hear it.

'I'll leave you now,' she said. 'But you'll call me when you've finished the book, won't you? I've got some champagne in the fridge. I don't know much about wine and things, but the man at the shop said it was the best. I want us to have the best, Paul.'

'That sounds lovely, Annie. But there is one other thing you could do for me, to make it special.'

'What's that?'

'I'd really like a cigarette – just one, when I finish. There were some cigarettes in my suitcase.'

'But cigarettes are bad for you.'

'Annie, do you really think I have to worry about dying from smoking now? Do you really think that?'

She didn't say anything.

'I just want one cigarette. I've always relaxed with a cigarette immediately after finishing a book.'

'All right,' she said. 'But long before the champagne. I don't want to drink expensive champagne with my favourite author with all that dirty smoke in the air.'

81

She left and a while later came back with a single cigarette and a box of matches – with only one match in it. She put them quietly on the table and crept out of the room, not wanting to disturb her favourite author.

Several hours later Paul wrote the two words which every author loves and hates most: THE END. He sat back in satisfaction.

Then he bent over to the loose board in the floor.

Chapter 25 'You Can't Burn Misery'

He called her five minutes later. He heard her heavy steps coming down the stairs. The room smelled strongly of fuel.

She stopped at the end of the hall and shouted out, 'Paul, are you *really* finished?'

Paul looked at the huge pile of paper in front of him on the table. It was wet with fuel.

'Well,' he shouted back, 'I did the best I could, Annie.'

'I can hardly believe it!' she said. 'After all this time! I'm so excited. I'll go and get the champagne. I won't be a minute!' She sounded like a little girl.

He heard her crossing the kitchen floor. The fridge door squeaked open and then shut again. She started down the hall.

He reached for the box of matches and took out the single match. He scratched it against the side, but it didn't light. She was nearly at his door. The third time, the match lit and he watched the yellow flame carefully.

'I just hope this –'

She stopped. Paul was holding the burning match just above the pile of paper. Paul had turned the top page around so that Annie could see it when she came into the room: MISERY'S RETURN, by Paul Sheldon. Annie's mouth dropped open.

'Paul, what are you going?'

'I've finished,' he said. 'And it's good. In fact, Annie, I think it's the best thing I've ever written. Now I'm going to do a little trick with it. It's a good trick. I learned it from you.'

'Paul, no!' Her voice was full of pain and understanding. Her hands reached out and she dropped the champagne bottle and the glasses on to the floor. They broke: there were pieces of glass and champagne everywhere.

'It's a pity that you'll never read it,' Paul said, and smiled at her. It was his first real smile for months. 'Actually, I think it's better than a good novel: I think it was a *great* novel, Annie.'

The match was starting to burn his fingers. He dropped it on to the pile of paper. For one awful moment he thought it had gone out, but then pale blue fire rushed across the top page and down the sides of the typescript. The flames grew taller and stronger when they met the little pools of fuel which lay on the table on both sides of the typescript.

'OH, GOD, NO!' Annie screamed. 'NO! NOT MISERY! NOT HER! NO!'

Paul could now feel the heat of the flames on his face.

'PAUL, WHAT ARE YOU DOING? YOU CAN'T BURN MISERY, YOU DIRTY BIRD, YOU!'

And then she did exactly what he had known she would do: she seized the burning pile of paper. Then she turned round, intending to run to the bathroom with it and put it under the tap. As soon as she turned her back on Paul he picked up the heavy old typewriter and lifted it over his head. The side of the typewriter was hot and blisters sprang up on his hand. He ignored the pain and threw the typewriter at her. It hit her in the middle of her back.

'OO-OW!' Annie fell forward on to the floor, on top of the burning pile of paper.

Paul stood up on his one good leg. Tongues of flame began to play at the edges of Annie's clothes and he could already smell burning skin. She screamed in pain. She rolled over and struggled to her knees. Now he could see broken glass in her arms and face, too. Some of her clothes had melted on to her skin. He did not feel at all sympathetic or sorry.

'I'm going to kill you,' she said, and started to get to her feet.

Paul let himself fall on top of her. This pushed her down on to the hard typewriter. She screamed in pain again and tried to push him off. She rolled over on to her back. He grabbed some paper, which was lying in a pool of champagne, and squashed it into a ball.

'*Get off me!*' she shouted, and her mouth opened wide. Paul pushed the ball of paper into her mouth.

'Here's your book, Annie,' he gasped, and he grabbed some more paper. She struggled under him and his left knee hit the ground. The pain was terrible, but he kept his position on top of her and fiercely punched more paper into her mouth . . . and more and more, until the first balls of paper were deep in her throat, making it impossible for her to breathe.

She fought back with all her strength and managed to push him off her. Her hands reached for her swollen throat. There was little left of her clothes at the front of her body and he could see that her flesh was red and covered with blisters.

'*Mumpf! Mark! Mark!*' Annie said. She struggled to her feet. Paul pushed himself backwards along the floor, his legs straight out in front of him. He watched her carefully.

She took one step towards him, choking on the paper. Drops of champagne from the paper ran down her chin. Her eyes looked at him with a question: *Paul, what happened? I was bringing you champagne. Why did you do this to me?* She took another step and fell over the typewriter again. Her head hit the wall hard as she fell down and she landed heavily on the ground like a loose sack of bricks.

Chapter 26   Annie Everywhere

Annie had fallen on the main pile of burning paper; her body had stopped it burning.

Paul crawled towards his wheelchair. He had strained his back, there were blisters all over his right hand, his head ached and his stomach rolled with the sick-sweet smell of burned flesh. But he was free. The Dragon Lady was dead and he was free.

He was halfway to his wheelchair when Annie opened her eyes.

Paul watched, unbelieving, while she got slowly to her knees. Perhaps she could not be killed! Her eyes were staring and horrible. A huge wound, pink-red, showed through her hair on the left side of her head. Blood poured down her face.

'Durd!' Annie cried through her throatful of paper. She began to crawl towards him.

Paul turned away from her and started to crawl for the door. He could hear her behind him. He started across the broken glass and then he felt her hand close around the stump of his left ankle. He screamed.

'Dirt!' Annie cried. Paul looked round to see whether she had spat out the paper, but she hadn't, and her face was starting to turn purple.

It was easy for him to pull his leg out of her grasp because there was no foot for her to hold on to. But she reached out again and seized him higher up the leg. Some broken glass stabbed into his elbow as he continued trying to crawl away.

'AW... GAW! OOO OW!'

He turned again and now her face was nearly black. He reached for the doorframe and pulled hard on it to try to escape, but her hand closed on his thigh.

'No!' he cried in fear and desperation. He felt her hands run like spiders up his back and reach his neck. He felt the weight of her body on his legs, pinning him to the floor. She moved further up his body, trapping him. It was difficult for him to breathe.

'GAW! OOO... BIRT! DIRT!'

The Dragon Lady, on top of him. She seemed dark and immense. The air was driven out of her lungs as she fell on to him, and her hands dug deep into his neck.

He screamed: *'Die! Can't you die? Can't you ever die?'*

Suddenly her hands went loose and she lay heavily on top of him.

He pulled himself out from underneath her body and crawled into the hall. Annie lay silent and face down in blood and spilled champagne and pieces of green glass. Was she dead? She *must* be dead. Paul did not believe she was dead.

He shut the door and reached up to turn the key in the lock. He lay down, in pain and exhaustion, on the floor. He stayed there, only half conscious, for an unknown period of time. He only moved eventually when he heard a scratching sound. At first he thought it was the rats in the cellar. Then Annie's thick bloodstained fingers crept under the door and tried to seize the end of his shirt. Paul screamed and punched at the fingers with his fist. The fingers did not disappear back under the door, but at least they lay still.

Paul crawled further down the hall, towards the bathroom. He was in terrible pain now, from his legs, his back and his burned hand. As soon as he was inside he found the packets of Novril and swallowed three tablets. He sat with his back against the door and slept.

When he woke up it was dark. He listened carefully for any noises outside in the corridor. The more he listened the more he seemed to hear slight noises. *This is crazy*, he told himself. *She's dead . . .* But what was that? Was that a light footstep in the hall?. . . *and she is in a locked room.*

She could have escaped through the window.

Paul, she's DEAD!

Paul had a problem. He needed to check on something. He wanted to make sure that the typescript was safe . . . the *real* typescript. What Annie had seen and tried to save was just a pile of blank pages and old, uncorrected pages which he had collected. He had put the title-page on the top so that Annie would believe it was the book; but the real typescript was in his room, under the bed. He wanted it safe, he wanted people to read it. He knew it was the best book he had written. That was the problem. Did he have the courage to go back into the room to get the typescript? Suppose Annie was still alive!

He crawled slowly down the hall towards his room. In the shadows he imagined Annie everywhere: waiting for him in the sitting-room or further down the corridor. The boards on the floor made a noise behind him and he turned round. Nothing . . . this time.

Outside a car door shut and he heard a man's voice say, 'God! Look at this, will you?'

'In here!' he screamed. 'In here! I'm in here!'

It was the two policemen from the day before. When they managed to understand what Paul was saying they looked in his room. Paul stayed in the corridor. They came out again and the detective said, 'There's no one there. There's a hell of a mess – blood and wine and stuff – and the window's broken, but there's no woman in there.'

Paul was still screaming when he fainted.

They told him later that they found her in the barn. She was dead, but she was grasping the axe tightly in her hands and was on her way back towards the house.

Chapter 27   *Misery's Return*

Paul's legs slowly recovered in hospital and the doctors made him an excellent left foot. *Misery's Return* sold millions of copies . . . but Paul still sees Annie Wilkes waiting for him in corners, in shadows on the streets, in every woman who ever tells him that he is her favourite author.

ACTIVITIES

Chapters 1–4

Before you read

1   Look at the pictures on pages 6, 37 and 57. What do they tell you about the story and about the woman? Do you think you will enjoy this story?

2   Study the Word List at the back of the book. Which words connect with these topics a–j?

   a gardening

   b written work

   c feelings (two words)

   d celebrations

   e photography

   f injuries and treatment (four words)

   g sounds (three words)

   h violence (two verbs)

   i bedroom furniture

   j picnics

3   Read the Introduction to the book and answer the questions.

   a What kind of books does he usually write?

   b Have you read any of his books or seen any of the films?

While you read

4   Number these events in the correct order, 1–9.

   a Paul finishes writing *Misery's Child*   .....

   b Paul crashes his car   .....

   c Paul sees Annie Wilkes for the first time   .....

   d Paul writes the first Misery Chastain book   .....

   e There is a heavy snow storm   .....

   f Paul stops breathing   .....

   g Paul hears a woman's voice   .....

   h Paul's car is out of control   .....

   i Paul leaves his hotel in Colorado   .....

5 Circle the correct endings.

    a Paul wakes up in *hospital / his car / bed on a farm.*

    b Every four hours Annie gives Paul *coffee / tablets / a sandwich.*

    c Paul thinks Annie is *mad / attractive / pleasant.*

    d Annie has tied splints on to Paul's *arms / legs / neck.*

    e Annie has *started / finished / not enjoyed* reading Paul's last book about Misery Chastain.

    f Annie doesn't like the *title / language / people* in his typescript.

    g She makes Paul drink *dirty / hot / green* water.

After you read

  6 Why do you think Annie was in court in Denver?

  7 What else can you guess about her from the clues in these chapters?

Chapters 5–8

Before you read

  8 Annie wants to finish reading *Misery's Child*. Is this good or bad for Paul, do you think? Why?

  9 What would you do in Paul's situation?

While you read

10 <u>Underline</u> the wrong word in each sentence and write the right word.

    a Annie's favourite character leaves at the end of *Misery's Child*. ....

    b She nearly hits Paul's head with a heavy water glass. ....

    c Paul hears Annie run away from the house. ....

    d Annie pushes a kitchen stove into the bedroom. ....

    e Annie wants Paul to rewrite *Fast Cars*. ....

    f Paul thinks he will report Annie. ....

11 Are these sentences right (✓) or wrong (✗)?

a Paul wakes up as Annie is putting him in the wheelchair.   .....

b The snow is starting to melt.   .....

c Annie tells Paul she thinks he'll recover from his injuries.   .....

d Annie has bought an old typewriter.   .....

e There is no letter 'n' on the typewriter.   .....

f Annie wants Paul to write a new novel.   .....

g Annie starts locking Paul's door each time she leaves.   .....

h She brings Paul the most expensive paper.   .....

i Paul tells Annie the typing paper is the right kind.   .....

j Annie puts Paul back into bed before she leaves.   .....

After you read

12 Complete the first part of each sentence a–j, with the correct ending 1–9.

a Paul picks up some of   .....

b Paul learnt to open locks when   .....

c He manages despite the pain because   .....

d He also wants to get   .....

e First, he wheels himself   .....

f He finds the medicines   .....

g He puts the packets of tablets   .....

h He hears the sound of a car   .....

i He reaches the telephone   .....

1) Annie's hairpins from the floor.

2) down the front of his trousers.

3) but it isn't working.

4) he was writing *Fast Cars*.

5) into the bathroom.

6) underneath the shelves of towels.

7) he needs some tablets.

8) but it doesn't stop.

9) an extra supply.

Chapters 9–11

Before you read

13   Which of the following things do you think would be most useful to Paul now? Why? Discuss this with another student.

   a   a motorcycle?

   b   an axe?

   c   a box of matches?

14   What do you think happened in Denver to Annie?

While you read

15   Who says these things? Write P (Paul) or A (Annie).

   a   'Come on, come on.'   .....

   b   'I'm sure you'll learn.'   .....

   c   'It's not right.'   .....

   d   'What do you mean? Don't you like it?'   .....

   e   'I used to go to the cinema every week.'   .....

   f   'Then you know what to do.'   .....

16   Answer Yes or No to these questions.

   a   Does Annie like the first chapters of the new typescript?   .....

   b   Does she want Paul to continue?   .....

   c   Does Paul want to continue?   .....

   d   Does he want Annie to stay while he writes?   .....

   e   Does Paul usually show his work before it's finished?   .....

   f   Does Annie want to fill in all the 'n's?   .....

   g   Does Paul continue writing after she has left him?   .....

After you read

17   How are these important for Paul's survival?

   a   the thick snow   **d**   *Misery's Return*

   b   the wheelchair   **e** $400

   c   hairpins

18   What is Annie's threat to Paul to make him keep quiet? Do you think she would carry out her threat?

19   Can you understand why Paul feels 'curiously happy'? (page 34). Do you think his situation has improved? Why, or why not?

Chapters 12–15

Before you read

20 How do you think the rain will affect the writer's relationship with Annie?

21 Look at the picture on page 37. What do you think has happened to Annie?

While you read

22 Put these words in the correct sentences.

rat death jam hit spilled killing locks
determined scream

   a Annie's clothes are messy with .... food.

   b Paul hears her .... herself in the face.

   c Annie has been eating .... with her hands.

   d Annie has a large, grey .... in a trap.

   e Paul knows he is very close to ....

   f Annie goes to her Laughing Place to ....

   g Paul is .... to escape.

   h There are strong .... on all the outside doors.

   i Paul thinks about .... himself.

23 Make correct sentences about Annie.

   a In 1954 .....   **1)** she moved to Colorado.

   b In 1959 .....   **2)** she was chief nurse in a hospital department.

   c In 1978 .....   **3)** she was happy for a while.

   d In 1979 .....   **4)** she killed Andrew Pomeroy.

   e In 1980 .....   **5)** her husband left her.

   f In 1982 .....   **6)** she killed her neighbours.

   g In 1984 .....   **7)** she killed a student.

After you read

24 In chapter 15 Annie is missing from the farm for several days. What things does Paul do while she is away?

Chapters 16–18

Before you read

25 Why do you think Annie has given Paul an injection? What do you think she plans to do next? Why?

While you read

26 Circle the words that describe how Paul feels in chapter 16.

happy   dull   optimistic   alarmed   sad

angry   afraid   disappointed   sick   unlucky

27 Which of the following items of equipment is *not* used in the 'little operation' on Paul's foot?

blowlamp   bottle of liquid   axe   water   knife   match

After you read

28 Answer these questions.

a What does Paul decide to do when the old typewriter loses its letter 't' and then 'e'?

b Why does Paul think he'll never forget all the details of the 'little operation'?

c Why does Paul continue to write the book?

d Why does Annie bring him the ice-cream?

e Why won't Paul tell her how the story ends?

f How does Annie punish him?

29 Explain the phrase 'he had skated on thin ice'.

30 Think of two reasons why Paul is surprised at the birthday cake.

Chapters 19–22

Before you read

31 What do you think will happen next? If you were Paul, what would you do first?

While you read

32 Put the correct names in each sentence: Paul, the policeman, or Annie.

a Paul realises how frightened of .... he is.

b .... pauses not far from the window.

    c .... hears Paul.

    d The policeman has been staring at .... so he doesn't see .... until it is too late.

    e .... stabs ....

    f Paul is sure .... will kill him next.

    g .... drives the tractor over ....

33 Are these sentences true (T) or false (F)?

    a Paul feels envious of the young policeman. .....

    b Annie throws the glass vase under the lawnmower. .....

    c Annie thinks Paul is responsible for the policeman's death. .....

    d Annie has forgotten to clean under the lawnmower. .....

    e Annie wants them both to hide in the cellar. .....

    f Annie has put a mattress on the floor. .....

    g There is no food or water in the cellar. .....

After you read

34 Find *five* examples of Annie's behaviour after she kills the policeman that show Paul that she is not angry with him.

35 Explain what you think Paul plans to do with the can of fuel. Do you think his plan will work?

Chapters 23–27

Before you read

36 Both Paul and Annie know the police will come. How do you think they will behave when this happens? Why?

37 Think back to the beginning of the story. Have either Annie or Paul changed in any way? How? Why?

While you read

38 Put these sentences in the correct order, 1–10.

    a Annie brings Paul a cigarette and one match. .....

    b Annie drops the champagne bottle and glasses. .....

    c Two different policemen ask about the cuts on her face. .....

    d A TV news crew arrives. .....

    e Annie brings the champagne. .....

    f Two older policemen come to the house. .....

g Annie falls onto the burning paper. .....

h Paul throws the typewriter at Annie. .....

i Paul finishes the book. .....

j Paul lights the papers. .....

After you read

39 What role do these things play in Paul's revenge?

    a barbecue fuel   **d** *Misery's Return*

    b a floorboard   **e** balls of paper

    c a typewriter

40 Why does Paul want to go back to his room (pages 86–87)? Why don't the police find Annie there?

41 What did you like or not like about this story? What were the best or worst things about it? Would you like to read more stories by Stephen King?

Writing

42 How does Stephen King build up both the physical appearance and character of Annie, step by step, in the early chapters of the book?

43 Write Annie's letter of application for the job of chief nurse in the childbirth department of the hospital in Boulder, Colorado. Give full details of your background and experience, and say why you think you would be suitable for the job.

44 Describe the importance of Annie's training as a nurse in the story. How would the story have been different if she had had a different background?

45 Write a short story about Annie's short marriage from Ralph Dugan's point of view. Begin with: *I loved her the first time I saw her...*

46 You are the visitor in chapter 11. When you get back to your office you have to tell your boss what happened at the farm. Write your conversation.

47 You are one of the police officers who finally finds Paul. Write your report, describing your previous suspicions and investigations and the actual discovery of Paul in the house and Annie's body in the barn.

48 Write a newspaper article about Annie's history of madness and murder. What mistakes did the police and hospital authorities make? What should they have done? What should they do in the future to prevent such things from happening again?

49 You are the person who has the job of selling Annie's farm after she has died. Write your sales details. Be careful not to give any clues to the horrible events that happened there!

50 It is two years after the end of the story. You are a TV presenter and you are going to talk to Paul about his life and his latest book *Dragon Lady*. Plan your interview and write the questions you want to ask Paul.

51 Stephen King wrote *Misery* in 1987. What changes would he make to the story if he were writing it today?

Born in East Africa, Uganda, A. A. Wise moved to England, UK, when he was very young. He has been interested in fantasy books from a young age. Beyond reading and writing, his hobbies include travelling, keeping up with current events, watching movies and playing video games.

To my loving mum. Thank you for the care and support.

A. A. Wise

BLACKWOOD CHRONICLES: INOCK TEHAN AND THE RETURN OF THE IMMORTAL WITCH

AUSTIN MACAULEY PUBLISHERS™

LONDON • CAMBRIDGE • NEW YORK • SHARJAH

A CIP catalogue record for this title is available from the British Library.

ISBN 9781398408951 (Paperback)
ISBN 9781398403291 (ePub e-book)

www.austinmacauley.com

First Published 2022
Austin Macauley Publishers Ltd®
1 Canada Square
Canary Wharf
London
E14 5AA

Book Synopsis

Sixteen-year-old Inock is a demon with special powers. He lives in a magical world filled with witches, demons and wonderful mysteries yearning to be uncovered. There is a diabolical immortal witch that he has to prevent from rising to power. The struggle leads Inock and his friends to many dangerous situations and battles with dark witches and the hateful venators.

Character Names and Descriptions

Inock Tehan:
Inock is a sixteen-year-old boy living in a magical world filled with witches and demons. He is the main character of the story. He is a demon himself with very special powers. Inock gets involved in an ancient mystery that leads him into dangerous situations.

Andre:
Andre is a sixteen-year-old black boy who is also a demon with supernatural powers. He can transform himself into any animal he pleases. Andre lives with Inock and his family, and likes to tell the truth; he respects his elders.

Lalita:
Lalita is a very clever sixteen-year-old girl who is a good friend of Inock's. She is also a demon with special powers and is a young witch learning magic.

Rozanthia:
Rozanthia is a female ghost who died when she was twelve and so never grew any older. She has been the same

age since she died many, many years ago. She is Inock's secret friend since not many people know about her. She can turn and stay invisible for as long as she likes. This way, she follows Inock around without anyone knowing she is there.

Tehan:

Tehan is Inock's father. He is a demon with supernatural powers and a very famous power-trainer who teaches other demons how to use their powers properly. He owns a Power-Training school.

Esttia:

Esttia is Inock's mother. She works at Tehan's Power-Training school as a receptionist and also mixes magical potions.

Torend:

Torend is Inock's big brother. He is also a demon with special powers. He, too, is a power-trainer at Tehan's Power-Training school who teaches other demons how to properly use their powers.

Laden:

Laden is Lalita's big brother. He is a demon with special powers and a known troublemaker.

Tharah:

Tharah is a very beautiful girl who lives in Inock's world. She is older than Inock and is a demon with the power to telepathically communicate with animals.

Mabiyah:

Mabiyah is an oracle who sends Inock and his friends on many dangerous missions. A demon with very special powers, she can see the future and is also an unnaturally old witch. She is very clever and helps a lot of people in Inock's world because of her powers.

Esmatilda:

Esmatilda is a good witch who lives in the Haunted Valley ruins. She is a good friend of Inock's.

Dentas:

Dentas is an ex-dark witch. She was arrested by the venators and Inock needs her help to defeat Immotshap, a long-lost immortal witch.

James:

James is a friend of the Oracle's. He is a male witch with a dark past. He was killed but returns from death due to his immortality.

Ms Strict:

Ms Strict is Inock's and Andre's schoolteacher. She is a witch and she teaches the two boys upstairs in the power-training school next door to their home.

Villad:

Villad is a young demon with the power to turn himself and others invisible. He is a friend of Inock's.

Rukia:

Rukia is a young woman who works in a potions shop in Kasama Market.

Rikelle:

Rikelle is Rukia's younger sister. Inock starts going out with Rikelle.

Barnarbo:

Barnarbo is a male witch who co-owns and works on a farm that Inock, Andre and Lalita often visit.

Radock:

Radock is a venator who works in the Kasama venator lookout. Inock meets him when he starts working at the lookout.

Maliki:

Maliki is a young demon who Inock has issues with. He has the power to teleport himself.

Adem:

Adem is a descendant of Immotshap. He is a loyal supporter of Immotshap and is praised and worshipped by witches. He grants Rozanthia her body back.

Barla:

Barla is a dark witch who was killed by James. She plans to return Immotshap, a long-lost immortal witch, back to power.

Anandre:

Anandre is a male dark witch who was also killed by James. He also plans to return Immotshap back to power.

Immotshap:

Immotshap is an ancient immortal dark witch. He disappeared many years ago, and a group of dark witches want to find him and make him their leader once more.

Chapter One
Inock's Birthday

Inock and Andre were in the Oracle's chamber. Mabiyah, the Oracle, had summoned them there to do a job for her. Mabiyah was a good friend of Inock's and Andre's, and she was a very old witch who could see the future, the present and the past. She was tiny, barely five feet tall, with many wrinkles and a hunchback, and needed a small, crooked walking stick to stand and move around. She usually wore a cloak with the hood off and had thinning, white hair that was often tied back in a bun.

You see, Inock and Andre live in a very special world; a magical world filled with witches, demons and all kinds of wonderful creatures. Their world has many things different to ours; for example, their sky is green, not blue.

And in Inock's world, there are many people who have special powers; people who can do magical things. Those people are called *powerfuls* and there are three types of powerfuls. There are demons; these are people who are born with all kinds of powers. There are witches; those are people who are not born with powers, but learn to use magic and witchcraft. (Just so you know, in Inock's world, male witches are also called witches, not wizards.)

And finally, the third kind of *powerful* is a natural witch who does not necessarily need words of power or spells; witches who can affect the world around them by willing special things to happen.

Inock and Andre were themselves demons. Inock had the ability to use other demons' powers when they were close by, but when those demons went away, Inock could no longer use their powers. But he had to know what their powers were and how to use them in order to do it right.

Andre was Inock's adopted brother. He was a red-haired black boy about Inock's age, and he could transform himself into any animal he wanted. Right then, he was dressed in brown shorts and a red T-shirt and black sandals.

Many months had passed since Inock and his friends had defeated the dark witch Dentas and got her captured by the venators. (Venators were like the police of Inock's realm.) Inock and his friends had grown and changed much since then.

Standing next to Andre, Inock looked excited. It was Wednesday, February the sixteenth, and today was Inock's birthday; his sixteenth birthday. Inock's family had an exciting day planned for him. They would later take him to a powerfuls-performers-only circus in the big city, Unatia, or Unatia district, as it was sometimes called.

Inock and Andre had been getting ready to go to the circus when the Oracle had summoned them with a peculiar clone of Inock. The clone knocked on Inock's front door; Inock answered, and the clone went on to tell him—in Mabiyah's small voice—that Mabiyah wanted them in her chambers immediately. (When the Oracle summoned Inock and Andre to her chambers, she often used strange means of doing it.

Sometimes, it was odd clones of Inock, Andre, Lalita, or strangers that would then vanish before their eyes; at times it was talking animals and sometimes it was flying notes or talking paper aeroplanes.)

And the Oracle's chamber was a weird and interesting place to be indeed. The whole space was lit by a turquoise light coming from a large glass bowl filled with a glowing, bubbling turquoise goo set on the only table in the small room. The table, accompanied by two chairs, was by the wall to the left of the space. Mabiyah was sitting in one of the chairs. In a grey cloak, she was smiling kindly at the boys.

'Young ones, I have a special mission for you today,' the Oracle said to Inock and Andre in her small voice. She had wished Inock a happy birthday then got straight to the reason she summoned them. There was no time to waste.

As always, all outside noise coming into the room was muted, even though the door was wide open. This was because of a magic spell cast by Mabiyah a long time ago.

You see, the Oracle's chambers were inside a market, the Kasama Market, which is also where Inock and Andre lived. So, Inock was always pleased when he entered her chamber and the rest of the market noise was shut out.

Excited about the mission that the Oracle had for them, Inock was grinning, and had his hands in his black shorts pockets. (Most men and boys in Kasama—that was the district Inock and Andre lived in—wore shorts and T-shirts or vests since it was almost always hot in Kasama.)

Inock passed a hand through his black hair, which was in the shape of a perfectly round bowl with several strands sticking up at the crown; he'd been trying to get these strands

to stay down for many months with hair gel but it seemed a tad impossible.

'What's the job, Oracle?' Inock said, his voice clear. You see, Inock's voice had had that funny sound to it as though it would break but never did. And about six months ago, it had finally broken, sounding more mature. And let me tell you, Inock was ever so pleased about this. He looked very happy indeed in his bright green T-shirt and sandals, and on top of his voice finally breaking, like Andre, Inock had grown about two feet in the last few months.

'I need you to go to Omulilo Village to deliver a potion,' said the Oracle. 'There is a young witch there who needs it. But be warned, the village is a battlefield for powerfuls. I recommend you transform yourselves and fly there. Do not take gante.' (Gante were the main means of conveyance in Kasama. They were wonderful creatures that looked like giant tigers with black and white stripes like zebras. They were generally over five feet tall and had long, wide tails that looked like platypus tails. Inock and Andre owned their own gante, which were kept at the market stables.)

'Why can't we take gante, Oracle?' Andre asked. 'Wouldn't it be faster?'

'I know it would be, young ones,' Mabiyah said. 'But I have foreseen that it is best for you not to take gante to Omulilo Village. It would be best if you both used your powers and flew there. You will find out why soon enough.'

'Okay, Oracle, we'll do as you say,' Inock said grinning. He enjoyed going on missions for the Oracle very much.

The Oracle looked at the space between her and the boys, and a small glass bottle filled with a clear liquid appeared there, revolving in mid-air.

16

'This is the potion the young witch needs,' Mabiyah said. 'It will transport her to a safe place. Take it, please. We have little time to waste.'

Inock grabbed the potion and pocketed it.

The Oracle then gave the boys directions to the village and the exact location of the witch.

'Hurry, young ones. Leave urgently. The young witch is in great need of that potion,' she finished by saying.

So Inock and Andre left the chamber and emerged into the bustling market. (The Oracle's chamber was located somewhere in the south-eastern part of the market, along the market perimeter wall.)

Kasama Market was like a city within walls. The whole market was enclosed within towering, white stone walls, and had four main entrances. Each entrance was a great black gate. The market had grey concrete stalls that were permanent. The stalls were built in chains, so each stall was actually a small segment of a ring of stalls. And there were many rings making up the entire market.

The market had two bricked roads that dissected it into four equal quarters and ran straight through to the four market entrances. The roads were called "The Divider".

Many people lived in the market. Some of the flats at the centre of the market and along the market boundary were shops, some were storage rooms, and others were people's homes.

Like many in that district, most people in the market wore bright colours. Some were in shorts and sandals, and some wore hooded cloaks, which were usually to shield themselves from the scorching sun. And the people in the market were a

mixture of colours, but on the whole, there were more dark-skinned people than not.

As always, the market was loud and busy with people moving in all directions, buying things, talking, or eating at the many stalls that sold ready-to-eat foods, and children playing here and there. And to add to the clamour, there were animals too.

Kasama was like a tropical country where sometimes the days were so hot, you could barely breathe. But sometimes it was cloudy. Sometimes, it was windy. And sometimes, it rained for a long time. But it was almost always hot.

Inock and Andre descended the white steps leading from the Oracle's chamber, weaved through crowds, passing stalls laden with all sorts of goods—food, clothing, fabrics, shoes, potions, books and small pets—until they found a quiet spot behind a parchments stall.

'Okay, let's transform here and fly to Omulilo Village,' Inock told Andre from behind the stall.

Andre nodded, then without a single word, transformed into a large red bird and took off into the sky towards the valley, making a passing woman in shorts and a white vest jump in fright.

Without hesitation, with his powers to copy other demons' abilities, Inock transformed into a large green bird and took off after Andre. It was a strange feeling being a bird. Inock's thoughts were all funny, his view was all different, his whole body still ached a little from the change, and he felt much smaller, but overall, it was an amazing feeling; he felt ever so light and free.

Up, up and up, bird Inock and Andre soared, riding the winds. They simply flew. Across the district they went,

passing other birds and piercing the clouds, flying over numerous villages, forests, towns and rivers and lakes.

It took Inock and Andre over an hour and a half to reach Omulilo Village. Andre landed first at one of the village entrances, followed seconds later by Inock. They morphed back into themselves, clothes and all, and proceeded into the obviously rundown village.

The two boys passed many houses that looked like they badly needed repairing. Even the streets were dirty and the pavements broken in many places. And the villagers didn't look all that friendly either. The people Inock and Andre passed looked grubby and standoffish. The boys passed two groups of teenagers who looked as though they might attack them at any moment. A boy from one of the groups was menacingly juggling a bluish energy ball the size of two footballs—he was an energy manipulator, someone who could mould magical energy into different things like energy ropes or lethal energy spikes or even energy shields that could block any projectile, not to mention energy bolts that could either stun or kill.

The closer they got to their destination, the more Inock got a bad feeling. They passed many houses that looked as though they were damaged in a raging war and seconds before they got to the mansion the Oracle had described to them, the boys passed a house blazing in green flames. Yet, it still stood wholly intact!

And as soon as Inock and Andre reached the three-storey mansion, they could tell something was off about the place. There was a faint dark energy billowing up all around the house and indistinct screams could be heard coming from inside.

Inock and Andre walked to the front door, expecting to have to knock but found it slightly ajar and it was covered in scorch marks.

Inock looked at Andre and Andre looked at Inock.

'Do you think we should knock?' Inock asked.

There was another feeble scream from within the house.

Andre frowned worriedly.

'No. I think we better hurry up and go in,' Andre said. 'I think she's in trouble. That was a woman screaming!'

'Well, let's just hope she's not evil or something,' Inock said.

'The Oracle wouldn't have sent us to help her if she was evil, Inock!'

So, they pushed the door fully open and just as they entered the house, both Inock and Andre heard the Oracle's voice loud and clear in their minds and all over:

Young ones, deliver the potion as soon as possible. Make sure you get it to the young woman. Her life depends on it!

'Okay. We will, Oracle,' said Inock quietly.

The pair found themselves in a spacious entrance hall with a set of stairs to the right and many doorways leading deeper into the mansion.

'We should hurry, Inock,' Andre whispered after hearing yet another scream coming from somewhere upstairs.

'Yes, but where do we go first?' Inock asked.

'I say we check upstairs. I think she's upstairs and she's in trouble!'

'Okay,' Inock said running for the set of stairs, Andre tailing him.

And it was as they were hurrying up the stairs, that the business went all wrong.

Two men, one with dreadlocks and the other with a shaved head, both in vests and shorts, appeared from a hallway halfway up the stairs.

'Hey! What are you two ones doing in here?' yelled the one with dreadlocks. ("One" was short for "young one". Something that young people in Inock's world sometimes called people younger than themselves.)

But the other man wasn't so inviting. He held out a hand and muttered a spell in a funny language. A dagger materialised out of thin air above it; he grabbed it and hurled it at Inock who was in the lead.

Inock dived sideways, the knife missing him by inches. Andre, too. Inock then broke into a run at the witch and at reaching him, shoved him over the banister to the floors below.

The second man—the one with the dreadlocks—scowled at Inock and held out a hand as an energy ball appeared above his palm. The thing was bluish in colour with a pulsating centre that fed energy into the rest of it through flailing tendrils. The whole thing was contained within a perfectly round roaring energy and it glowed. He hurled it at Inock.

But Inock was fast. He also held out a hand, and with his powers to copy other demons' abilities, conjured an energy ball of his own and quickly launched it, sending it crashing into the other demon's energy ball with a thunderous bang that shook the stairs. Wisps of energy showered down onto the stairs where the energy balls had collided. (And he was lucky it had hit because his aim was sometimes unreliable.)

Then it was Andre's turn. He transformed himself into a gomorah, a creature unique to Inock's world. A yeti-like beast that in its adult form was over twelve feet tall and five feet wide with dark blue fur and hands the size of boulders.

Gomorah Andre then made a run at the man, crashed into him, knocking him over the banister.

Andre then transformed back into himself.

'Come on, Inock! Stop looking down at them and let's go up!' Andre yelled.

So, the two boys ran up the stairs to the topmost landing and crashed into the only door in sight.

They found themselves in a spacious attic that looked like a studio flat with a bed, a wardrobe, kitchen and bathroom all in one room.

And in the room was a young woman with long black hair in a black dress crouching on the floor. There were three black, three-dimensional shadows around her, a clear sort of energy emitting from the witch and feeding into the shadows.

The woman jumped up from the floor seeing Inock and Andre in the room, the strange shadows retreating away from her.

'What are you two doing here?' she whimpered. Then she went on to scream: 'COME TO COLLECT MORE OF MY POWER? GET OUT! LEAVE ME BE! HAVEN'T YOU TAKEN ENOUGH?'

'Inock, I think this is the witch the Oracle sent us to help!' Andre said.

'We can't leave,' Inock said, locking the attic door behind him. 'We came to help you!'

'Yes, we can't leave, miss. We have a potion for you,' Andre said gently. 'The Oracle sent us.'

Fast footsteps could be heard coming up the stairs outside the room.

The young witch looked more carefully at the two boys before her and managed a feeble smile.

'Thank Existence,' she said. 'They've been draining me of my power and consciousness for ages ... It cannot grow, they just keep draining me! I can't do anything ... no spells! I can't even leave the house. I spend most of my time being scared!' (There was a bang at the door and the sound of two men yelling for the door to be opened immediately.) 'I've been praying and hoping that someone or something would come and save me. I sent out my already weakened mind to look for help in my sleep and I'm not sure but I think I found an Oracle from Kasama Market. Did she send you? Please say she did.'

'She did. Her name is Mabiyah.'

'I know her name, ones,' the witch said, managing a smile. 'She told me in my sleep, you see.'

'Are you the one we heard screaming?' Andre asked, almost in tears. It was just a very sad situation.

'I am. I'm always screaming out,' the young witch said, tears trickling down her pretty face. 'You see those things?' She pointed to the three shadows that had retreated from her when the boys entered the room. The strange creatures were now at the room's perimeter, half of their oddly three-dimensional bodies in the walls. 'They leech on me every single minute of every single day! They feed on my mind and energy and power and magic! It's disgusting and it is terrible ... you have no idea! And it is very painful! It is the reason I'm always screaming out ... because I want it to stop ... but it never does! Never! Ever!'

'Why don't you just run away? You're a witch!' Andre cried, arms thrusting out in utter desperation.

'Because the house is always guarded by powerfuls, ones, and the door to this room locked,' replied the witch. 'The same stupid powerfuls that take the power those ugly demons steal from me for themselves! And I told you, they drain me all the time so I have no power to help myself! Oh, it's just terrible!'

'Oh! That's really awful!' Andre said miserably.

The bangs on the attic door continued mercilessly; the two men were yelling for the door to be opened at once.

'Not to mention that they're constantly driving me insane!' the witch wailed on, looking to the vibrating door fearfully, wiping away tears. 'The shadows are always playing with my mind and emotions, confusing me all the time, installing dreadful fear into me. They seem to do it by playing with the very matrix of my making! I can barely do anything! I can't even think right!'

'Yes, well, that's all over now! Mabiyah sent us to give you this potion to drink,' Inock said hurriedly. (The banging on the door continued, the door almost breaking off its hinges.) He handed the potion over to the woman. 'It will get you to a safe place; the Oracle said it would.' He looked to the door uneasily to see it shaking, almost broken in from the torment the men on the other side were inflicting on it. BANG! BANG! BANG! it went on and on and on.

'What do I do with it?' the witch demanded, frightened.

'Just drink it!' Andre urged. 'We need to escape!'

So, the young witch did as she was told and uncorked the potion, downed it all in one and her whole body was slowly, at first, bathed in a clear energy that began to quickly billow

24

up and all around her with rustling whooshing sounds. The three shadows zoomed at her, giving off odd, terrible screams, and she was gone in a flash. She simply vanished, leaving her tormenters behind. And at that very moment, the door to the room crashed down with an angry smash, three angry men inching into the room; the two from before and a dark-skinned man with close-shaven hair.

'You did it, didn't you? You freed the filthy witch!' the man with dreadlocks seethed, pointing an accusing finger at the boys.

'You will *die* for what you've done, ones!' the dark-skinned man bellowed. 'We needed her! Do you have any idea how strong she made us? There's a war going on in this village!'

'Well, that's just too bad!' Inock exploded, almost in tears. 'You are all bad men and you didn't deserve her!'

The one with the dreadlocks fired up an energy ball and hurled it. Realising Inock was too fired up to react in time, Andre grabbed him by the arm and dragged him behind the bed where they crouched down, the energy ball missing them and flying into a wall with a disgusting bang.

'So, boys, what do you think we should do with these little young demons?' the man with the dreadlocks asked, a sinister grin on his face. 'We could play with them.'

'I'd rather you didn't, sir!' Andre protested from behind the bed. 'I don't bend that way!' He turned and hissed to Inock, 'We need to escape! The Oracle wouldn't have sent us if she didn't know we'd escape, would she?'

'I don't think she would have, Andre. My father would kill her. What should we do? They have us surrounded!'

'I know exactly what to do to them!' the dark-skinned man said, a look of great focus coming across his face.

'What do you have in mind, Tubaq?' asked the one with the dreadlocks. 'I think we can really have some fun with them! They helped our power source get away and she was a natural witch too!'

The one with the dreadlocks conjured and fired off an energy ball at the bed, breaking it in half, making Inock and Andre scream and run behind a tall wardrobe.

'Just watch what I do to them!' said the one called Tubaq.

And as soon as he'd said that, both Inock and Andre began to suffer dizzy spells and confusion, making the both of them drop to the floor.

Then, the man with dreadlocks fired another roaring energy ball at the wardrobe, breaking it in half too, the top half tumbling to the floor with a loud crash.

Andre hissed, 'Change into a rat, Inock!'

Even with Tubaq's powers confusing him, Andre managed to change into a green rat, quickly followed by Inock who found it a little difficult to morph, feeling too dizzy, and together they scurried behind the fridge.

Two other energy balls hit, smashing the fridge to bits, making rat Inock and rat Andre run from it behind a bathtub.

'It's no use hiding, you two! I know a nifty trick that allows me to hear a fly from a mile away!' Tubaq roared furiously. 'And oh, are you enjoying your minds being muddled? Ha! That's another trick I know!'

Rat Inock and rat Andre kept running from one piece of furniture to the next, and Tubaq just kept telling his companions where they were hidden: 'Now they're behind the chair … now that cabinet … now the bed! Get them!' Until

almost every piece of furniture in the room was completely destroyed.

'Just come out and let's end this now!' the man with the shaved head jeered. 'Let us play with you, young ones!'

With no more places to hide, both rat Inock and rat Andre morphed back into themselves.

Peering about the room, Andre whispered to Inock, 'Follow me to that window, Inock.'

He crept to the barred window, the three men in the room laughing vociferously.

'What are you doing over there? Planning to jump out of the window? You'd die on impact!' the one with dreadlocks barked with a wicked smirk.

'The window's got metal bars, anyway! You cannot escape! You think you can free our power source and not be killed for it, ones?' the one called Tubaq yelled.

'So go on then! Fire at us and end it, you fools!' Andre barked, to Inock's great surprise.

The effect of Tubaq's powers was wearing off now. The demon had stopped doing it to them.

'What are you saying?' Inock hissed out of the corner of his mouth at Andre.

'Just let him fire one more energy ball at us!' Andre said loudly, ignoring his brother. 'Go on then, you witch-leeching losers! Fire!'

'Are you mad, Andre?' cried Inock.

But the man with dreadlocks was already all fired up. He conjured and aimed a particularly large energy ball, and oh, it roared hungrily! He hurled it at the two boys, and at the same time, Andre grabbed Inock by the arm and yanked him down, the energy ball just missing them both and crashing into the

window, breaking the bars clear off. Only a great hole of melted metal was left.

'NOW, INOCK! TURN INTO A BIRD AND LET'S FLY OUT!' Andre screamed before jumping out of the window and morphing into a large red bird in a flash.

Inock followed his brother's lead and dived out of the window and quickly transformed into a green bird, flying after Andre into the shimmering emerald afternoon sky, deadly energy balls whizzing past them.

The three men at the attic window screamed out in great frustration; their prey had escaped.

Chapter Two
Dead Witch at the Circus

Inock and Andre landed right outside the southern market entrance and transformed back into themselves, the guarding venators barely flinching at the sight of two boys turning from birds to humans; they were used to that sort of thing.

However, one of the two venators slid a hand to his venator's whip just in case the two demons would be troublesome.

All venators wore a uniform of dark green, knee-length silk jackets with long black sleeves, black trousers, black boots, had black whips on their waists, and each venator wore a green metallic brace around his neck. All venators were bald black men with green eyebrows; eyebrows that were usually furrowed in displeasure. I should tell you, venators absolutely hated powerfuls, so any whiff of trouble from a witch or demon and they were right there to arrest and incarcerate.

And their four onis certainly kept watchful eyes on the two boys as they proceeded into the market. Onis were large black creatures that came up to a man's waist. Venators used the ugly beasts to patrol the streets; they looked like gigantic dogs, petrifying to look at! Like a bull terrier with large red eyes, no ears and two very long, scaly tails that writhed like

serpents behind them. The nasty animals had long jaws that resembled a crocodile's, with lots of sharp, stained teeth. You could never see a venator without onis.

The venators were always watchful, and not just with powerfuls, but with regular people too.

Inock and Andre moved into the market and onto The Divider, and raced home after Inock suggested they collect their payment from the Oracle another time. They needed to get home and meet their family to go to Unatia city for his birthday celebrations. (At the very centre of the market was a tall tower made of white stone and had three huge spheres along it. At the bottom of the tower was a ring of flats built around it. Inock's and Andre's home was one of these flats.)

It was late in the day now, the sun just setting, throwing an orangish-red glow on anything its light touched. The market lamps were slowly lighting up to give light to the night shoppers and those that lived in the market.

Inock and Andre found the rest of the family and Lalita waiting at the white steps outside their home.

'Hello, you two, we've been waiting for you for quite some time now!' Tehan, Inock's father, said in his deep voice. Tehan was a very tall man. He had long, white hair that was usually loosely tied back and had broad shoulders. He was dressed in loose grey trousers, a loose grey shirt with no collar and white sandals.

'And why are you both covered in filth and panting?' asked Esttia, Inock's mother. Her thin lips looked even thinner in anger, her thin-rimmed spectacles catching the light of the setting sun. As always, her greying hair was tied back loosely in a bun. 'I told you we'd be leaving soon and you simply just vanished off!'

'Well, now isn't the time to argue. Let us depart,' said Tehan, leading the way. 'Boys, do clean yourselves up a bit.'

Esttia followed Tehan, who was succeeded by Torend, Inock's big brother, who grinned back at Inock and Andre as he went. Inock liked his big brother quite a lot; he usually let him off when he caught him doing something he shouldn't be doing.

Torend was in his twenties. He had a powerful looking face like his father and had close-shaven, black hair. He was tall with broad shoulders, again like his father. For the occasion, he wore dark shorts and a dark shirt.

Lalita, too, was grinning at Inock and Andre smugly. Inock quite liked her but she could really be trouble sometimes. Inock and Andre had been friends with Lalita for a long time now; they both rather enjoyed her company, but she could be difficult at times. She was bossy and liked adventure and danger. Though she was the same age as the boys, Lalita didn't go to school. She had no parents and lived with her older brother Laden.

And another cool thing about Lalita, Inock thought, was that she was also a demon, an energy manipulator. And what's more, she was a young witch. In fact, she'd taught Inock his first spell.

'So, what kept you?' Lalita whispered to Inock out of the corner of her mouth, taking his arm as they followed the rest of the family down the crowded Divider, her blonde pigtails swishing as she walked. She was dressed in a knee-length black dress and black trainers with bright red socks.

'Don't you worry about that, Lalita,' Andre said, catching their conversation.

Lalita adjusted her round glasses. She always wore round glasses.

'Oh, go on, tell me,' she said. 'I bet it was fun!'

'Danger isn't fun, Lalita!' Andre said for perhaps the millionth time since meeting Lalita. Then, he lowered his voice and added, 'If you must know, we were on a job for the Oracle; it turned nasty!'

Lalita cackled.

'Blood-sucking succubus! I missed out!' she said.

'Danger isn't fun, Lalita!' Andre screeched, making Tehan, Esttia and Torend look back.

'What's going on with you three?' asked Esttia.

'Nothing, Mother,' replied Inock.

'We're just talking,' said Lalita, innocently.

Chatting excitedly along the way about all the amazing acts they'd witness at the circus, the group headed towards the eastern market gate and proceeded through to the tree-lined path lit by streetlamps that would lead them straight to the Kasama venator lookout. Venator lookouts were like police stations but were used for so much more.

Just twenty minutes later, they reached their destination.

The Kasama venator lookout was seven storeys high, brown-bricked and had a black spire shooting from the top of each corner of the rectangular structure. It had grey windows. There was a colossal, black sphere floating high above it, with a pulsating, spiralling beam of emerald energy that shot up from the structure below, and into the bottom of the sphere. The emerald beam glowed in the evening light.

Inock, his family and Lalita walked past the two venators standing guard at the path end straight to the ethereal entrance, which looked like a large grey door that was hazy. It gave

each one of them that funny, tingly feeling that you got when you walked through an ethereal barrier. It was like walking through a wall of grey smoke.

Inside, they were met with a black and green affair.

The lookout lobby was rather expansive. A big semicircle, it had a long, green, curved wall that ran from corner to corner, lined with black archways leading deeper into the lookout and a black granite floor. Far across the entrance, right in the centre of the room, was a large reception booth where a venator sat waiting. Tiny balls of light hovered high above the space, giving light to all and everything below them; similar balls of light illuminated the entire lookout.

Inock and his family were in the lookout to use the transport chambers that would teleport them instantly to the Unatia city venator lookout.

Tehan led the way to the reception booth where the venator, not looking happy to see them there, greeted them.

Tehan explained what they were there to do, paid the green-eyebrowed man and after the venator handed the power-trainer receipts, the group proceeded across the lobby and through an archway. They found themselves in a long corridor lined with even more archways. Several archways down, the group turned into a room full of wide bays filled with a greenish glow. People and venators were entering and leaving the chamber, appearing and disappearing within the bays.

Tehan handed the receipts to a venator waiting in a booth, and after carefully checking them, the man grunted for the group to proceed.

'All right, everyone, follow me in,' Tehan said, leading the way into a bay. 'I understand you all know what to expect?'

'We certainly do, Father,' said Inock merrily.

So, they all followed and once all in, the power-trainer looked at a board on the wall with a long list of figures that, if keyed in, the contraption would lead you to any lookout in the world. Tehan then reached for a small black ball that hovered by the corner. The shiny ball had the numbers zero to nine engraved in it; they glimmered green. Tehan pressed a set of numbers he read from the board into the shiny ball, there was a short beep, and the group vanished when a wide beam of green energy suddenly engulfed them. They reappeared in a similar space.

'Cool, we're here!' screeched Lalita, following Tehan out of the bay, followed by the others.

The group left the Unatia lookout, which was far bigger and grander than the Kasama venator lookout, and were finally in Unatia city, the big city!

It was a splendid city of towering glass skyscrapers that kissed the clouds, tall art sculptures and monuments, fast cars and colourful people, some in suits, some in casual attire and some in quirky clothes. And unlike the roads in Kasama, the city roads were tarmac with concrete pavements. There were no animals on the streets either like there were in Kasama.

It was now night time, the streets illuminated by tall black lamp posts. Tehan led the way down a busy street, passing kiosks and scintillating posters. He hailed a large green and black car; a Unatia city taxi.

The group got in—Esttia, Torend, Inock, Andre and Lalita in the back and Tehan in the front seat—and after greeting and

telling the male driver dressed in a black suit their destination—Pafoma Town—they were off.

Traffic was light. The ride lasted just under thirty minutes, with Inock, Lalita and Andre chatting excitedly about their destination and pointing out breath-taking buildings that seemed to be made entirely of glass, green and white double and triple-decker buses, bullet trains on golden tracks, moving statues, not to mention some funnily dressed characters they drove past.

The circus was to perform in Pafoma Stadium, so the driver pulled right up to it and after Tehan paid, the group got out and proceeded to the crowded entrance.

Pafoma Stadium was titanic and oval shaped, surrounded by bright lights and soaring trees and parks.

The Tehans and Lalita queued up, chatting amongst themselves. Reaching the ticket booth, Esttia looked into her brown bag for the tickets, which she promptly presented to the bespectacled lady inside the booth and they joined a faster moving queue.

Minutes later, the group were off to find their seats, with Lalita asking, 'Can we go and get something to eat and drink?'

'The box I hired comes with a lot of food, Lalita. Let's wait and see what they prepared,' said Tehan gently. 'If it's not to your liking, we'll get something else.'

And good seats they were. Tehan had booked one of the private boxes at pitch level not far from the pitch itself. Inside the space were reclining leather seats and tables loaded with all sorts of refreshments including boxes of sweets, to Inock's and Andre's great delight.

'You can see the whole stadium from in here!' Lalita squealed, pressing her face to the booth's glass as soon as they

were in. Inock and Andre joined her, while Inock's father, mother and brother took seats behind them.

'Yeah, nice work, Father!' Torend cheered with a grin. He gave a little clap. 'Really nice work!'

'Lalita, you're right!' Inock sort of shouted banging on the hard glass. 'We'll see everything! Oh, and look at all those cameras! Do you think they televise their performances?'

'What do you think those tall poles with wires are for?' Andre asked, pressing his face to the glass. 'I've never seen the circus before! And what about those nets?'

'Come now, boy, try to behave yourself. You're sixteen now!' Esttia scolded Inock, passing her husband a crustless sandwich and a hot beverage.

'Yeah, Inock. Come on, you're a man now,' Torend said with a cheeky wink at Inock. 'Behave!'

'Sorry, Mother. Torend, shut up!'

'Ha! That's the man of the day, everyone. Nice way to talk to your older brother, Inock!' Torend laughed, also taking a sandwich from the food tray.

'The poles are for the trapeze acts, son,' Tehan said after taking a sip of his drink. 'Always a fun part of the show, I think. So are the nets, though the nets are used for more acts than just the trapeze acts.'

Outside the Tehans' private box, people were gathering and taking their seats excitedly, and before long, the stadium was jam-packed.

Soon, the lights dimmed.

A male announcer walked onto the pitch in a spotlight, dressed in a yellow, red and green pinstriped suit and yellow bowler hat; he held a microphone.

'Welcome, ladies and gentlemen, boys and girls, and assorted animals!' The man boomed into the microphone reaching the centre of the pitch, his voice echoing all around the stadium. 'welcome to our hundredth show in pafoma stadium! I hope you all brought your lungs and handkerchiefs because tonight you will be wowed. You will laugh, you will cry, you will scream and you will clap! I hope that every single one of you will have a merry time and come back to see us again! What's the sticky red stuff between a giant gampe's toes, boys and girls? What's that? You don't know? Then i'll tell ya, boys and girls! It is slow-moving performers! So, ladies and gentlemen, boys and girls, and assorted animals, let's not be slow and get this show on the road!'

Inock, Lalita and Andre ran to the refreshments table and each grabbed sandwiches, sweets and bottles of fizzy drinks.

'I can't wait to see it!' Andre shrieked.

Meanwhile, the plump man walked off the pitch and the show began.

The show started with over two hundred clowns doing rounds around the pitch, juggling big balls, daggers and small animals, while doing funny little dances all in different coloured spotlights.

Then, things kicked into high gear when performers in black, skin-tight outfits came out juggling flaming daggers that vanished if not caught. They also juggled energy balls and multi-coloured fireballs that vanished mid-air at the end of the act.

'I could do that! I bet I could do that!' yelled Lalita.

Then came an act of men hurling flaming swords at three boys who would teleport out of the way just before the swords struck. Then, an act of performers spinning large energy

plates that would explode if they stopped spinning, which made the spinners do crazy dances in pretend fear. Inock really liked that act. There were magically shimmering human pyramids that reached heights of tower blocks, trapeze acts of flying witches, gampe tamers who did acrobatics on top of the moving animals (Gampe were similar to gante; they looked like massive tigers with red and black stripes like zebras; they were generally over five feet tall), clowns riding elephants the size of small houses and other fantastic creatures that did all sorts of acts, which Esttia seemed to enjoy a lot, clapping loudly as she watched the marvels.

All around the stadium, the lights came on and the announcer in the yellow, red and green pinstriped suit walked onto the pitch holding a microphone, while the last acts walked away.

'Ladies and gentlemen, boys and girls, and assorted animals,' the man addressed the stadium, 'we will now take a short intermission. Take this time to stretch your legs and get some refreshments. The wonderful performances will continue shortly!'

The whole stadium broke into applause. Many people got up from their seats, moving in all directions, some walking to kiosks for food and drinks, while some stayed put.

Straight away, Inock and Andre shot up from their seats and went to the food table and collected bags of sweets.

'That was brilliant!' cried Lalita. 'Did you see those human pyramids? They were so tall! Oh, and oh, what about the animal tamers?'

'I thought that last gampe tamer would get eaten!' said Andre taking his seat, his mouth full of candy. 'And did you

see those trapeze acts? Those witches and clowns were really flying!'

'They were very impressive!' said Inock, giggling. 'I can't wait to see the rest! Thank you for the birthday present, Father! I really like it!'

'That's quite all right, son,' Tehan responded, with a pleased expression. 'I am glad you are enjoying yourself.'

'Swallow before you speak, boy,' scolded Esttia. 'Remember your manners!'

'Sorry, Mother.'

Not long after that, fresh performers walked onto the pitch, along with the announcer.

'Ladies and gentlemen, let the show commence!'

First came the shape-shifters that mutated into all sorts of wild creatures that raced all over the pitch, did tricks and even roared frighteningly, the powerfuls transforming into countless other things, also making themselves thin as rakes or tall as tents. It started raining during this act. Then, there was an act of invisible hide-and-seek where invisible children—though the circus audience could see them as bluish blobs—would seek out others in a magically conjured maze and every time one touched the other, there would be super explosions and the children caught would shoot high up into the air screaming. There were then flying witches and demons and many more enchanting acts.

Inock left the private box once with Andre to use the toilets, and it was on the way back from the toilets that he saw something strange, or rather someone strange … someone whom he thought had died months ago … the dark witch

called Barla! A thin-faced woman he'd seen killed in a vision conjured up by a friend.

As soon as he spotted her, Inock grabbed Andre's arm.

'Let's follow that woman,' Inock said. 'She looks exactly like that dark witch Barla!'

The pair ran after the woman, but she soon turned a corner, her long black coat billowing behind her, her brown ponytail swishing as she went. And when the boys quickly turned the same corner, the witch was nowhere to be found. It was like she'd simply vanished into thin air.

'Do you really think that was her?' Andre asked, panting and bent over double. 'She's supposed to be dead, Inock!'

'I am one hundred percent sure about it, Andre!' Inock said. 'It looked just like her! But how can it be her? She's meant to be dead! She killed the Oracle's friend James! Then he killed her just before he died!'

'I know, Inock, but we really should get back to the box before they start wondering where we went,' said Andre. 'And besides, I don't want to miss any acts, the circus is awesome!'

So, the boys returned to the box in time to see the start of an act that involved a witch who would grow instant full-sized multi-coloured trees by throwing seeds all over the pitch; trees that dancing clowns would then comically chop down with giant axes. Inock quite enjoyed this act and noticed it rained no more.

At the conclusion of the final act, which was a young boy using his powers of telekinesis to juggle fifteen laughing, giggling and screaming clowns all at once, the announcer in the yellow bowler hat returned to the pitch one final time.

'Thank you! Thank you, ladies and gentlemen, boys and girls, and assorted animals for coming to see us!' the man boomed. 'i do hope you have enjoyed yourselves! Now, i have one last question for you, boys and girls: why don't cannibals eat demon entertainers? Give up? Okay, i'll tell ya: because they taste powerful funny!' there was a roaring of laughter and applause from all around the stadium. 'get it? Because they are powerfuls and are amusing!' he went on to say. 'didn't i tell you you'd laugh? Please come and see us again soon! A good night to you all!'

And that was the end of the phenomenal magical show, which left the whole stadium clapping ecstatically. Inock and his family were certainly doing some vigorous clapping of their own.

Inock, his family and Lalita left the stadium shortly, all yawning with sleepy eyes and full stomachs, and returned to Kasama where Lalita separated from them and went home, and the Tehans headed for Kasama Market, to their home. Inock and Andre couldn't stop talking about all the wonderful acts they had witnessed on the way.

Chapter Three
Power-Training with Tehan Tehan

The next day, Inock and Andre had school. They'd been allowed yesterday off for Inock's birthday.

The boys still studied at the power-training school next door, taught by the witch Ms Strict. Except, it was now called Last School, the school year before university level education or employment. Last School had started sometime in September as the previous school years, but it would be longer than a year, six months more. Along with the usual school holidays, Inock and Andre would get four weeks off in July. Inock would be seventeen years old at the end of it.

It was the morning and the two brothers were in the sitting room enjoying cereal and orange juice for breakfast.

Their sitting room was a fusion of red and black, with a large, black leather sofa and two matching armchairs, two big, black glass cabinets on either side of the sofa, tall, stylish glass lamps in all the corners of the room and the room centred with a long, black glass coffee table. The 3D television on a wall, that when turned off changed into a painting of a forest, was muted and turned onto a channel showing a *Power Trials* repeat, Inock's and Andre's favourite show where witches and demons took part in challenging trials using their powers.

The two boys had matured somewhat over the last few months and therefore did not worship the *Power Trials* contenders so much anymore; they only watched the show from time to time.

After breakfast, Inock and Andre grabbed their backpacks and left the house. Tehan, Esttia and Torend had already left for the power-training school next door where Esttia worked as the receptionist and Tehan and Torend worked as power-trainers. Both men had a power like Inock's where they could emulate other demons' powers, which they used to train demons wishing to learn or excel at their gifts. Tehan owned the school and was one of the best power-trainers in the world; he was well known around the world for it too.

Outside, Inock and Andre descended the white steps that led down from their front door. From their flat, you could see all the way along The Divider to the southern market gate far in the distance.

It was a sunny and crisp morning, and the market was already busy with shoppers and various animals, including gante and gampe. The two boys turned left and walked through light crowds to the power-training school, up the white steps, and entered the wide, glass sliding doors.

The school reception was small with a row of ten chairs lined along the wall, with five students sat waiting. To the left of the space was the receptionist's desk where Esttia sat writing in a large black book, and beyond the row of chairs, the reception narrowed into a corridor that ended just a few paces further on.

After a quick 'hello,' to their mother, Inock and Andre moved to the staircase, which was past the receptionist desk, leading to the next floor up.

Upstairs, they hurried to the classroom since they knew Ms Strict didn't like to be kept waiting.

The classroom had two desks with chairs by the window overlooking the market. Inock and Andre were her only students; she taught them privately. There was a big desk at the front of the classroom, Ms Strict's desk. And behind that was a big blackboard.

Ms Strict was sitting at her desk, waiting with her eyebrows furrowed in irritation.

'What explanation do you have for being late this time, boys?' Ms Strict tutted and commented in her harsh little voice. 'You live next door!' The loose bun of grey hair on top of her head was swaying comically as she said this, making Inock fight back a smile.

'Sorry, miss,' Andre said following Inock to the two chairs by the window. 'We didn't realise we were late.'

The boys sat down and each extracted a business studies textbook from their bags, ready for the lesson to begin.

'Well, all right. Just try not to be tardy anymore, boys. You know I don't like to be strict.' Inock knew she did very much like to be strict. And Ms Strict certainly looked like a strict boring schoolteacher, though she was a witch. She was old and usually wore long dull-coloured skirts and cardigans. 'But good time-keeping is important in life. Note that!'

'Yes, miss,' chorused the boys.

'Good. I am sick and tired of having to remind you of this!' Ms Strict said brandishing her crescent-shaped spectacles at them. 'Now let us begin the first lesson.'

For Last School, Ms Strict taught Inock and Andre maths and number reading, science and alchemy, languages, world history, business studies, media studies, theoretical

44

agriculture and hospitality and law. (With Ms Strict's guidance, Inock and Andre had chosen the last four subjects to prepare for university. The boys would take their end-of-school-year exams in the Kasama venator lookout.)

The day's first lesson was business studies. Ms Strict had the boys read a section in the set textbook then asked them to answer questions at the end of said section after a lengthy discussion.

Halfway through answering the case study questions, Ms Strict had a strange request for Inock. She was sat at the front of the classroom marking the boys' homework while they worked, when suddenly she looked up.

'Inock, boy, I have a favour to ask of you,' Ms Strict said.

Inock was shocked to hear this. Ms Strict had never before spoken to him so casually, let alone ask a favour of him.

'What is it, Ms Strict?' Inock asked.

'Well, boy, it is to do with a rather delicate matter,' Ms Strict answered. 'There was a robbery you see.'

'At your home?' asked Andre, who was also looking at their teacher with mild shock.

'No, boys, not at my home. It was a grave; my grandfather's grave to be exact.'

'That's terrible!'

'I know,' said Ms Strict. 'Terrible business!'

'And disgusting! What was stolen?' asked Andre, looking horrified. 'Not the corpse, surely!'

'No, not the corpse, young ones, but something from the corpse. A ring,' Ms Strict explained. 'You see, I recently visited the grave and was told by the graveyard caretaker that it'd been desecrated. And on further investigation, I learned

that something was taken from the corpse, only one thing, the ring I mentioned.'

'Was it an expensive ring?'

'No, but it was a magical ring. My grandfather requested to be buried wearing the ring and that wish was met. Now his grave has been vandalised and the ring stolen. Hence the favour I need to ask of you.'

'What do you need me to do, miss?' asked Inock.

'Well, I can't imagine it'll be easy, but I need you to investigate, find out who broke into the grave and stole the ring. It is rather important that the ring be recovered. My grandfather was ever so dear to me and my family.'

Ms Strict laid a hand on her chest and seemed to force herself to carry on talking.

'I have attempted to investigate myself and found out from the graveyard caretaker in Ettaka Village that teenagers were seen idling at the gravesite. Would you boys manage to speak with the caretaker and see what you can learn? Perhaps you might get further than I have. Do you think you can do this for me, boys?'

'Yes, that's fine, miss, we'll try,' Andre answered politely.

'Excellent, boys!' the teacher said, seeming to cheer up somewhat. 'I am indeed pleased to know that you'll help.'

Inock and Andre turned back to their work but their teacher went on to say, 'Furthermore, there is another matter I wish to discuss with you two.'

'What is it, miss?'

'It is to do with your further education,' said Ms Strict. 'I understand you both intend to tour Unatia University soon as a potential university. I mean to advise you, you must be fully

prepared. Ask the right questions, meet the right people and be thorough in your investigation of the place. You do not want to choose Unatia University and later feel dissatisfied with your choice. Do you understand?'

'Yes, miss. I think we've prepared well for it though,' Andre said. 'We've already checked out Kasama University and—'

'Yes, we did, but it's not in a great city like Unatia,' interrupted Inock. 'And it was small and not at all impressive. There were cows and sheep on campus!'

'I'm glad to hear that, boys,' Ms Strict said with a smile.

'Yes, Inock, it was small, but I thought it was okay,' spoke up Andre. 'Their curriculum looked okay to me … And it is a lot closer to home.'

'Yes, I suppose,' said Inock.

'Then very well done, boys,' said Ms Strict. 'And do remember to be thorough in your investigations of the universities you visit. Big and flashy doesn't equal quality, remember that. As they say: Wake up to make up!'

'What does that mean, miss?'

She answered: 'You must rise to the occasion to achieve. That is all it means. Do you understand, boys?'

'Yes, Ms Strict,' chorused the boys.

'Are you ready, Inock? Time for another power-training lesson,' came Tehan's voice.

It was lunchtime and Inock, Lalita and Andre were sitting on the school steps enjoying homemade vegetable cakes when Inock's father appeared through the school doorway. (Lalita knew the boys' timetable so she usually found them on the school steps having lunch to hang out.)

Tehan had been power-training Inock for months, but did not do it very often. (Esttia had taken Inock off the power-suppressing potion some time back.)

Inock's father had trained him in many powers, and he was getting quite good with them. With energy manipulation, he could now fire off multiple bolts of electricity from his fingers that could knock a being, human or animal, unconscious for a while. He could create and hurl energy balls but his aim needed work, and he could conjure up reasonably powerful energy shields. Tehan had tried to teach him to fly but Inock could only hover over short distances. With Andre's power, Inock could now turn into many animals. He learned how to create strong winds and manipulate water. Inock was really pleased to learn how to will darkness into existence that could overpower sources of light, and how to enhance light sources to make them shine brighter! (That power was quite rare.) And of course, Torend had taught Inock many powers before like invisibility and telekinesis. Tehan always encouraged Inock to train hard, saying he could be really powerful if he mastered most power types.

Inock rose from the steps with vigour.

'Yes, Father. I am ready!' he squealed, making Tehan smile at his eagerness.

'Come then,' the tall man said. 'Let us head into the orbiis.'

So, the power-trainer led the way into the school reception, past two waiting students and through the door past the staircase into his power-discovery room. Torend had a similar room upstairs. The power-discovery room was a spectacularly long, windowless room. It was split into eight equal sections, each about the size of a bedroom; each section

48

was a different colour. There was a tall wooden cupboard full of boxes of potions, books and other power-training gizmos in the far corner of the white section of the room. Next to that was a table and two chairs.

But this wasn't the space they'd train in today. They would train in a far more impressive space, the orbiis!

After giving Inock a potion to drink that would temporarily enhance his powers, the *Validus Valeo* potion, Tehan led the way to the other end of the room, uttered '*ESRA-IN!*' and something simply wonderful happened.

A huge, circular chunk of the violet wall began to slide slowly out towards them, bricks loudly scraping against each other. The wall stopped moving after several inches, then it cracked down the middle, splitting into two halves. Each half slowly slid aside revealing a dark, empty space. A round hole just big enough for Tehan and Inock to enter had been created, with bricks poking out around its edges.

'Follow me in, son,' Tehan said to Inock before walking through the hole.

Inock did as he was told and followed his father into the exciting darkness.

The dark space ahead of Tehan and Inock slowly illuminated, and at the same time, the wall behind them slid back into place, sealing them in.

They stood at the edge of a great silver dome the size of two football pitches. The wall behind them was a curved silver one. The ground beneath them was the only flat surface in the whole space and it felt a little colder than it had been in the power-discovery room.

A ball of light hovered at the centre of the dome, its light reflecting on the polished walls, making the vast space glisten

incredibly; Inock knew the light ball in the distance worked by magic. It was always wonderful to behold, like the light balls in venator lookouts.

Tehan led the way further into the great chamber.

'Son, today's lesson is energy manipulation,' Tehan turned and said after a minute or so. 'Take twenty paces away from me and fire an energy ball at me. Let us improve your aim, then perhaps, time allowing, move onto energy shields.'

The lesson had begun!

Inock did as he was told and walked twenty steps away from his father. He then turned around and conjured up a decent-sized energy ball twice the size of a football. As always, Inock got a thrill conjuring the sizzling ball of energy. It always got him excited to focus and will the energy to gather above his palm; then he had to maintain the shape of it keeping it spherical with just his mind, not to mention he had to regulate the constant energy flow into the deadly ball, and it was certainly mesmerising to look at; the thing sizzled and the energy all around it roared.

Inock hurled the bluish ball at the power-trainer. He missed him by five feet.

'Try again, son,' Tehan said aloud, his voice echoing off the silver walls.

So Inock tried again and again and again. But he just kept missing. The first two flew to Tehan's left and the third zipped past his right.

The power-trainer walked to his son, and laying a large hand on his shoulder, gently said: 'You need to focus, son … concentrate. You did well on the third try but you overshot. Remember what I told you about your wrist work. Do not twist the wrist just before you release the ball. I do believe

that's why your energy balls have a slight curve to them. Now, let us try again.' And he walked about twenty paces away from Inock. 'Conjure and fire, son!'

Inock did as he was told and summoned an energy ball above a palm and fired it, keeping in mind his father's advice. It took him seven tries to hit the target, though the power-trainer simply conjured up a blue energy shield between himself and the hurtling ball of energy just before it hit him and it exploded there with echoing bangs, showering the silver floor at his feet with sprinkles of energy.

'Well done, Inock!' Tehan bellowed. 'You succeeded! Let's keep the rhythm going and try that again!'

So, they practiced like that for the next half an hour; Inock managed to hit the target many times more, though disappointingly, he missed more than he struck.

Then, before you could say, 'a venator and his onis,' Tehan announced they had run out of time. The lesson was over.

'I'm afraid we won't have time to practice energy shields today, son.'

'Already?' Inock sulked.

'It's okay, son,' his father said with a slight smile. 'We'll try energy manipulation again soon.'

The power-trainer then led the way to the orbiis entrance, and at uttering *'ESRA-IN!'* a large chunk of the curved wall slid towards them, split in half, and the two halves slid aside revealing the long, multi-coloured room beyond, the power-discovery room.

'And don't worry, Inock,' Tehan said when they were back in the school reception. 'You're getting better each time we practice together.'

'Thank you, father,' Inock said with a giggle and a grin.

'And do be careful when you practice with your friend Lalita. I don't want either one of you to get hurt. Remember what I told you when we started your power-training; always use your powers responsibly. And always keep the Three Fundamental Demon Laws in mind when doing so.'

'Yes, father.'

'Can you remind me what the laws are, Inock?' asked Tehan, looking at him.

Inock recited, 'One: You shall not harm yourself by demon nature. Two: You shall not harm another by demon nature. Three: You shall not cause disorder by demon nature.'

'Perfectly done, son,' said the power-trainer. 'Now head to class.'

Tehan then walked to the reception desk and asked his wife which student was next.

Inock went upstairs to afternoon class, feeling significantly elated.

Chapter Four
Mind to Mind Spell Versus Imperiuo Fenestram

The Oracle summoned Inock and Andre to her chambers with a talking aklonas for a mission one late afternoon just as they walked up the steps to their home. (Aklonas were large, orange, monkey-like beasts with razor-sharp teeth, sharp claw-like nails and two long tails.)

The creature sneaked up behind the two boys, hurled a stone at the back of Inock's head, and Inock shouted, 'Hey! Who did that?'

The creature then howled with laughter before straightening itself; then it spoke clearly in a deep man's voice.

'The Oracle requires your presence in her chambers post-haste, young ones. Please attend.' It grinned its stained teeth before vanishing in a white flash.

The two boys wasted no time and headed to the Oracle's place.

'Oracle, why did you do that?' Inock demanded as soon as they entered the glowing chamber. 'That aklonas threw a stone at me! It really hurt!'

Andre snickered.

'Don't laugh, Andre,' barked Inock. 'It was really irritating and painful!'

'Sorry, Inock,' said Andre, straightening up.

Sat at the only table in the room, the Oracle smiled a wrinkly smile.

'I'll try a different method next time, young one,' she said. 'Perhaps a blood-sucking succubus? Might you prefer that?'

Succubi were nasty, gargantuan insects that could paralyse a person with just one sting then suck you dry! Usually black, hairy and very much resembled dragonflies. They buzzed, struggling to hover.

Andre laughed at Mabiyah's comment, making Inock punch him in the arm.

'But back to why I summoned you,' said the Oracle. 'I need you both to make a delivery to Mateete Village to a small house near the village boundary with the olive tree at the front.'

She looked at the space between her and the boys and a small golden envelope magically appeared there; it floated in mid-air. Inock took it and pocketed it, at the same time massaging the back of his head. 'That really hurt … not funny,' he grumbled.

'Take the envelope to Mateete Village, young ones,' the Oracle said next. 'I've already given you the directions to the house you need to deliver it to.'

'We'll do it right away, Oracle,' said Andre.

So Inock and Andre left the chamber, collected their gante from the market stables and once out of the market, mounted the creatures and sped away. (The stables were located in the south-eastern section of the market.)

Gante were as fast as horses, or even faster. Sat in his comfy black saddle and holding the soft leather reins, Inock couldn't imagine a better feeling. He really loved riding his gante; it always gave him such exhilaration being up so high looking down at pedestrians and speeding away.

The journey to Mateete Village took just under half an hour; they didn't make any stops on the way.

The village was small and quiet with small houses with red tiles for roofs, and tree-lined streets. The boys wasted no time and rode straight for the house the Oracle had described.

They dismounted and Andre knocked on the brown door.

A young woman with blonde hair answered and the boys introduced themselves as messengers from the Oracle of Kasama Market; the woman seemed to understand why they were there; but when Inock reached into his pocket and took out the golden envelope, something comical but also very annoying happened.

A small white animal that looked like a lemur but with two red tails flew out of nowhere, grabbed the envelope in its mouth, and scampered off down the street with it.

'Oh no! That's my grandmother's!' the young woman cried, hand on mouth. 'A sixonas cat just stole it!'

'Don't worry, miss, we'll get it back!' Andre said before grabbing Inock by the arm and taking off down the street after the creature, leaving the woman behind, blinking in surprise.

'Andre, we have to catch it!' Inock cried as they turned a corner after the bounding sixonas cat. 'I've never failed a delivery before!'

The pair chased the small creature down two streets and along two alleyways, until it ran into the back garden of a small house.

Inock and Andre entered the green garden with a single tree and were both surprised to see none other than Laden, Lalita's older brother, stood there at the back door, holding the thieving animal in his arms.

'Hello, boys. What are you two doing here?' Laden asked with a grin. He looked to be in his early twenties, had short, blonde, spiky hair, wore dark shorts and was topless, showing off his flat stomach and muscles.

'Is that animal yours?' Andre asked, pointing an accusing finger.

'No,' said Laden with a mock pout, cradling the creature at his chest.

'Yes, it is, Laden, do not lie to them!' said another voice; a girl's voice. And she came into view from inside the house.

Inock and Andre were only mildly surprised to see it was Lalita.

'What are you two doing here? Inock, you remembered where I live?' Lalita asked, pointing a finger, a hand on her hip.

'That sixonas cat stole something from us!' said Andre. 'A package from the Oracle. We need it back, Laden!'

'Laden! Did you get that thing to steal again?' Lalita asked accusingly, her round glasses catching the afternoon sun.

'Sorry, I didn't know Sixon would steal from you lot, did I?' said Laden.

'Then give it back!' Andre hissed. 'The woman is still waiting for us!'

Laden laughed, his spiky hair shining in the sun.

'You're always so serious, Andre!' he said. 'Relax a bit. Sixon didn't know not to steal from you.' He scratched the animal's head and it purred softly.

'This is no laughing matter, Laden! We're on a mission from the Oracle!'

'Okay, okay … I understand,' said Laden. He carefully removed the golden envelope from Sixon's mouth and handed it to Andre, saying, 'Bad Sixon! No more stealing!'

'The Oracle's business is serious, you know!' said Andre. He pocketed the envelope then grabbed Inock by the arm and led him away, back to the envelope's true recipient.

'Come and visit me after you deliver that thing,' Lalita called as Inock and Andre left.

The two boys returned to the young woman's house where they found her waiting nervously, and after apologising generously, Andre handed her the envelope and he and Inock left her alone. They returned to Lalita's home on gante.

The size of the house was reflected on the inside; it was cramped, with wood floors and shabby old furniture. Lalita led Inock and Andre through a messy, cluttered sitting room, up a narrow set of stairs and into her bedroom, which was also small with a single bed, a wardrobe and a desk and chair.

'Wow, Lalita, your room's a mess!' Andre said, whistling.

And it was true, the bedroom floor was dotted with dirty laundry, plates and cups and magazines.

'Well, I don't have a mother to tidy up after me like you two have,' said Lalita, shooting Andre a mock-angry expression. 'Laden's right, you need to relax more.'

'Oh shut up, Lalita. I'm plenty relaxed!'

Inock let off a small laugh which was mirrored by Lalita.

Then Inock spotted something interesting on the desk in the corner; an open leather-bound, brown book that appeared to be a spell book; a section of the open pages was covered in multi-coloured socks. He walked over to it, brushed away the socks and turned a page, confirming his initial assumption; it was indeed a spell book.

The page he was looking at was titled:

Mind to Mind Spell
A Spell to Link Minds

'Lalita, where did you get this?' Inock asked.

Lalita came over to the desk.

'Be careful with that, Inock, it was my mother's spell book,' she said.

'Wow, so you have your own spell book?'

'Yes, but it is encrypted,' said Lalita. 'I've been trying to decrypt it one spell at a time using a small handwritten dictionary mother created in her own self-invented language but-!'

'Wow, she made up her own language?' Andre asked disbelievingly, also moving over to the desk.

'Yes, she did. I have only decrypted a few spells, but I can't work them. I don't know whether that's because I decrypted them wrong or if I'm just not executing the spells right.'

'Looks like the spell names are not encrypted though,' said Andre, turning page after page.

'Well, I rewrote some in English,' Lalita told them.

There was a spell to turn things and people to stone; spells to levitate things; spells to transfigure bodies and things; spells to manipulate the weather; a spell to create insects and many more. Inock was excited just looking at the strange handwritten book.

Until Andre turned to a page that made Lalita gasp.

'Check out this spell!' the girl said. 'It sounds interesting. I've decrypted it but cannot work it.' She sat at the table reading the spell instructions.

They were now looking at a page titled:

Imperiuo Fenestram
A Spell to See into Another Location

'I think this is the kind of spell witches use to view another place, like a fly on the wall.'

'Oh, like the one Barnarbo uses?' asked Inock. (Barnarbo was a male witch who co-owned and worked on a farm that Inock, Andre and Lalita often visited.)

'Yes, exactly!' Lalita said triumphantly. 'Maybe we can try it out together? It might work if we all try.'

'Okay, what do we need to do?' Inock asked. He loved doing magic.

'Are you sure we should mess with this stuff, you two? It sounds complicated,' said Andre looking closely at the spell instructions. 'I know magic and witchcraft sounds cool, but do you ever really know what you're getting yourself into by exploring the stuff?'

Lalita yawned very noticeably.

'Oh, relax, Andre. *Existence*, you sure do preach! I think it's worth a try,' she said. 'Let me get what we need for it.' Then she got up and left the room. She returned a minute or so later with a glass bowl of clear water, which she placed on the desk after clearing away more socks.

Lalita then sat down and took the spell book from the desk.

After moments of reading, she said, 'It says to execute the spell we have to visualise the location we want to see, recite the incantation and at the same time *will* the reflective surface to display the place we wish to view.'

'What's the incantation?'

'It's right here; I just hope I decrypted it right.' She pointed to the incantation.

Both Inock and Andre looked down at the five-line spell written neatly in the spell book.

It read:

Ostendo mei locus
Ostendi mei locus
Ostendo mei locus
Ostendi mei locus
Ostendi mei locus optare promo

'It says here that we have to say the words correctly and keep chanting until it works,' Lalita told the boys. 'Oh, and we have to look at the chosen surface. I guess that means the surface of the water. And we need to remember to visualise the location we want.'

'What location should we choose?' Inock asked.

'How about Dwayne's and Barnarbo's farm?' asked Andre.

'Oh, look who's getting into it all of a sudden,' said Lalita and then chuckling.

'Oh shut up,' said Andre.

'Well, you're always so serious, Andre!' said Inock. 'You are not very humorous, and I think you know that.'

'I am plenty humorous!' said Andre, stung. 'I like jokes too, you know!' Then worriedly: 'You don't find me boring, do you, Inock? And you, Lalita?'

Inock and Lalita swapped brief furtive looks, but neither answered him.

'All right, the farm is easy enough,' said Lalita, stopping herself from smiling. 'Let's get started.' She laid the spell book on the desk and said, 'Alright, ready? Everyone, look at the water and chant the spell. And remember, visualise!'

So, all three of them stared at the water and began chanting the incantation.

On the fourth completion of the chant however, Inock found his mind wandering, not to mention he felt a bit silly doing the thing altogether.

But their perseverance paid off as at the end of the sixth chant, the surface of the water shimmered with a transparent sort of energy and a distorted image appeared there; Inock thought it was like looking at a small round television set with bad reception: but it wasn't Dwayne's and Barnarbo's farm; it was a vision of themselves in Lalita's bedroom staring down at the bowl of water.

'Wow! It worked!' howled Lalita, jumping in her seat. The motion was reflected on the surface of the water.

'Well, that's great, Lalita, but that's not the farm, that's us!' whined Andre. 'It went wrong! We really should be careful what we try.'

'Come on, Andre, we achieved something at least. I wonder what went wrong though? Were you both thinking of the farm?' inquired Lalita.

'Actually, I sort of lost concentration and kept thinking of myself looking like an idiot doing the spell,' Inock said, scratching his ear nervously.

Then Andre let off a minute laugh.

'So did I!' he said. 'So, I don't think we concentrated enough. What did you think of, Lalita?'

'I thought of the farm of course, I'm no amateur,' Lalita said in a dignified sort of voice, adjusting her glasses.

'Ha! No amateur? How many spells do you know, Lalita?' Andre asked her with a grin.

'I know more than you, idiot!' said Lalita, and then smiling in his face.

'Ha!' said Andre. 'I don't care, I'm good with my powers, anyway.'

'Okay. Maybe I don't know many spells,' said Lalita, punching Andre in the arm. 'Actually, Inock, I think you probably know more spells than me by now, what with *ghost girl* being your best friend and all.' (Lalita referred to Rozanthia, Inock's oldest friend who was a ghost.) 'Why don't we try again?' she finished, rubbing her hands together excitedly.

'Oh, not again!' Andre said. 'I feel stupid doing this!'

'Come on, Andre, it'll be fun!' argued Lalita.

It took some arm-twisting on Lalita's part, but Andre was finally convinced. And so they tried again. It took them four

rounds of the chant to cause an effect this time; but once again, the highly distorted image on the water surface wasn't a farm, but of Laden sat on the toilet, stroking the sixonas cat in his arms. And what's more, the image gave off sound.

'Ha! We have sound now!' squealed Lalita.

'Good boy, Sixon,' Laden was softly saying to the animal. 'You did very well today. Remember, anything shiny, you take. And always come straight home when you take something, we don't want anyone following you and stealing you. I love you, boy.'

Then the magical vision vanished; only clear water was left.

'Existence, that thief!' cried Andre. 'He trained that thing to steal from people? It knew what it was doing all along! Lalita, you need to have a good word with him!'

'I've had enough,' said Lalita. 'This spell isn't working out. I'll have to recheck the encrypted version. Maybe I missed something when I decrypted it.'

'Great. I'm glad,' said Andre. 'I've had enough too.'

'No, no, you misunderstand me, Andre,' said Lalita. 'I've had enough of *this* spell; I don't think we'll get anywhere with it if I didn't decrypt it correctly. But I want to try the *Mind to Mind* spell; that one needs more than one person. I couldn't try it before because no one else but Laden knows about this book.'

'Okay, great!' Inock said cheerily, rubbing his hands together in anticipation. 'What does it do?'

Lalita picked up the spell book and turned to the page titled: *MIND TO MIND SPELL.*

'This one's simpler. It lets us communicate with each other telepathically!' she said with relish. 'I've never tried it

before because I've never had anyone to try it with. Laden doesn't do spells, you see.'

'What do we need to do?' Inock asked, mirroring Lalita's gleeful expression.

She looked down at the book in her hands and read out loud: 'This spell allows two or more people to communicate telepathically with each other. Simply by thinking of a person, then that person's name loudly in your mind, then thinking thoughts at the intended person. The spell requires the users to enter an agreement where they can think to one another whenever they want to. And I think, initially, we need to touch each other's temples, then...' She turned a page. 'Look, there's a ritual that we need to undertake in order to enter into the covenant!'

'Covenant? What covenant?' Andre asked with doubt in his voice.

'Oh, don't worry so much, Andre, it's just a few words to say that we all know what we're doing and that we're doing it willingly,' Lalita said on further reading. 'Look, read it for yourself if you don't believe me.' She handed Andre the book.

Andre took it with obvious uneasiness on his face and read out loud: 'The ritual requires each member to touch the other's temples with both palms and recite this incantation:

> *I command a link of minds that's right*
> *As I link my mind to yours this night*
> *I Promise to handle our connection right*
> *To abuse this connection is to forfeit*
> *I swear I know what this is*
> *You may break this bond at anytime*
> *I may break this bond at anytime*

This bond I promise to respect
And from you respect I expect
So be it.

Andre seemed to look closely at the page then with a happy smile read on: 'To break the bond between minds, simply speak out the other person's name and then say: Mental Bond Be Broken!'

'See? That doesn't sound so bad. Does it, Andre?' Lalita said forcefully. 'You can break the bond whenever you want. Just say mine or Inock's name and then "Mental Bond Be Broken"!'

'Okay. But I still think we need to be careful what we try,' Andre said. 'You never know what might happen to us.' And then at noticing Inock and Lalita swap a meaningful look he hastily added: 'Maybe it will be fun. I like humour. I saw a very funny joke on the television yesterday—!'

'Oh Existence, this will be painful!' said Lalita. 'Shall we just get on with the—'

'What do you mean by painful?' Andre asked her.

'Shall we please just do the spell,' said Lalita. 'Andre, I promise you, everything will be fine. And yes, you are plenty humorous—' smiling broadly, Andre went to say something and Lalita said gruffly, 'Just don't tell us the joke from the television right this second!'

'Fine, I won't!' said Andre, with a confused frown.

And so they took it in turns to place their hands on one another's temples and recited the spell that would activate the telepathic bond between them.

Then Lalita said, 'Okay. Inock, I'll think to you first.'

She seemed to concentrate for a moment then next thing, Inock heard loud and clearly in his mind: *Hello, Inock. It's me, Lalita! I'm thinking to you!*

Inock jumped back in shock, knocking into Andre.

'*Wow!* It actually worked!' Inock yelled. 'It really worked! Now you, Andre! Go on, think something to me.'

Andre too got a look of focus, then two seconds later, in his mind Inock heard: *Hey, Inock. Can you hear me? Oh, I feel weird doing this!*

'Did it work?' asked Lalita.

Inock concentrated, thought of Andre, and then his name loudly in his mind before broadcasting: *Yes, I heard you, Andre! Can you hear me?*

'What's going on, you two? Is it working or not?' Lalita asked once more, annoyed she was being ignored.

She was answered when Andre beamed from ear to ear, clapped powerfully, and said, 'Yes, it worked, Lalita! I wonder how close we need to be for it to keep working.'

Lalita picked up the spell book once more and read from it. Her eyes lit up like full moons.

'My Existence! It has no limit!' she screeched. 'We can be anywhere in the world and it still works!'

'Amazing!'

'That is pretty amazing,' even Andre had to admit. 'So should we break the bond now?'

'No, wait, let's leave it for now. I promise I won't abuse it,' Lalita said with a giggle and a mischievous grin.

And Inock suspected she might abuse the bond; however, he found the whole business exciting.

'Let's wait to break the bond, you lot,' Inock said. 'I want to have some more fun with it!'

Andre seemed to think for a moment then he too said, 'Okay, let's wait.'

And so it was settled. They'd wait to break the psychic connection between them.

Then in his mind, Inock heard Lalita's voice say: *A man was holding two crystal balls.*

Inock thought of Lalita, thought her name clearly in his mind and sent back: *Then what happened?*

Lalita replied: *An angry woman kicked him in the crotch. The man dropped the crystal balls.*

And then what happened, broadcasted Inock.

Lalita sent: *Another man watching them said: "watch your balls, buddy."*

And then what happened? Inock thought, already giggling.

The angry woman said: "I hope that hurt," sent Lalita. *Then, the first man said: "Yes it did, thank you very much!"*

Inock laughed aloud.

And then? he communicated back.

"Yes, but which balls did it hurt?" said the other man, broadcasted Lalita, now giggling too.

'What's going on? What did she say?' said Andre.

Then thinking of Andre and his name loudly in his mind, Inock thought: *Hey, Andre, listen to this: A rat took a shower. His owner sniffed him and said to his friend: "Why don't you smell him? I think he could do with another shower yet."*

And then what? sent Andre, already laughing. *Rats don't shower, you silly!*

Inock broadcasted back: *The friend took the rat and smelled it and said: "You see, I don't know, I think it smells just fur-ine!"*

Andre burst into laughing fits at that.

'That is funny!' Andre screeched.

Then next, in his mind, Inock heard Andre's voice: *Hey, Inock, try saying this very fast and over and over: A gaggle of girls giving off girlish giggles!*

'A gaggle of girls giving off girlish giggles,' said Inock quickly. 'A giggle of girls giving off girlish giggles. A gaggle of giggles giving off girls giggles!'

All three friends giggled at that.

'That's funny, Inock!' said Lalita, also saying out, very fast, the phrase: 'A gaggle of girls giving off girlish giggles!' And then: 'That's not bad at all for someone like you, Andre!'

'I can enjoy a joke too, you know!' argued Andre.

Looking at each other, they all howled with laughter.

The threesome spent the rest of the afternoon thinking all sorts of things to each other; puns, jokes and funny stories they were once involved in, all laughing away.

Inock and Andre left Lalita's home that evening with the mental bond still active; they chose not to break it just yet.

Chapter Five
Magic Lesson

It was a cloudy but warm Friday afternoon and Inock, Andre and Lalita were atop gante, riding to Dwayne's and Barnarbo's farm, Inock and Andre having just finished school for the day. Lalita was arguing they hurry to get there and ask the male witch Barnarbo how to perfect the *Imperiuo Fenestram* spell.

'Oh, don't worry so much, Andre,' said Lalita. 'I'm sure he'll tell us how to work the stupid spell! It's similar to the spell he used to show us that witch James and his dark witch friends.'

'But I heard witches are all secretive. They don't share their spells,' argued Andre.

'Actually, I heard the same thing,' said Inock. 'Witches are secretive.'

'Don't worry, boys, I'll make Barnarbo tell us how to work the spell properly,' Lalita said with a sly smile. 'I rechecked the original spell in my mother's spell book. I'm now sure I decrypted it right. And anyway, I'm sure not all witches are so secretive. Look at me and you guys, we're not so secretive. And we're witches, aren't we?'

'Are we?' Andre asked, looking behind him at a pretty girl who just zoomed past them atop gante; otherwise, the grass field-flanked path was secluded.

'Hmm, what is a witch, anyway?' Inock wondered out loud. 'What makes a witch a witch?'

'I think we are,' Lalita said, placing stray blonde hairs behind an ear and grinning at the boys. 'We practice magic and spells; we're not just demons.'

'I think there might be more to it than just that, Lalita,' said Andre. 'What about beliefs and rituals and who you worship and all the rest of it?'

And they discussed the differences between witches and demons and what made a witch a witch all the way to the yniqem farm. By reaching the place, they'd concluded that indeed they were witches as well as demons, inexperienced though they may be.

The threesome found Dwayne and Barnarbo feeding the many yniqem cubs on the farm. Yniqem were fire-breathing dragon-like creatures with feathers instead of scales all over their bodies, two very long feathery tails and they only ate coal and charcoal. Dwayne and Barnarbo bred and sold the brilliant creatures.

Though they were partners, Dwayne and Barnarbo certainly were different; Dwayne was an old but fit man with short white hair and Barnarbo was an incredibly handsome mixed-race man with a bright smile. All who worked on the farm were usually friendly with Inock, Andre and Lalita when they visited.

After the two brothers and Lalita helped the two farmers and a handful of farmhands feed the yniqem, Barnarbo had Inock, Andre and Lalita follow him to the toolshed to a

wooden barrel full of clear rainwater to show them how to properly work the spell they had come to perfect. (As soon as they arrived, Lalita straight away announced to Barnarbo why they'd come.)

'It's not the spell I usually use to achieve *Remote Sight* but it's one of the easiest to use for the task,' Barnarbo said. 'In fact, it's far easier than the ones I usually use. But then again, I can achieve more with my spells.'

'But this one's easy, right?' Lalita asked the cheerful man.

'Yes, most witches would argue it's the easiest,' said Barnarbo. He turned to the barrel of water, a look of deep concentration coming across his face. 'Now, watch and listen very carefully,' he said.

And he began to chant:

> *Ostendo mei locus*
> *Ostendi mei locus*
> *Ostendo mei locus*
> *Ostendi mei locus*
> *Ostendi mei locus optare promo*

Right away, a beautiful top-down vision of Kasama Market materialised on the water surface; the image was very clear, as though the group were in a helicopter looking down at the bustling market glowing with the late afternoon sun, with sound and all.

'Wow! That was easy!' cried Lalita. 'You make it look so easy, Barnarbo! Hey look, guys, I can see your house!' She was pointing at the base of the tower at the market centre, where indeed, Inock's and Andre's home could be seen.

'I can see it too!' said Inock. 'And the image is so much clearer than when we did it!'

Barnarbo touched the water surface making the vision disappear.

'Right, now it is your turn,' he said. 'Lalita, you first since this spell came from your spell book. Remember, focus, visualise and will, as I'm sure you are already aware to do.'

And so Inock, Lalita and Andre took it in turns to cast the spell on the water surface.

Lalita achieved a blurred vision of the market with muffled sound, Inock got a similar vision but without any sound at all, and Andre didn't even get a picture.

After Andre had had his go, Barnarbo seemed to think for a moment.

'Remember, in spellcasting it's not just about what you see and hear,' he said. 'There is a lot more going on; like willing … desire … concentration … chanting … and even mental chanting. It all has to come together perfectly for the caster to achieve the desired result. From what I've observed so far, Lalita, I believe you and Inock are too excited to focus properly, and Andre I don't think your heart is in it at all. You don't want it enough.'

'But I do. I really do,' argued Andre, shoving his hands in his shorts pockets.

'Don't be discouraged, you lot,' said Barnarbo. 'This sort of magic isn't for beginners. You've done really well so far considering you've already managed to conjure a vision, and with sound too. That's really brilliant for novices!'

'What do you think we're doing wrong, Barnarbo? I was concentrating really hard,' Lalita said. 'The image is all fuzzy and the sound isn't that good; not like when you do it.'

'Well, I normally use a different, more complex spell for *Remote Sight*,' said Barnarbo. 'Usually, the harder spells are the better spells. You can achieve more with them.'

'Can you teach us your spell for *Remote Sight*?'

'I'm afraid I cannot, children,' Barnarbo said, laying a hand on Inock's shoulder. 'The process would take too long and it is a rather tricky spell. Stick to this one.' He beamed a brilliant white smile at them. 'It's clearly working for you. Just remember, practice, practice, practice if you want to master it. It is a lot to do with your focus; you need to concentrate and get every step of the spell right. Say the words of the spell clearly and correctly and even hear them in your mind; give attention to the chosen surface, and not to mention the location you want to view. And don't just wish for the spell to work, you have to also will it, want it and see it already happening!'

Barnarbo had Inock, Andre and Lalita try out the spell a few times more, and at each repeated attempt their conjured visions got clearer and the sound a little better; even Andre managed to bring about a decent vision.

The threesome left the farm feeling rather pleased with themselves.

'And don't be afraid to ask me for more help with your spells if you need to,' Barnarbo called out to them as they rode off.

'See? I told you Barnarbo would help us,' Lalita said.

'It was cool!' said Inock.

And things seemed to get better for Inock since mere days later, his father found him in the sitting room one evening doing his Business Studies homework with Andre, quietly took a seat, and told him he had some good news for him.

'Inock, I've got some good news for you, son. I've decided to power-train you on a more regular basis,' Tehan said.

'Awesome! Thank you, father! When do we start?' Inock was positively over the moon.

'Yes, well, son, you've been learning so well that I decided to direct attention to the growth of your powers. Starting next week, I will train you twice a week straight after school, and perhaps from time to time during your lunch breaks. I've arranged it all with your mother.'

'Oh, wow! Thank you, father!'

'Well, son, you've earned it with all your hard work,' said Tehan. 'Be sure to keep it up. Andre, you are doing very well with your powers too. I will test your progress in another four months or so. You do not need as much training as Inock. Now, back to your homework both of you.'

'Thank you, Tehan,' said Andre with a smile.

Tehan got up and left the room.

'This is really, really cool!' said Inock, ignoring his homework. 'I'm going to get so powerful!'

'Not more powerful than me though, Inock, so don't get so excited, brother,' said Andre, grinning at him.

Inock laughed at that.

'Of course I'll be more powerful than you, Andre! You just wait!'

'All right, all right, it's very good news but we really should get back to work, Inock,' said Andre. 'You know how Ms Strict hates it when your homework is incomplete.'

And they got back to work, though Inock found it very difficult to concentrate after the very exciting news.

Therefrom, Inock's powers progressed well in the weeks that followed. He power-trained with his father in the expansive orbiis, and power-trained as well as practiced spells with Lalita and Andre.

And let me tell you, there was absolutely no way the Oracle could summon Inock for errands during lessons with his father, and certainly not by terrifying Tehan with a scary monster or tricks like the Oracle often did to Ms Strict.

Although, Inock was often distracted during both power-training lessons with his father and his school lessons by the disturbing memory of seeing that dead witch Barla. Could it really have been the same woman? Inock was sure it had been. He just hoped he was wrong about the matter since he knew she was a terrible evil witch; she and a companion had killed the Oracle's friend James without a second thought. Not to mention that her and her companion were trying to reunite their long separated dark clan of evil witches.

What's more, there was something else on Inock's mind, something he had been putting off doing for some time; looking into the matter of Ms Strict's stolen ring. Inock knew he had to investigate very soon; especially since Ms Strict kept asking him for updates and he always had to lie and say he was working on it.

It was the first week of April, a Monday morning, and Inock and Andre were in the sitting room enjoying a breakfast of cereal and juice. Today was the day they would go to Unatia city to tour Unatia University. The pair would go on their own straight after breakfast.

After the meal, the two boys said goodbye to their parents at the power-training school next door then walked to the venator lookout, where they used the teleporting contraptions

to get to Unatia; once there they hurried through the busy city, chatting animatedly about all they would see and do at the university.

The university wasn't far from the Unatia venator lookout; it was a twenty-five-minute walk, if you walked at a decent pace, and the boys were happy to walk there, gawking at the various sights the city had to offer; they passed shopping centres, walked through a splendid park with beautiful tall trees with orange bark and countless towering statues, passed museums and brightly coloured triple-decker tourist buses.

Inock and Andre did a double take when they reached the university campus.

Unatia University was awesomely beautiful. It looked like a big fort with many smaller buildings surrounding it, numerous soaring ancient trees around the campus and parks with comfortable benches. A green and white flag flapped at the highest point of the main building. There were students sat around the many well-manicured fields and small groups of students moving about the place, chatting spiritedly and tittering amongst themselves.

Inock and Andre approached the main building, passing a grand bicycle parking area, and entered into the main reception area, which was littered with students, some in queues and some going about their business, the space abuzz with chatter.

The duo approached the reception desk queue and joined it.

'This is amazing!' Andre murmured, looking at Inock. 'It's so exciting, so many people. And to think we could be students here.'

'And did you see the outside of this place?' Inock asked, grinning. 'It feels like I'm in a wondrous magical story! It's a castle, Andre! We're in a massive castle!'

After that, the boys went into a lengthy chat about the lecture they would attend about their chosen subject and what it would be like to live on campus.

At reaching the front of the queue, Inock told the receptionist why they were there. The woman offered them visitors' passes that they wore around their necks, and then she handed them a schedule of their stay on campus.

First, the visiting students were allocated into small groups led by current students. The groups then each got a tour of the university, which included the student cafeterias, shops, sports centres, a very wide power-training arena, students living quarters, finance department, lecture halls and classrooms with memory orbs on the tables which were crystal balls hovering over golden chalices that could record memories; then they sat through a two-hour lecture about the university, its history, as well as what courses they offered, though Inock and Andre were mostly interested when the lecturer spoke about the Law courses they taught focusing on powerfuls' affairs; they found the rest of the speech and electronic presentation a tad boring.

After the lecture, Inock and Andre attended a shorter seminar, which was led by the head of the Law department; a pasty-faced, squat man with a shiny bald head; there was a Q&A part at the end; but all Inock's and Andre's questions were answered by the lecturer during his speech, so they didn't put up their hands to ask anything.

After that, the boys had lunch in the main cafeteria and were free to roam the campus on their own.

As they walked through the main building corridors, reading notice boards and collecting flyers of activities they might do while attending the university, Andre found something interesting.

'Oooh! Inock, look,' Andre said pointing to a flyer just outside the Student Union, 'it says here the Student Union represents student demons and witches. Can we go in and see if we can find out what they do?'

'Yeah, okay,' Inock said, now reading the notice. 'It says they have meetings to discuss student powerfuls' issues. Sounds exciting. Let's go in and see. Then home, I think.'

So the boys entered the Student Union department; they were in a moderate-sized room with desks and cabinets. There was a casual sitting area in a corner, where a handful of students sat talking.

A boy of about nineteen approached the pair from a desk and greeted them warmly. Inock and Andre introduced themselves, mentioning they might be attending the university in the future, and asked a few questions about what the Student Union did to represent student witches and demons and the boy explained briefly; which included powerfuls meetings with active participation from student powerfuls, One-to-One Counselling sessions, and managing the power-training arena, then he handed them a flyer each.

The front page of the flyers was in bold letters.

It was titled:

WELCOME STUDENT POWERFULS

Unatia University welcomes all manner of Powerfuls.
All variety of Witches, Demons and Learned Ones.
Read below and on the back to learn more on what we can
do for you.
We hope to see you soon.

(Inock knew Learned Ones were natural-born demons with a specific power but then also learned to do magic and witchcraft.)

Minutes later, Inock and Andre left the department feeling informed and excited about Unatia University altogether; the university seemed to encompass a lot, Inock thought.

They left the university campus and commenced the walk back to the Unatia venator lookout.

And it was as they neared the lookout that they were approached by two boys and a girl, all in black jeans and vests; they looked to be in their late teens or early twenties.

The trio had been walking in the opposite direction of Inock and Andre, who were both busy reading the Student Union flyers, and had stopped right in front of the boys.

Inock had been busy reading the section on One-to-One Counselling.

So far he read:

Come to our One-to-One Counselling sessions and speak
with our counsellors!
They are willing to listen to any problem you may have with
your powers and magic, big or small!

They will not judge and will really listen and even give you advice on what to do about your unique problem!
All counsellors are professionally trained, and if you desire, you may have a student volunteer present; someone who really knows what you are going through; someone who has been through similar situations and problems!
You can have your pick of volunteers!
They do not judge and truly understand your problems!
Please, do come and try out our One-to-One Counselling service!
All powerfuls welcome; we do not judge!
Please do come and see us!

'Hello there. What is that you're reading? Are you students at the university?' the girl asked with a bright, pretty smile.

'But more importantly, are you powerfuls?' asked one of the boys. He had a trendy hairstyle with a blue fringe. The other boy had close-shaven, brown hair.

'Who's asking?' inquired Andre.

'Be not afraid, we're friends,' said one of the boys in a near whisper. 'We're powerfuls too.'

'Yeah, guys, we just want to see if you'd be interested in our organisation,' the girl said, still smiling cheerfully, her black ponytail swishing happily.

'And what organisation is that?' Andre asked, sounding ever sceptical.

The girl leaned in close to Inock and Andre and whispered, 'The AVC!'

'The what?'

'A-V-C! It's short for Anti-Venator Clan!'

'Thank you, but I don't think we're interested,' Andre said, making to walk away. 'Come, Inock, let's go home.'

But Inock was curious.

'What does your organisation do?' he asked.

Andre stopped and turned back, frowning.

The trio of older teenagers smiled conspiratorially.

'Follow us and we'll show you,' said the boy with the close-shaven hair. 'But first, I have to ask, are you in fact powerfuls?'

Inock grinned.

'Yes, we are,' he said proudly.

'Perfect! Follow us,' the boy with the blue fringe said, rubbing his hands together and beaming as though he'd just found a fifty ryza note on the ground.

'No, Inock! Don't go with these people!' Inock heard a girl's voice whisper into his ear, and at the same time the three older teenagers began walking away down the street.

Of course, Inock knew who had spoken. It could only be his ghost friend Rozanthia, and he knew she was floating right next to him, invisible. (Rozanthia sometimes followed Inock throughout the day, and could turn invisible at will. Inock assumed she must have followed him to Unatia from Kasama and hadn't told him she was there.)

'Rozanthia, what are you doing here?' Inock asked, barely audible, looking to his right; that's where the voice had come from.

Andre looked quizzical, but only for a second; he seemed to understand what was going on.

'I followed you, Inock,' said Rozanthia in an undertone, still invisible. 'I wanted to be here for you. To help you if you needed me.'

'That's great but you didn't need to,' said Inock. 'I want to go with them, they're interesting.'

'You should listen to her, Inock,' Andre said, having watched Inock debate the issue. 'This idea smells bad to me. They don't seem like our sort of people!'

'Look, you two, I'm going,' argued Inock. 'Feel free to go home if you want to. I'm not forcing you to do anything!' And he took off after the darkly dressed trio.

'But you don't even know those people!' Andre yelled in frustration at Inock's back.

'Whatever you say, buddy!' Inock called back over his shoulder.

Chapter Six
The Anti-Venator Clan

Andre seemed to wrestle with his thoughts for a moment or two, then scowling and cursing under his breath, ran after Inock.

Inock, Andre and an invisible Rozanthia followed the AVC members into a less developed area of the city; the journey lasted just under half an hour and the AVC trio stayed ten paces ahead of Inock and Andre all the way.

Eventually, the two older boys and girl stopped outside what appeared to be an abandoned theatre on a deserted rundown street. They looked back at Inock and Andre and the girl beckoned the boys to follow them inside, before entering.

Inock followed straight away, succeeded by a reluctant and irate Andre.

Inside the theatre foyer, they were in near-darkness. The girl soon mumbled a spell and a small ball of yellow light came into existence; it hovered before them all, lighting the space rather well, Inock thought.

Thereafter the threesome led Inock and Andre across the space and through decaying, foul-smelling corridors and into the main auditorium, the light ball always floating several paces ahead of them.

What lay before the group was a sort of shabby settlement; there were tents and beds all over, even a rust-covered cooker on the stage; the space was littered with dirty laundry, unwashed plates and cups, food wrappers, cigarette butts and empty beer cans, benches and chairs lined along the walls. There were over twenty people there, teenagers and some older men and women hanging about, chatting between themselves. The whole space was lit by a bright light ball the size of a fist floating high up just below the mouldy ceiling.

The girl who'd invited Inock and Andre took to the stage. And as soon as she did, the crowds in the theatre all gathered before her. Inock and Andre fell in behind the large group, Inock intrigued by what would happen next.

'Settle down, everyone!' the girl on the stage called out at the top of her voice. Everyone went quiet. 'It's time to begin today's meeting. Kano, Chris and I have recruited well this week; there are a few new faces with us today and we've just now found two more. So, I'll begin by telling the new people—' she smiled at Inock and Andre '—what we're all about and what we do. We are the AVC: The Anti-Venator Clan! And our goal is to overpower the venators so powerfuls all over the world can practice and use their magic and powers freely!'

'But we do use our powers freely!' Andre called out.

The girl on the stage smiled a sly smile at Andre and emphatically continued: 'That is an illusion, my friend! You may think you are free, but you are not! All powerfuls around the world have to abide by the Three Fundamental Demon Laws. These are: One: You shall not harm yourself by demon nature. Two: You shall not harm another by demon nature. Three: You shall not cause disorder by demon nature! Yes,

these laws keep demons and witches who might misuse their powers in check, but we are still too afraid to use and enjoy our powers openly! Those of us who use responsibly are still too afraid of the venators!

'And with good reason; the venators are cruel to witches and demons! One toe out of line and they send their vile onis after you, and let's not forget about their disgusting energy-sapping whips! No, my friends, we only appear to be free! So I will say this: we need powerfuls from all over to aid in our goals. We need you to dedicate yourselves to helping our cause, whatever the task at hand may be. When you are called to participate, we hope you will answer!' Then she bellowed out: 'we are all still too afraid! We are oppressed! It is time people stood up to the venators and this is what we're here to do! Join together and oppose! The avc intends to bring down the venators in any way we can! This is our mission!'

The girl nodded her head to signal her speech was over.

There was a round of applause from the crowd, and Inock found himself hollering and clapping along. He knew very well how cruel and vicious venators were to powerfuls. The girl was right, he thought; one toe out of line with the venators nearby and you were doomed.

The crowd dispersed into smaller groups that started chatting away to themselves, the room abuzz with a mixture of sounds.

The girl who gave the speech on stage came over to Inock and Andre, accompanied by the two boys from the street.

'Hello, you two, I am Erin, one of the founders of the AVC,' she said to Inock and Andre. 'You already met Kano.' She pointed to the boy with the trendy hairstyle and blue

fringe. 'And this is Chris.' She gestured to the one with the close-shaven hair.

'Why do you hate venators so much?' Andre asked the trio. 'They're just doing their jobs! If you behave, they leave you alone.'

Kano's brow shot up.

'Well, aside from everything Erin just told you about them,' he said, 'let me tell you something you probably don't know. And I'm sure that after hearing it, you'll be on our side all the way. All venators and onis are beings from another realm. Although, many onis escaped from them and bred in the wild.' He gazed at Inock and Andre defiantly as though expecting them to say he was lying. When the boys didn't argue, he went on to divulge, 'They don't originate in this realm—in our world; this is truth, my friends! They even have a magical gateway in every venator lookout leading to their home realm. And we all just hate them! They're too cruel to powerfuls!'

'We've learned there are a number of ways one can travel between realms,' added Erin. 'And there are more other realms than we even knew!'

Inock didn't find the concept of other realms so strange since he already knew other realms existed; he went to Samuel Blackwood's realm after all.

'That puts new meaning to the saying, *a venator and his onis*, eh, Inock?' Andre said with a small laugh. He too knew of magical gateways leading into other realms.

'But enough about the loathsome venators,' said Kano next. 'I'm sure everyone in this room will tell you plenty about them in due course. What are your powers?'

'I have the power to emulate other demons' powers and Andre here can turn into any animal he wants, and because of my power, so can I,' said Inock.

'That's incredible!' said Chris in a near yell, unable to contain himself. 'Are you any good with it?'

'My father is Tehan Tehan of Kasama,' replied Inock proudly. 'He trains me. I'm getting pretty good with it. He teaches me many powers!'

'Incredible! Absolutely incredible!'

'He could be the strongest one here!'

'My thinking exactly, Kano, but since they're newbies, I think they'd be more suited for onis release missions to start with … beginner's work,' the girl Erin said. 'Then maybe trickier missions later.'

'What's onis release missions?' Inock asked.

'I'll tell you … but first, what's your name? Did your friend call you Inock? We know his name is Andre.'

'Yes, I am Inock. Andre here is my brother.'

'Oh nice, brothers,' said Erin. 'That should come in handy when we try to find you for missions. Anyway, the AVC sometimes sneak into venator lookouts and smuggle onis back into their realm using their gateways. We figure the less of those disgusting creatures they have in this realm the better for all us powerfuls.'

'And not just for powerfuls but other people too, Erin,' Kano added. 'Let's not forget that venators police them too. In fact, we have an onis releasing mission in a week. You two should come and help us. Come to the theatre around the same time.'

'We'll think about it,' Andre said dryly.

'Great. Well, ones, we'll let you mingle, get to know the others. And hopefully we'll see you back in our lair soon.'

And the trio left Inock and Andre alone.

As soon as they were out of earshot, Andre insisted they leave the place and head home. Inock agreed, but only reluctantly; he was fascinated by the whole business.

On the way home, Inock had a considerable amount to ponder; being a powerful himself joining the AVC was definitely something he was interested in, no matter how much Andre seemed to oppose to the idea.

'The venators are just doing their job, Inock!' Andre kept saying every time Inock brought up the idea of helping out the AVC.

But Inock had made up his mind. He knew for sure he wanted to aid the AVC; he decided he would attend the onis releasing mission in a week's time.

***

The AVC were hard on Inock's mind. He thought about helping the radical group for days since meeting with them. He'd been racking his brain trying to figure out how to support their cause. And one thing kept coming to mind; the Demon's Amulet of Power.

Inock first heard of the Demon's Amulet of Power when Mabiyah the Oracle informed him it was stolen from his father's school. Inock had recovered the amulet from the thieves and kept it for himself, trying to figure out how it worked but never did; he'd eventually given it back to his father. If anything, Inock knew it was a contraption that enhanced a witch's or demon's powers; so he thought perhaps

it might help him be strong enough to help the AVC. And what had the girl Erin said? That he was a newbie who only deserved beginner's missions? Well, this newbie would certainly show her. If he could only decipher how the Demon's Amulet of Power worked, he would be powerful enough to help in their more important missions.

At that very moment, Inock was stood right before his father's magical collectibles cabinet in the sitting room; it had all sorts of wondrous magical items in it, the Demon's Amulet of Power being one of them.

Inock made a decision; he opened the cabinet and took out the amulet. It was a golf-ball-sized silver pendant with a large clear crystal in the centre that glowed with power when worn by a demon, hanging on a black leather chain. Inock put the amulet around his neck and under his T-shirt. He just knew if he figured out how to work the thing, he could use it to help the AVC.

But was that a good idea?

The next day, Inock and Andre were forced to use their *Mind to Mind* link when the Oracle sent them on an errand to a distant forest to deliver a satchel of potions to an old witch. (They hadn't severed the mental link between them just yet.) On the way back from the witch's hut, still in the forest, the boys ran into a fifteen feet tall cannibalistic, partially blind giant hunting for food. The creature was aggressive as soon as it spotted Inock and Andre in the trees and fired off immense energy bolts at the two brothers, that shattered thick trees to splinters. Inock and Andre had to repeatedly hide behind trees and could only contact each other through their psychic link, since every movement made by them alerted the mad giant. (*No, not behind that tree, Inock, he's already*

headed that way, Andre once sent into Inock's mind, making Inock dive behind another tree. And Inock next sent: *Oh look out, Andre, he's firing off humongous energy bolts again!*)

They finally managed to escape the forest, skulking from tree to tree, the giant constantly not far behind them, listening to their footsteps; it appeared the mammoth being had acute hearing, which was very bad for the boys. At reaching the forest edge the boys hopped on their gante and were speeding away, leaving the nightmare behind.

Inock took the Demon's Amulet of Power with him everywhere trying to figure out how to work it, no matter how much Andre urged he return the thing to the sitting room before the rest of the family found out, which was essentially what Rozanthia told him to do, but he never listened. Lalita on the other hand was impressed Inock dared take it without his father's permission.

'I can't *wait* till we figure out how to use it!' Lalita said. 'We'll be so strong! And I'm coming with you to that onis mission, Inock! I can't believe I missed going to Unatia with you!'

Inock took the amulet to class, to bed, on Oracle's missions and to power-training sessions. He would say random words while holding it, hoping it might somehow activate, like 'On!' and 'Fire!' He would squeeze it hard, press it to his forehead and pray for it to work, but sadly, it never did.

Until one evening at the conclusion of a power-training session with Lalita, Andre and Villad the ex-thief in Gante Forest. (Villad was a sad-looking boy the gang met many months previously. He was a demon with the power to turn himself invisible. He looked Indian and was about Inock's age

or younger, and was timid with messy hair and a small voice.) Inock was getting really good at aiming energy balls, firing off multiple bolts of lightning from his fingers, creating energy shields and turning into more complex animals. Lalita too was getting much better at her powers, considering she wasn't professionally trained. And as always, Andre was perfect at his powers.

While Inock was fidgeting with the Demon's Amulet of Power for perhaps the millionth time, Rozanthia took pity on him.

'I can help you with that thing if you want,' she said.

'Rozanthia, is that you?' Inock asked, looking up into the trees. They weren't too deep into the forest; the sun was setting, a golden glow kissing everything in sight.

'Yes, I've been here all along,' came Rozanthia's voice once more and she materialised right in front of Inock. Rozanthia was greenish and transparent. Inock could see right through her. Only the top half of her body was visible; there was nothing below her waist, just air. She had long, green hair and wore a greenish dress. She was still clutching that teddy bear that she always held. 'Though dangerous, and although you didn't ask your father for permission to borrow it, I think what you intend to do with it is noble, Inock, so I'll help you. At any rate, if you go up against the venators you will need all the help you can get. I can tell you how to work the amulet.'

'How can you, *ghost girl*, what would *you* know,' said Lalita. 'You were what—ten when you died?' She was leaning on a thick tree; they had been hanging back in the forest, waiting while Inock tried to activate the amulet yet again.

'Don't be so rude to her!' demanded Andre.

'Actually, I was twelve when I died,' Rozanthia said resentfully. 'But Atheva the Ghost Oracle still teaches me many things … things your mortal brain probably couldn't handle!'

'Ha! You wish, *ghost girl!*'

'Oh shut up, Lalita!' said Inock. He turned to Rozanthia. 'What can you tell me about the amulet, Rozanthia?' he asked.

'Well, I know it is a magical amulet that is imbued with limitless power, and the wielder, witch or demon, can tap into that power to amplify their powers,' Rozanthia said confidently.

'Yes, but how? How do we tap into that power?'

'Just squeeze the amulet and clearly say these words: *Vis Release!* As long as you're wearing it, all spells and power executions are amplified. When you're done with it just squeeze it again and clearly utter: *Close!* But be careful, Inock, that sort of power shouldn't be messed with; it can be very dangerous!'

'Thank you, Rozanthia, I will be. I'll try that now.'

'It would have been nice if *ghost girl* had told us that sooner!' Lalita said grudgingly, crossing her arms and pouting.

'I told you never to call me that!' screamed Rozanthia.

'Honestly, Lalita, what does it matter! She told us now, didn't she,' raged Andre.

'Oh come down, Andre, I'm only teasing her!'

Inock didn't dither. He squeezed the amulet in his right hand and said clearly: '*Vis Release!*' The crystal in the amulet glowed bright red.

As soon as he'd done that Inock felt a surge of energy go through him; it was like being enveloped in a cocoon of power; he felt really energised … felt like he could fly just then. He thought the incantation must have worked.

Inock next aimed a hand to the skies and with all his might fired off a torrent of bluish bolts into the air, but what came out wasn't quite what he expected. Instead of just a few electric bolts, he fired off a mass of bright scorching bolts that reached further into the sky than he ever reached.

'Ha! That felt great! What a feeling!' Inock cried.

'WOW! DID YOU SEE HOW FAR THEY REACHED?' yelled Lalita, excitedly. 'I want to have a go. I say we go deeper into the forest and test it out on some gomorah!'

'But the forest is really dangerous if you go in too deep,' said Villad in his small voice.

But before you could say, 'blood-sucking succubus,' the group heard a continuous ruckus; a series of howls and screams coming from somewhere in the forest that seemed to be getting closer. Straight away they knew that could only be one thing; wild aklonas were coming their way.

'Oh no!' cried Andre. 'They must have seen the lightning! We should run!'

'No, I say we have Inock fire crazy bolts at them!' said Lalita, positively bursting with delight. 'It'll be so much fun!'

And Lalita certainly got her wish because within seconds a horde of over twenty aklonas came charging and swinging into sight.

Villad went invisible at once.

Inock got an idea. He pointed a finger at the approaching beasts and cried, '*GERRUDUS CILICIA!*'

Something amazing happened. Inock felt a tremendous rush of energy go through him, then all the aklonas turned to grey stone; the ones on the forest floor and even the ones high up in the trees. (*Gerrudus Cilicia* was a spell Rozanthia had taught Inock; a spell to temporarily turn anything to stone!)

'Oh boy, what a shot!' cried Inock, punching fists into the air and dancing on the spot, Lalita mirroring him.

'Well done, Inock! Well done!'

'Good shot, indeed, Inock!' came Villad's voice. He was still invisible.

Even Andre managed a feeble, 'Ha! That was brilliant!' And then more seriously: 'But we should run before they unfreeze! Quick!' And he took off.

This time, Inock, Lalita and Villad listened; they ran off after Andre and out of the forest.

They laughed all the way to the lamplit market; it had been an exhilarating experience.

And wonderfully, Inock now knew how to use the Demon's Amulet of Power!

Let the AVC come, he thought.

Chapter Seven
The Venator Realm

Weeks had passed since Tehan started power-training Inock on a more regular basis. The power-trainer introduced and taught Inock many, many more powers. Tehan would sometimes transform the entire orbiis into a battlefield with many buildings and obstacles that Inock had to overcome, battle silver clones of himself as well as battle his father. (The orbiis was very magical indeed; once activated with a password it would create a silver liquid-like substance called orbiis matter that melted from the ceiling and walls before settling on the chamber floor in a glimmering shallow pool; this is the substance Tehan used to create the buildings, obstacles and moving clones.)

Using his powers, Inock could now conjure small objects out of thin air with a mere thought, control others' thoughts but he was terrible at it, and even animate objects amongst other things.

At that very moment, Inock was stood twenty paces away from his father in the massive, glistening orbiis; they had practiced energy manipulation, specifically aiming energy balls, for the last twenty-five minutes or so, the power-trainer

insisting that Inock get a good handle on the most basic and most common power; energy manipulation.

'Now we move onto energy shields,' Tehan said, and then holding out an arm before his body, palm facing up, and an energy ball triple the size of Inock's head appeared there. The sizzling, crackling thing gave off bluish light, making the power-trainer's entire front, especially his arm glow that colour. 'Will a shield into existence, son. And this time, make it your strongest.' Tehan's voice bounced off the curved silver walls, the weird effect distracting Inock somewhat.

Inock did as he was told and felt the power inside him and all around; he then focused, and gathering that power, willed a wall of bluish energy as tall as himself and five times as wide as himself right before his body and waited for his father to fire.

And Tehan surely did fire. The deadly ball of energy whooshed at Inock—he hastily ducked down in fear—and it crashed into his barrier with a thunderous bang. Sprinkles of energy rained down at Inock's feet but the shield was more or less intact, apart from several cracks around where the energy ball had hit.

Inock quickly stood up, inspected his shield and grinned at his father.

'It held, father!' he called to the power-trainer. 'I'm getting better!'

'Yes, you certainly are, son!' Tehan said, walking to Inock. He inspected the shield and smiled at his son, proudly ruffling his bowl hair. 'Good work, Inock! A very good job indeed.' Then he walked back into position, saying, 'Now let's do that again. But first, focus on your shield and replenish any damage done to it. You know what to do.'

Inock did as he was commanded. He focused on the cracks in his energy shield and gathering energy, willed them to be healed.

Tehan then conjured, aimed and hurled another energy ball at the shield and again the shield held, but this time with less cracks.

'It held well, father! It held! It held!' Inock yelled, jumping five feet into the air, at seeing how well his shield had done.

And so, father and son trained that way for another fifteen to twenty minutes, until Tehan suggested they train Inock's ability to create energy discs beneath his feet that he could then will to lift up with him still on them, therefore levitating and moving himself around high in the air. Inock was quite exhausted at the end of the lesson and was rather pleased when his father called an end to the session.

Tehan congratulated Inock on a job well done.

**

Inock was at the Anti-Venator Clan's lair in Unatia city; he'd gone to the abandoned theatre with Lalita and Villad to meet with the AVC and had taken the Demon's Amulet of Power thinking it might come in handy during the onis release mission. Andre had flat-out refused to come. Though Erin had said it was a beginner's mission, Inock figured he might need the amulet's power.

The theatre was populated with half the crowd of people as before, and Erin, the girl with the black ponytail who'd given a speech last time was on stage addressing everyone.

'You all know the deal with onis releasing missions. We get in, rescue a few onis from their animals holding chamber then sneak to the gateway room and use it to go into their realm. Once in the venator realm we meet with our man who will lead us to the forest, hopefully unseen. Those of you who want to participate in today's mission should assemble around Kano now.' She left the stage.

Without further ado Inock, Lalita and Villad walked over to Kano, the older boy with the trendy hairstyle and blue fringe.

'Hello, Inock, I didn't see you enter the lair,' Kano greeted. 'Where's your brother? Are these your friends? Are they powerfuls too?'

'Hello, Kano. Andre couldn't come. Yes, these are my friends. This is Lalita and this is Villad.'

Lalita let off a kind of giggle, batting her eyelashes and smiling wider than Inock had ever seen her smile.

'Hi there, Kano,' she said. 'I'm an energy manipulator, plus I know a few spells.'

'Hello,' said Villad, timidly. 'I can turn invisible.'

'That's great, Lalita! You too, Villad,' said Kano, enthusiastically. 'It's nice to meet you both. Will you join us on the mission? We need all heads on board.'

Lalita giggled again.

'Yes, I will if that's okay,' she said.

'Yes, me too,' said Villad. 'I'd like to.'

'It's more than okay,' Kano said, flashing Lalita a handsome smile. 'The more the better for us. You too, Villad. The AVC is always looking for more powerfuls. There is a lot to be done.'

At that point two older boys came to Inock, Villad, Lalita and Kano, one of them being Chris with the close-shaven hair; the other boy Inock had met last time. The second looked to be in his late teens and had neat black hair, and was wearing black jeans and a vest.

'Hey, Kano, me and Maliki will come with you today,' Chris said. 'But it looks like that will be it for this one; no one else is willing today. Last night's mission took it out of them.' Then looking at Inock he said, 'Oh, hey, Inock. Thanks for coming. Where's Andre?'

'He couldn't come today, I'm afraid,' said Inock.

'That's too bad,' said Chris. 'Like they say, you cannot have everything, eh? I see you brought some new ones to us though. Hello, I'm Chris and this is Maliki. What are your names?'

'Hi, I'm Lalita, Inock's friend.'

'And I'm Villad.'

They all shook hands with the new arrivals.

'Right, now that introductions are done, we might as well get moving. Everybody, follow me,' Kano said and made for the room exit, the others following. 'We're liberating at the Unatia lookout today. We'll walk there.' He magically conjured a small yellow ball of light as they moved through the theatre corridors. 'Inock, Villad and Lalita, you've never done this before so I'll tell you what will happen: I own an Onis flute and so does Chris, and we know how to use them well. We'll get into the lookout, sneak some onis from one room and into the chamber with the portal in it and go through it to the venator realm.'

'But won't the venators see us?' Lalita asked.

'They never do,' Kano said, chuckling and turning a corner. 'I have the gift of premonition which means I can look ahead to see if we'll run into any trouble then decide on another route; one of the better demon gifts, I think. If I do my job right, we can expect minimal friction.'

'Sounds good,' said Inock, wondering how the older boy's power worked.

'Anyway, once in the animals holding chamber,' Kano continued, 'Chris'll use the Onis flute and get about five onis to follow us to the venator realm … in essence, that is the usual procedure. Sound good?'

'Simple.'

'Sounds good,' said Lalita beaming. She seemed to really be enjoying herself. 'What are your powers then?' She referred to Maliki and Chris.

'I can teleport, which comes in handy if things go wrong and I need a quick escape,' Maliki said with a toothy smile. Inock noticed he had neat white teeth.

'And I can morph myself into anybody I've come across, which can be very useful on these missions into the venator lookouts. I will turn into a venator and collect the onis. The venators don't bother us then,' Chris explained as they walked. 'Actually, I trained with your father, Inock. I really like him and his training methods. My mother paid for the whole thing. It was great!' He finished with a wink at Inock.

'Wow, really?' asked Inock.

'Oh yes.'

'I don't have a power-trainer,' Lalita said a little glumly. 'But I'm still good with my powers.'

'Me neither,' said Villad quietly.

Then Inock remembered he had a golden goose egg hanging at his chest; the Demon's Amulet of Power! He chose to show and tell the group about the gizmo.

'Wow! Where did you get that? I've heard of it. I hear it has got almost infinite power!' said Maliki, unable to take his eyes off the device.

'It's my father's.'

'Wait till you guys see what it can do!' said Lalita. 'It's absolutely amazing!'

'How do you work it?'

'I know how to work it, don't you worry, buddy,' said Inock, placing the amulet back under his red T-shirt; Maliki simply couldn't take his eyes off it.

'Okay, Inock, just make sure you use it if we need you to,' Kano said.

'I will,' said Inock, though he wondered what sorts of trouble they were headed into going up against the venators.

They were now outside; Kano killed his light ball.

'Just give me a second to change,' Chris said quickly before walking down a deserted alleyway. Inock was shocked to see a venator in full uniform walk out of the same alleyway, and what's more, the black man grinned at them all and said, 'Well, don't look so shocked. It's me, Chris.'

Lalita was first to burst into fits of laughter followed by Inock and Kano and Maliki. Villad just looked scared.

'Do you know your first mistake?' Lalita cried, bent over double from uncontrolled laughter. 'Venators never smile and they certainly don't grin!'

'Oh, sorry, I forgot,' said Chris replacing his smile with a sort of scowl.

'That's better.'

After composing themselves, the group proceeded to the venator lookout, Chris staying several paces ahead of the rest, pedestrians sidestepping out of the way at the sight of him, many of them looking fearful. Kano and Maliki told Inock, Villad and Lalita more about the AVC, what they stood for and the various other activities they engaged in, which included sneaking into venator lookouts and tampering with their computers and paperwork, freeing captives in lookouts who they believed did not do anything that wrong to be arrested in the first place, and trying as much as they could to gain more intel on the venators and their origins.

Inock found the whole business rather interesting and exciting.

The plan went off swimmingly. Chris led the group into the Unatia venator lookout, down a series of corridors, not a single venator they passed showing them any kind of interest, and into the lookout's animals holding chamber.

All around them were all manner of animals in different-sized cages arranged in floor to ceiling columns; the cages seemed to move in all directions to suit the venators' needs.

Many of the animals were restless and making a great commotion in their cages; some were as big as mammoths and others as small as rats; and there were onis, aklonas, gomorah, red shadow bats, ice bats, gampe, multi-coloured birds, snakes, and many more varieties. (Red shadow bats with their wings spread out each spanned about ten feet wide, had frightful glowing red eyes with pointy fangs, sharp claws and very long tails with pointy edges to them.)

There were only three visible venators in the vast warehouse; one was sat at a desk near the room entrance and the other two were inspecting the animal cages and making

notes on plastic pads. (Inock and Lalita had encountered a similar chamber in the Kasama venator lookout, months before.)

Venator Chris walked to the desk, while the rest hung back by the entrance so as not to be seen, and told the venator there he would be taking five onis out on patrol. Luckily, the man didn't seem to suspect a thing and just pointed to the cages with onis in them.

Chris walked over to the onis section and opened two cages, freeing five onis, blew into his Onis flute—a small, dark green, metallic flute, giving off a high-pitched ringing sound, and the onis followed him out of the chamber.

Venator Chris then led the way to the gateway chamber, which was in the basement, the five onis directly behind him and the others at least ten paces behind him all the way.

Kano stopped the group several times and used his powers of premonition to look ahead in time, saying things like 'A venator is coming, quick, hide,' or 'It's clear, we can go now,' and 'It's okay, it's not venators this time,' and they waited around corners for whoever it was to pass. Inock thought Kano seemed to really know how to use his powers.

A little while later, Venator Chris stopped outside an unmarked ethereal door and looked back at the group behind him.

'Right, this is it,' Chris said. 'Kano, can you look and see if there is anyone in there, there usually is.'

Kano seemed to focus for a moment then grimly he said, 'Yes, there is, one venator guarding the portal.' Another look of concentration and a little more cheerfully he said, 'He will come out in about two minutes. You wait here and look like

you're just passing when he comes out. The rest of us will hang around the corner.'

So Inock, Kano, Villad, Lalita and Maliki hurried and waited around the corner.

Then about two minutes later, they heard a venator greet another one.

'Okay, guys, he's gone. Hurry, let's go in!'

Inock and the others came out from around the corner and proceeded through the ethereal entrance after Venator Chris and the onis.

The chamber they entered was a circular room with a great gateway on a giant dais; the portal itself was sort of oval and looked as if it contained clear water with lots of ripples. The group made for the thing, but just before Chris, who was in the lead stepped through, Kano called out:

'Oh no! Someone's coming! And it's a venator!'

And soon after he'd said that a venator entered the space.

Inock was lightning quick. He grabbed the Demon's Amulet from under his T-shirt, uttered, '*Vis Release!*' then took Kano's and Lalita's hands and made himself and them invisible.

Villad seemed to have vanished too.

Maliki too was fast. He teleported out of the chamber so that Venator Chris and the five onis were the only ones left visible in the room; his body and clothes turned a shade of black and then he dissipated, vanishing completely with a hiss.

Then it was Chris's turn to react.

'Are you here for guard duty?' Chris asked the venator.

'Yes, I am. What are you doing in here?' It seemed the venator hadn't seen the others.

'The rota has changed,' said Venator Chris. 'I'm supposed to take the next watch … you can go on outside patrol.'

'Okay … but what are those onis doing in here?'

'They just came through from home.'

'I see … I'll take them to animals holding.'

'No, no, that's okay, someone else just went through the gateway, he will be back in a second to take them to animals holding, don't worry about it.'

Inock watched as the venator's eyes narrowed ever so slightly … he waited nervously for what would unfold … but the venator said nothing more and just turned and left the chamber.

Inock willed himself visible again, Kano and Lalita following suit; he let go of their hands.

Villad too was visible once again.

Maliki teleported back into the room and Inock thought the effect was quite something; at first, he was a sort of shadow that quickly turned three-dimensional then solidified into the boy, clothes and all.

'Existence, that was close!' said Maliki with a grin. 'I waited outside till I saw him leave. Nothing like lookout infiltration to make the heart beat fast, eh?'

'I'm sorry, I miscalculated how long it would take for him to come into the chamber,' Kano said.

'I thought it went really great!' beamed Lalita.

'That was totally crazy and insane!' said Inock, his heart racing. 'We were almost caught!'

Villad just coughed nervously.

'All right, but we really shouldn't stand around discussing it, we should go through, now!'

And they all walked through the rippling gateway, the five onis following after Venator Chris blew into his Onis flute.

Moving through the portal was a strange though familiar sensation for Inock; he went through something similar many times with Samuel Blackwood. Everything seemed to go dark, he felt like he'd dived into a warm swimming pool, his ears popped, then just as quickly, his vision cleared.

They emerged into a circular chamber similar to the one they left behind, with a rippling gateway on a dais.

However, Inock's blood soon froze when he noticed there was a venator in the chamber. And he was even more surprised to see the handsome man smile then come over and shake Kano's hand.

'You finally made it through,' the man said. 'I was getting worried you got caught.'

'We almost were caught, Kallam,' said Kano smiling, returning the handshake with vigour. 'We have some new members with us; this is Inock, this is Villad and this is Lalita.'

'Hello,' Inock and Lalita greeted in tandem.

Villad just coughed, mumbling something inaudible.

'Hello, glad to meet you all,' Kallam greeted, shaking Inock's, Villad's and Lalita's hands in turn.

'Now that we are all introduced, I say we go before we're almost caught again,' Venator Chris suggested.

So, the man Kallam led the way out of the chamber and into a light-ball-lit corridor, the five onis following in tow. The group made their way through a series of corridors, not coming across anyone, then across a black and green entrance hall manned by one venator in a booth, through an ethereal entrance and they were outside.

Inock couldn't believe he was in another realm yet again and it was the venator realm of all realms!

It was daytime, around three o'clock in the afternoon. Inock looked up to see a ruby sky and two moons close together, one huge, the other about the size he was used to; he thought the view was stunning.

They were outside a building that resembled the venator lookouts in Inock's realm, it was surrounded by woodland and had a gravel compound.

'I can't believe we're in another realm!' Inock heard Lalita say. He was busy staring up at the red sky and moons.

'*Blood-sucking succubus,* it's a red sky!' said Villad, looking up.

'It's incredibly amazing!' said Inock, turning on the spot. 'They have a red sky and two moons! This is so amazing!'

'But I think our sky is better, Inock,' said Lalita. 'And our moon has revolving rocks which one might say is more beautiful.'

'Well, now that you lot have taken in the sights,' said Maliki, 'let's go before we're discovered!'

'Already?' complained Lalita.

'Yes, let's just go!' said Maliki, forcefully.

Kallam led the group away from the building and along a tree-lined dirt road.

'Where are we going?' Lalita asked.

'We are going to Kallam's farm, it's not far from here,' Kano said, smiling at her. 'We'll leave the onis there then head back to our realm. Kallam will take care of the rest.'

'Ah, okay, but how did you know we were coming?' Lalita asked Kallam.

'We always plan these things in advance,' Venator Chris said, as he walked. 'Kallam is always waiting for us when we come. He's been working with the AVC for a while now. The venators leave us alone when we are with him.'

'So, you don't hate powerfuls like the other venators?' Lalita asked the man.

'No, I do not,' Kallam answered. 'Witches and demons are rare in this realm but are always frowned upon. They are not celebrated here like they are in your realm.'

Then Inock thought of the prefect question; something he was always curious about.

'Why do venators hate powerfuls so much?' he asked.

And Kallam certainly answered: 'A long, long time ago, powerfuls from your realm invaded this realm and tried to take over with their powers and magic.'

'Wow, really?' Villad gasped.

Kallam continued: 'A great hate grew between my people and those that invaded. We fought back. And let me tell you it was a close struggle, we almost lost. The warring went on for years! That is why venators hate powerfuls.' They walked another minute in silence before Kallam carried on with the tale: 'When the authorities from your realm found out about the struggles between the powerfuls from your realm and the men in this realm, and they saw how well we fought back and how well we used onis to fight, they decided to take men from this realm to police the witches and demons in your realm. In the beginning, our government forced men to travel to your realm and work, though some went willingly; they knew they had to do it in order to oppress the powerfuls that so wanted to conquer our realm.'

'That is crazy!' said Inock, whistling. 'Or like Musa would say, it is totally bonkers!'

'Who's Musa?' asked Kano.

'A friend of Samuel Blackwood's' Lalita answered. 'He's a funny guy, makes me laugh.'

Kallam carried on with the tale: 'The men who were taken into your realm to work were given land to build lookouts, and I know some lookouts were just renovated. We were a very peaceful people until those horrific, demented witches and demons invaded and tried to rule us. Do you know why the venators in your realm wear those metal bands around their necks?'

'You mean the green metallic braces every venator wears?' Lalita asked, fascinated. 'No, why?'

'Well, at first they wore the braces as a symbol of their servitude in your realm,' said Kallam. 'But as the years wore on, they kept the braces to remind themselves that your realm wasn't really their home; many of them do not really like being there.'

'Wow, that is something else,' said Inock.

'It really is,' spoke up Villad.

Inock said, 'So they were like slaves and they hate us! We invaded their world and now they have to work for us. It finally makes sense!'

'In a sense yes, they are like slaves, especially those who didn't want to go into that realm,' Kallam replied.

The tree-lined path ended onto a wide road busy with carts pulled by gante and other alien creatures Inock had never seen before. There were people walking along the road, women carrying large clay pots on their heads and children playing on the sidelines. Inock and the group stayed on the road edge

as they made their way deeper into the realm, headed for Kallam's farm.

It was a long while before anybody spoke again.

'Why are there no female venators?' Lalita asked suddenly.

'In this realm the men dominate,' Kallam said simply. 'Women do not have much say in anything, so it's not usual to find a woman in a position of power. That is probably why you don't see women venators.'

'Like Samuel Blackwood would say, that sounds rubbish!' said Lalita with a pout. 'I would hate to live here.'

'It's madness!' said Villad, quietly.

Again, the group walked in silence for some time.

'We're here,' Kano announced abruptly.

They had veered off the main road many minutes ago and walked down a narrow dirt path that ended into a sprawling green field. Beyond the field, Kallam's farm could be seen with a small brown-bricked cottage. Behind the cottage were plantation fields of all sorts of crops, and beyond that, a forest.

'This is where we leave you, Kallam,' Kano said, shaking the man's hand. 'It was good to see you again.'

'And you, Kano. Good to see you all. Until next time,' Kallam said. He shook hands with the rest of the team. Then he reached into his trousers pocket, took out an Onis flute, blew into it and walked towards the cottage, the five onis following behind him.

The gang made their way back to the gateway chamber safely and undisturbed, and after a quick check with his powers of premonition, Kano announced it was safe to go through the portal. They proceeded through the Unatia lookout and back to the abandoned theatre.

Back at the lair, Inock, Villad, Lalita, Kano, Chris—now transformed back into himself, and Maliki were congratulated by the AVC for a job well done.

'So how do you feel after your first mission?' Kano asked Inock, Lalita and Villad.

Kano, Inock, Villad, Lalita and Maliki were stood in a corner drinking juice from small plastic cups; the beverages had been given to them as congratulatory drinks.

'Just like Samuel Blackwood would say, I feel wicked great!' said Lalita, beaming.

'Yeah, me too,' cheered Inock. 'Well done everyone! To impeccable completion!' he cried, raising his cup. This was mimicked by the other four. Inock was certainly overjoyed about the whole thing. 'And we found out some interesting stuff too,' Inock carried on. 'You know, about those powerfuls that invaded the venator realm!'

'Well, if you found that interesting, let me tell you this: I heard some interesting information about the powerful that led the invasion into the venator realm to conquer it,' Maliki said with relish. 'His name was Immotshap! And he lived in your district, Kasama! Isn't that something?'

'That is amazing!' Inock couldn't believe what he was hearing. 'Absolutely incredible!'

'That's what I always say too!' Maliki said energetically. 'Immotshap was rumoured to be the most powerful witch of the dark clan of Kasama and was their leader. He disappeared many years before the ruined village's dark witches were all arrested. And let me tell you, I've heard some stories! Those dark witches sure knew how to get what they wanted! They embrace far more and wield greater powers. They don't care

111

about petty consequences or how the weaker, lesser masses feel.'

'Careful, Maliki, your dark side is showing through,' jested Kano.

Maliki laughed before saying, 'It's a shame we didn't get to see Inock's Demon's Amulet of Power in action more. I would have liked to see its true power. Can I take a look at it, Inock?'

'Yeah, sure,' Inock said taking the leather chain from around his neck and handing the amulet to Maliki. He was feeling elated and didn't mind at all.

The group discussed the amulet and whether the rest of the AVC would ever get to see the full extent of its power.

Inock, Villad and Lalita left the lair and headed back to Kasama not long after that.

Chapter Eight

James's Return

It was Saturday afternoon in Kasama Market and Inock, Lalita and Andre were moving through the sweltering crowded market, headed for the Oracle's chambers. Mabiyah had summoned them with a talking bird for a mission. But what they found there was quite the surprise; the Oracle wasn't alone. As always, the meeting room was alight with a turquoise glow emanating from the bubbling goo-filled bowl on the table. Mabiyah was sat at the small table with none other than James, the Asian-looking male witch who the trio had watched die in a vision months ago in the other chair. The man was dressed in dark clothes, though wasn't wearing his usual bowler hat; his short black hair was visible to all.

Inock, Andre and Lalita all gasped at seeing the man sat there.

Inock simply couldn't believe his eyes. He wondered for a second if he was dreaming.

James was in the middle of explaining to Mabiyah how he survived the death.

'... And after I gave up trying to detach that version of myself from them, I seemed to recall how to create gateways, and so I opened one and was able to return my existence to

this realm of existence. Unfortunately, they followed me back here,' James concluded.

'What is going on here?' Inock asked, his voice at a screech. 'You're supposed to be dead!'

'We saw you get killed!' Lalita said, manically waving her arms over her head. 'Barnarbo showed us!'

James smiled at her.

'Yes, Mabiyah has told me all about your visions with the witch Barnarbo,' he said. 'But let me assure you, young one, though Barla and her comrade managed to kill me, I returned from the dead whole and well. The first thing I did was go to my home and saw my wife and children of course.'

Mabiyah was nodding her head slowly in comprehension.

'This all sounds fascinating,' the old witch said. 'But, young James, with your permission, using the Time Window I would like to access your memories of the place beyond … the place you existed in for all those months.' (The Time Window was a magical device that with the Oracle's aid could look back in time, into the present and the possible futures.)

James appeared a little surprised at hearing this.

'Can you do that, Oracle?' the man asked. 'I thought your powers of *Extra Sight* could not stretch to other realms?'

'Young one, this I am sure I can do,' said Mabiyah. 'I simply have to access what you yourself have already witnessed.'

'All right, Oracle, if you think it will help in any way, I am happy to do it,' James said somewhat tiredly. 'But I feel I should warn you, it was a grim and dark business. I was just lucky, lucky, lucky to make it out of the miserable place.'

'Wonderful, young James, let us get started,' the Oracle said next. 'If you please, kneel before me when you are ready.'

James did as he was told, his black knee-length coat rustling as he knelt before the Oracle.

Mabiyah placed both hands on James's temples and began reciting a lengthy incantation under her breath, then after what felt like ten minutes to Inock, she pointed both hands at the large rectangular chequered patch on the wall opposite the small table—the Time Window—said seven words more, and magically, the patch turned into a vision of a dry, dusty islet with a violet sky. There was a huge sucking black-and-purple void with frightening blue lightning in the sky above the small island, violently drawing in what appeared to be dust and energies from below; but the whole scene was blurry as though Inock was looking at a television set with a thick layer of Vaseline smeared across the screen.

As they gazed at the daunting lonely scene on the Time Window, a man-sized, black, three-dimensional shadow materialised on the small island. The shadow was still and unconcerned by the environment. Mere seconds passed before two smaller but similar shadows appeared in the place. But unlike the first entity, as soon as they arrived, they began to float upward into the sucking black-and-purple void, which had started twisting and swirling more intensely.

The two smaller shadows shifted as they floated upward and touched for a second, and as soon as they did that began to slowly float back down inch by inch until they touched the islet surface once more. They then zoomed and attached themselves to the first shadow. And that point, Inock could have sworn he saw the smaller creatures breathe a sigh of

relief; it appeared they had been saved from the consuming void above by attaching themselves to the larger being.

But it seemed the larger shadow was greatly displeased by the situation. It zoomed left to right, up and down trying to lose the smaller beings but it could not; they simply would not detach.

Meanwhile, the void above the creatures continued to inhale energies from the space below it, and it seemed to Inock, with greater ferocity as time progressed, the swirling blue electricity increased and more aggressive.

Suddenly, torrents of orange flames emanated from the larger shadow and enveloped the two smaller ones. The creatures seemed to burn, but when the flames died out, though they appeared frayed around the edges, the smaller shadows were still glued to the larger thing.

And the terrible struggle continued on for some time. The larger being, as it appeared to Inock, discharged torrents of flames, slicing winds and jets of dark energy at the two smaller ones, but each time it relented, the situation was the same. They were still attached to it.

Meanwhile, the consuming void above roared and convulsed, hungry for the inhabitants below but it never received; its never-ending ferociousness was in vain, it seemed.

The passage of time seemed to speed up as Inock watched the endless fighting on the Time Window. Minutes turned into days and days turned into months … all the while, the first shadow fought and struggled to free itself. But it never succeeded.

Then something peculiar happened; the larger shadow drifted to the furthest corner of the islet, and once there a

massive disc of golden light appeared; it looked to Inock a lot like a gateway. All three shadows drifted towards the light and vanished into it, escaping the dismal place.

Next, the scene on the Time Window changed to a world Inock recognised; his world, with the shimmering emerald sky.

Three shadows similar to those they witnessed in that strange place were tumbling downward through the sky, and as they plummeted, they transformed into two men and a woman. Inock recognised one of the men to be James, and verily he recognised the other two as Barla and her companion Anandre.

The three figures finally hit ground, all half naked.

Barla was first to rise from the dusty ground of a quiet street lined with red-bricked houses, her long brown hair a total mess. She blinked as though just woken up from a heavy dream, and looking around memory seemed to come. She reached down and helped her companion off the ground, who was also just coming to, and within seconds they vanished into thin air. First, their silhouettes turned black, then into shadows and then they were gone.

James had watched them teleport away from where he lay, his eyes adjusting to the light. At realising he was naked followed suit; he too teleported himself away.

'And that's what happened,' James said, his voice cracking. He went and sat down in the other chair. 'I transported myself home immediately after my return. I realised I had missed my wife and two daughters too much.'

'Well … that was,' said Andre, his mind blank. 'That was … something … something … something more than I think I can handle. It was simply mad! And beyond me!'

117

'It certainly was intense!' said Lalita, with wide eyes and blinking.

'I don't even know what to say about all this,' said Inock, his mind also a confusing void. 'That was all so … What was that, a living nightmare?'

'It certainly was for me, dear Inock,' said James.

'Collect yourselves,' said Mabiyah. 'Calm yourselves. I realise what you saw was draining but you must know yourselves again.'

'You must, young ones!' said James. 'It will be okay, I survived it all after all.'

'Young James, you must have not moved on to the beyond because you are in fact immortal,' the Oracle said after a minute's silence. 'Your passing was not what was necessary to aid you to move on right. In other words, that was not the right way to kill an immortal. Do you understand my meaning?'

'Yes, Oracle, I do. I have thought the same,' said James.

'There is something more I feel I should share with you, Oracle,' James said next. 'Something you couldn't have learned from that vision of the place; Barla and Anandre have plans, terrible plans! I learned of this when they attached themselves to me in that realm. I could see into them as soon as they attached themselves to me. I could hear their every thought as simple comprehension. It was like what they knew became what I knew.'

'What is it, young one?' Mabiyah asked gently, but Inock thought he himself couldn't take any more. And Andre and Lalita too certainly looked drained by everything they had seen and heard since coming to the Oracle's chamber.

James said: 'They intend to find Immotshap wherever he may be and put him back in power!'

'Wasn't Immotshap the leader of the dark clan of Kasama?' Inock blurted out at remembering the AVC member Maliki's tale of the dark witch.

'But Immotshap vanished years and years ago, how do they intend to find him now?' Lalita asked. 'And isn't he dead?'

'He is immortal, Lalita,' James said with a grim smile. 'And he is terrible! He was worshipped by many and could grant immortality to others, so of course many liked him!' (Mabiyah too was immortal. Inock and his friends had learned this a long while back.) James carried on: 'Immotshap had one agenda; to subjugate the powerless masses! That evil witch had many meetings with famous powerfuls trying to recruit them to his side. He operated by his own laws! He did not follow powerfuls' accepted codes or laws, or the Three Fundamental Demon Laws, or even the rules of the immortal five for that matter!'

'Then suddenly he just vanished!' Mabiyah exclaimed uncharacteristically.

'But the thing that scares me the most is that before Immotshap vanished, there were rumours he had something grand planned,' James said, his loathing for Immotshap showing. 'Something that would change our world forever. Then he simply just vanished! We searched and searched but could not find him.' Looking directly at Inock he carried on: 'You see, we wanted to arrest him and stop him from abusing his power but, failing to locate him, the mission was aborted. The filth hated the powerless masses! He thought they were mere toys to be ruled; we knew we had to put a stop to that.

Only we could. It was our responsibility as the other immortals. Existence knows no other could stop him! You see, children, we felt responsible.'

'He was a very misguided young man fixated on conquering the world with an army of dark witches,' Mabiyah said. 'He had no compassion, killed mercilessly and earned the immortals a terrible reputation! Sadly, his whereabouts are hidden even from me, and not much is hidden from me so I realise something is amiss. He simply must be found and stopped, James!'

Inock had never seen the Oracle so fired up about anything before, so he knew this Immotshap must be something fierce, a great force to be reckoned with.

'You know, Mabiyah, I think I know a way to put an end to the evil witch,' James said next, appearing to be thinking. 'If we ever locate him that is. Immotshap always carried an amulet; his amulet of power. He called it the Demon's Amulet of Power. To strip him of his powers we simply need to steal and destroy the amulet. He talked about it many, many times, if memory serves me right.'

The Oracle smiled knowingly. 'I have thought similarly, young one,' she said. 'If the amulet can be found. I've heard of other similar amulets of course, so it would have to be the right one.'

At that point, Inock remembered something that made his blood turn ice-cold; he knew of the Demon's Amulet of Power, in fact he once owned the very thing, assuming it was the right one like Mabiyah said. But ever since going on the onis releasing mission for the AVC he couldn't remember what he did with it. The last time he remembered seeing the magical device was when he gave it to Maliki in the

abandoned theatre to look at. The amulet had been passed around, and when Inock returned home he realised it was not given back to him.

Inock glanced at Lalita, and judging by her expression, she was thinking the same thing he was; they actually possessed the very thing required to disempower the evil witch Immotshap, and had lost it!

'This Immotshap sounds just awful!' said Andre. 'He will have to be stopped, of course!'

Inock and Lalita swapped a meaningful look; they both knew it wouldn't be easy without the Demon's Amulet of Power. What if Immotshap somehow got a hold of it.

'Is it very likely that the mad witches will succeed in their mission?' asked Lalita.

'It's not impossible,' James told her. 'They very well may succeed, and then all will be lost. The world would fall into chaos!'

'Now, young ones, I believe we have kept you long enough,' the Oracle said next, yanking Inock from his contemplations. 'Please deliver this fireproof potion to Dwayne's and Barnarbo's farm.'

Mabiyah looked at the space between her and the children and with a tiny popping sound, a round glass bottle filled with an amber liquid appeared out of thin air right in front of Inock. (The potion made the drinker fireproof for several hours; it worked by surrounding your entire person with a reddish aura that was resistant to flames; Dwayne and Barnarbo needed it, what with the fire-breathing creatures they bred on their farm.)

Inock took the potion and he, Andre and Lalita left Mabiyah's chamber.

On the way to collect their gante from the market stables, Inock and his friends had plenty to talk about. All three of them thought Immotshap sounded diabolical and all three concluded it was imperative they retrieve the Demon's Amulet of Power from the AVC and destroy it.

At getting to Dwayne's and Barnarbo's farm the trio decided to tell the two farmers of James's and the dark witches' return from the dead. And after fulfilling a couple of farm chores with Inock's and his friends' help, which included feeding the yniqem and cleaning out the yniqem cages, curious to see what they got up to after they returned to the mortal world, with a cleverly incanted spell, Barnarbo summoned visions of what the sinister witches did after coming back.

The visions, skilfully conjured on clear water in a large barrel showed the two witches meeting with other witches in forests, poorly lit sitting rooms and drinking holes, for the most part discussing finding Immotshap, their plans to make the once famous dark witch their leader again, and how they would go about taking over the world. The witches also talked over Immotshap being missing for so many years.

After the magical visions, Barnarbo told Inock, Andre, Lalita and Dwayne how Immotshap was a dark witch who achieved immortality along with Mabiyah, James, Atheva the now Ghost Oracle of the ruins, and Demonios. (Demonios was a diabolical witch who lived in the valley village. Inock and his cohorts battled the witch's vengeful spirit when it attacked them.)

'He was a very evil and scary witch that relished the dark ways,' Barnarbo told his audience stood around the barrel of water outside the medicines shed. 'If these dark witches

122

succeed in finding him and bring him back to power, the result would be catastrophic! Many innocents will be killed and the powerless masses will be oppressed without a doubt! Someone has to stop them!' Barnarbo couldn't have looked more serious.

'But to be honest, I cannot think of anybody who would put aside their lives and go after them,' said Dwayne. 'Nobody wants to see them rise to power but as always, probably no one will rise to the challenge. They might succeed! It is a very difficult and tricky situation indeed!'

This got Inock thinking intensely. He knew he really had to recover the Demon's Amulet of Power. At that point he chose to ask Barnarbo about Immotshap's Amulet of Power; was the one he lost really the same one that the dark witch owned?

What Barnarbo had to tell the group chilled Inock to the bone. After Inock described the amulet, Barnarbo confirmed it was indeed the one Immotshap once owned, right down to the leather chain.

On the ride home, Inock, Andre and Lalita discussed getting the missing amulet back and how they would go about doing that. It was a desperate situation. The threesome concluded the first step was to return to the AVC lair and see if the rebellious group even still had the amulet.

**

'Have you boys thought about what you want to do after university? You should know, what jobs you're interested in should and will influence your field of study at university. I know you are both interested in Law, but I think you should

get part time jobs to give you an idea of what will be expected of you as employees.'

Esttia was lecturing Inock and Andre on career choices.

It was a Tuesday evening and it was dinner time at the Tehan residence. The whole family was present and enjoying a fried liver and kidney, boiled potatoes and mixed salad meal when Esttia had brought up the topic of employment.

Which got Inock thinking; perhaps it was a good idea to secure a part time job and find out what it actually felt like to work a serious job. But how would he go about getting a job? And what kind of job should he apply for?

'We've both been thinking about something in law enforcement,' said Andre while chewing on a piece of kidney. 'We have been applying to do Law, focusing on Powerfuls Affairs at universities.'

'Well, boys, I know you both applied to do Law, focusing on Powerfuls Affairs, but have you considered other options? You should already be thinking about your career paths,' said Esttia, after taking a sip of passion fruit juice. 'It is never too early to do so. What will you do after you graduate? Have you thought about any particular job positions in law enforcement?'

'I've been considering something in crime fighting,' said Andre to everyone at the table, after carefully chewing. 'I believe it is a noble profession and I find it really interesting. I've read some flyers.'

This got Inock thinking about a career in crime fighting. Could he handle such a thing? Perhaps join the RSA— Regulatory State Alliance? They used to do the jobs of the venators and still existed but on a smaller scale; a mixed police force of demons, witches and powerless others. Or

work as a Venator Liaison Officer? He read some flyers on it too. (Since the venators were a privately owned organisation, the government tried to keep a close eye on them, and one way it did that, was through Venator Liaison Officers.) And then there is the DDI—the Department of Demonic Investigations. If it involved his powers, Inock thought he could surely handle it. Inock certainly loved using his powers. On the other hand, he always fantasised about being a very famous power-trainer like his father and brother. He wondered if he would ever be as good as they at his powers.

To his mother, Inock said, 'Crime fighting sounds fun if I can use my powers; I've thought about that too. Or even work as a Venator Liaison Officer, or even as a power-trainer.'

'Very good, son!' said Tehan, cutting into a chunk of liver. 'Power-trainers are very well respected in this world.'

'And well paid, eh, father?' said Torend, chortling.

'That is all very good, son, you've clearly given it some thought,' said Esttia to Inock. 'Well done, both of you. The first, and possibly most important step is taking the time to consider your options and choosing what to do. And Torend, how many times must I remind you not to gloat about your wealth!'

'Sorry, mother.'

The answer to Inock's questions regarding employment came just days later when Esttia walked into Inock's and Andre's Thursday morning lesson, to Ms Strict's obvious annoyance, and informed them she had acquired part time employment for the both of them.

'I spoke to a friend who knows the Kasama Venator Liaison Officer and she put in a good word for you both,' Esttia said. 'Now guess what? The venators have offered you

both jobs working in their Records Department. Though the positions are unpaid I think you will both learn plenty from the work. You start work this coming Saturday.'

And so it was settled, the boys would start work that Saturday, no discussion.

Come Saturday morning, Inock and Andre woke early ready to start their jobs at the venator lookout. The pair washed and had breakfast, and after saying goodbye to their mother and father at the power-training school made their way to the Kasama venator lookout. They were both dressed in black shirts, black trousers and shoes; Esttia had prepared and ironed to a crisp their work clothes the night before. Even their shoes had a polished shine to them.

Esttia had told the boys to simply go to the lookout, introduce themselves, and say what they were there for at the reception. '… They will know who you are. The Venator Liaison Officer took care of everything,' she'd finished by saying the night before.

And the boys did just that.

They were now stood before the venator receptionist in the Kasama lookout, a queue of impatient people behind them.

'Take these badges,' the angry-looking receptionist told Inock and Andre, sliding two badges on the black counter towards them. 'You must wear them at all times when inside the lookout.' Inock took the badges and handed one to Andre. Like Andre's, Inock's was a green lanyard with a black and green plastic badge that read: *Records Department Volunteer* in white letters. 'Now go up to the records room on the fifth floor and tell them who you are, they'll find you something to do!'

The two boys took an archway somewhere to the right from the reception booth and emerged into a corridor lined with alcoves that had a greenish glow radiating from them. They entered into an alcove, which was one of the lifts. Once in the lift, the space filled wall to wall with a spiralling beam of green energy that shot up into a hole where the ceiling should be, the boys were instantly bathed in the greenish glow.

Inock reached for a small, black ball that hovered by the corner which had the numbers zero to nine engraved in it that glimmered green—and pressed the number five; it beeped, and within a heartbeat, they were on floor five.

Inock and Andre moved out of the fifth floor lift area and took a right. They walked seven doors down and they reached their destination; an ethereal door with the words: *Records Department.*

The ethereal words were a luminescent green in the grey ethereal matter of the door.

They entered.

The records chamber was a long room with thousands upon thousands of filing cabinets that covered all the walls floor to ceiling, and they seemed to move up and down and left and right, constantly rearranging themselves to suit the venators that were accessing them and there were desks with computers on them. Venators sat at almost every desk, toiling away, their desktops stacked with paperwork.

There was a large desk at the front of the room, the main desk; a venator sat there staring at a paper-thin computer monitor. Inock led the way to the desk and introduced himself and Andre as the new volunteers, and after the venator took

one look at their badges he got up and without preamble asked the pair to follow him.

The man led the two boys to the very back of the room and to two empty desks stacked with tens and tens of black folders.

'This is where you will work,' the venator told Inock and Andre impassively. 'I need you both to sort through these piles of folders and put them back into the right cabinets throughout the room. Each folder tells you which cabinet it belongs to. And don't worry about running out of folders to sort because I will bring you more as the day wears on. Begin!' He left them to it.

Each of the boys took a seat at a desk and got stuck in, first sorting the folders alphabetically.

Then, when Inock got up and took his first batch of folders to a cabinet, he couldn't quite work out how the moving cabinets worked. And when he looked to a venator for help, the man simply stared back at him and Inock could have sworn he heard the venator actually growl at him.

Andre came over, also holding a stack of folders, and they just stood there, staring at the cabinets move of their own accord.

They must have waited there for a full five minutes watching the cabinets manoeuvre endlessly before a venator approached them.

'Need some help?' the man asked.

The boys turned round to see a tall venator smiling down at them. He didn't however wear one of those green metallic neck braces all venators wore, and to top it off he had hair— short green hair. And what's more, he had a horrible scar across his neck.

'Yes, that'd be great,' said Inock though feeling a little afraid of the man. 'How do we get the right cabinet to come to us?'

'You just face the cabinets and read the folder name and the right cabinet will come to you. Or if you already know the cabinet you want, just utter its name and it will come to you.' The venator took a folder from the top of Inock's pile and read the folder name: 'William Aggon, Kasaman demon!'

And before you could say, 'galloping gante,' the cabinets before them began rearranging themselves until a cabinet labelled *Kasaman Demons* stopped before them.

The venator pulled open a drawer and inserted the folder then closed it. The cabinets began moving again.

'It's that simple,' the venator said in his husky voice. 'Are you the new volunteers?'

'Yes, we are,' said Andre. 'I am Andre and this Inock.'

'Good to meet you Andre and Inock,' said the venator smiling again. 'I am Radock. Volunteers don't normally last long in this department, or in the rest of the lookout for that matter, if I remember right.' He winked at the boys, a sight Inock found somewhat unnerving. And Inock glancing at Andre he clearly felt the same. 'But don't worry, I will look after you well. My lunchtime is at one o'clock. I'll come and collect you two and we'll eat together in the cafeteria. What do you say?'

Inock's and Andre's brows shot up at actually being invited by a venator to eat lunch with him.

'Yes, we could use all the help we can get,' Inock chose to say.

'Great, see you at one o'clock exactly!' Radock said with a bright grin then walked away.

As soon as the man was out of earshot, Inock turned to Andre and with a frightened expression on his face said, 'That was really, really, really odd, Andre! How weird!'

'Yeah, I didn't know venators could smile!' said Andre in a strained voice and with a grim smile.

And they burst into quiet laughter which earned them some angry stares from nearby venators.

The day flowed a lot more smoothly after the encounter with the friendly venator. The boys got a lot of filing done, placing many folders in the right cabinets, and at exactly one o'clock the venator Radock approached their desks and asked them to follow him to lunch.

Radock led the two brothers out of the Records Department and into the lookout basement. There he took them to the cafeteria, which was a wide room with tables and chairs, had fridges full of beverages and there were venators in hairnets serving hot and cold food.

Inock found the sight of venators in hairnets very strange, even comical.

Half the tables had venators sat at them enjoying their lunches and quietly talking away.

Radock led Inock and Andre to a serving station, picked up a black plastic tray and asked for a beef and vegetable pie and a hot tea, and not wanting to stand out any more than they already did, Inock and Andre each picked up a tray and ordered the same.

The three of them sat alone at a table at the edge of the room and tucked in.

During the meal, Radock informed the boys of what was expected of them while they were in the lookout; politeness, meekness, punctuality, responsibility, accountability and

being hardworking, and told them that truth be told they had nothing to fear from the other venators as long as they did their job right. '… Actually, I don't work here full time which makes a nice change from all the sour faces in this building. I also work at the Kasama Powerless-only School,' Radock was saying when none other than Chris from the AVC—the one with the close-shaven brown hair, turned up at their table holding a tray loaded with hot food.

'Can I join you, boys?' Chris asked with a cheerful grin.

'Yes, go ahead,' Radock answered.

Chris sat down next to Radock and tucked into his food without another word.

Inock thought the beef and vegetable pie was one of the best he ever had, and when he sipped his tea, it excited his taste buds like no other beverage ever did.

Andre seemed to really be enjoying his meal too, and like Inock, he cleaned his plate.

When Inock and Andre went to return their trays they heard Chris whisper, 'Radock, I came to find you for a reason; we think he is up to no good again…'

Glancing at each other, the boys slowed down, both intrigued by what they just heard. Did Chris already know Radock? Inock supposed it wouldn't be too difficult to come into the lookout and enter the cafeteria undisturbed, especially if you could actually morph yourself into any venator like Chris could with his powers. But who was Chris referring to? Who was up to no good?

'I know, I know. And I think I may have deduced what he is up to,' Radock whispered back.

'What is it?' asked Chris. 'How do you know?'

'Because I know darkness in a person from the moment I meet them,' Radock said in hushed tones. 'He is dark and will always be trouble to you.' He looked in Inock's and Andre's direction and they hastily scurried away.

The boys dropped off their trays, and when they returned, Chris and the venator ceased their whispering and went back to eating silently.

After lunch, the two brothers returned to the Records Department with Radock to find their desks loaded with even more folders that needed sorting. They got stuck into the task without delay.

The rest of the day flew by and Inock and Andre were told they could go home at exactly five o'clock in the afternoon. They went home feeling tired but proud of themselves for having coped well, what with working in a room full of irate venators.

Chapter Nine
The Inock's Elixir

It was lunchtime in Kasama Market and the place was heaving with shoppers, playing children and animals; the cacophony of sounds was at an all-time high, and Inock, Andre and Lalita were sat on the power-training school steps after enjoying hot sandwiches, chatting about the missing Demon's Amulet of Power and the cruel witch Immotshap when Rikelle, Rukia's sister walked up to them from within the crowds. (Rukia was an older girl who used to sell Inock the Demon's Elixir; a potion to counter his mother's power-suppressing potion.)

Rikelle was around Inock's age; she was black, extremely pretty with long and straight black hair. She was just then in a nice maroon dress dotted with black flowers, complemented with black sandals.

'Hello, you three,' Rikelle greeted the threesome cheerily. 'I haven't seen you in our shop in a long time. Inock, aren't you taking the Demon's Elixir anymore?'

'Nope, I'm not taking that elixir anymore,' Inock told the girl with a happy grin. 'My parents let me use my powers now. Actually, my father even trains me.'

'Oh,' said Rikelle looking somewhat disappointed. 'Does that mean we shouldn't expect you in the shop anymore?'

'I guess not,' said Inock, quite happily.

'What's that book you're holding?' Lalita asked at noticing Rikelle held a small brown book.

'Oh, this? It's a potions book. I was just wondering whether to keep it or not. I have three copies of it. Mother always says I should have an idea of our product, and makes me read books like this. Here, why don't you have it, Inock?'

Inock took the book with indifference; he was never interested in potions.

The book was titled: *25 Potions to Aid Demon Powers.*

Inock flipped through the pages without really reading any of it, though he noticed the book was artfully done. It had images of plants and potions preparation paraphernalia, not to mention the writing was beautifully done.

Then Inock's eyes fell on a page titled: *A Basic Potion to Enhance a Demon's Powers.*

That certainly piqued Inock's interest.

To Rikelle he said, 'Thanks, I'll keep it.'

'Great, I'm just glad I don't have to throw it away,' said Rikelle. 'I hate throwing away books. Come and visit us again soon. I'm sure you can find a potion you don't realise you need but actually do in our shop.' She left.

'We really need to get that amulet back!' said Andre. 'We need to get to that theatre and talk with those AVC people! One of them must have it!'

'I feel the same way,' said Lalita. 'It is really scary thinking of a world run by dark witches.'

'Immotshap sounds too terrible,' replied Andre. 'I wish I had come with you to the AVC that day, then maybe the amulet wouldn't have been stolen!'

Inock looked at the book in his hands and read a little on the chapter while Andre and Lalita carried on speculating how to recover the Demon's Amulet of Power, and what might happen if it ever reached Immotshap.

The chapter was of information on what exactly the potion did to a demon's powers, how it was to be prepared, and what ingredients were necessary. It required over fifteen ingredients and a long preparation process, and since he was missing the Demon's Amulet of Power, Inock thought the potion was worth a try. He wanted to be his strongest; or even the strongest demon in Kasama like his father and brother Torend.

After finishing the chapter titled: *A Basic Potion to Enhance a Demon's Powers*, Inock flipped through more chapters until the end of the book. He found two more potions that were interesting: *A Basic Potion to Make a Demon's Power Last Longer* and *A Potion to Copy Another Demon's Powers for a Short Time*. The second potion had a warning below the chapter title. It read: *Caution: To be taken rarely! Though fun, be careful not to overdose!*

After reading the information on what exactly all three potions did to a demon's powers, preparation instructions and what ingredients were necessary, Inock wondered what would happen if all three potions were combined. Judging by what the three potions did, he thought if he drank all three at the same time, he might be able to emulate other demons' powers permanently without them being near! He put the issue to Andre and Lalita, and after they too had a look at the three potions in the book, Lalita had something to say.

'Wow, that sounds really awesome, Inock! You could be super strong. You could be able to use other demons' powers all the time! You've got to do it, Inock!'

'Buddy, I think that is a very bad idea! Drinking all those potions together can't be good for you!' Andre commented, worriedly.

Inock thought there was one more person he could ask; or more accurately, a ghost—Rozanthia. She was a witch in training before she died after all.

'Rozanthia, Rozanthia, are you here?' Inock whispered.

And surely enough he soon heard the girl ghost whisper in his ear, 'Yes, I am. What is it, Inock?'

'Did you hear what we were just talking about, Rozanthia?' asked Inock. 'Don't you think it is a good idea to combine the potions and try it out?'

'Hmm, if you do it carefully and expertly it might work,' Rozanthia said loud enough for Lalita and Andre to hear, though she was still invisible. 'I saw the ingredients in the book while you were reading it and they seem the right mixture for what you want to achieve. But I think you have to mix them as one potion, not drink three separate potions.'

'See? Even *ghost girl* agrees!' said Lalita, triumphantly. She and Rozanthia rarely agreed on anything. 'I think the only reason that potion doesn't already exist is because Inock's power is really rare, so no one ever thought to make it! It's a good idea, I tell you.'

'Well, I still think it's a disaster waiting to happen,' Andre said, crossing his arms and gazing at a nearby crowd of people chatting spiritedly amongst themselves.

'So, what d'you say we get started on the potion tonight?' Lalita asked excitedly.

'No, I need to buy the ingredients first, tonight's too soon,' Inock told her. 'And I will need to borrow my mother's potions making equipment.'

'And you will need to find a place to do it all because your mother certainly won't let you do such a dangerous thing, Inock!' Andre said.

'Oh, yeah … well, that stinks!'

'What about the power-training school?' Lalita suggested, looking to think.

'Are you mad, Lalita?' screeched Andre. 'That's where his father and mother and brother work! They would see you!'

'Oh, Andre you're so dull,' said Lalita with a pitying look. 'I meant at night! We can sneak into the school at night and work on the potion then! What do you say, Inock?'

Inock thought about Lalita's suggestion briefly and it all sounded good enough to him.

'Okay, let's do it in the school after it is closed; without that there really isn't many other places we can do it without being seen anyway,' he said.

'So, when can you buy the ingredients?' Lalita asked.

'Saturday,' answered Inock. 'I think I can buy them from Rukia. She's bound to want to make some extra money, and then we can get started that night.'

'BOYS! It's time to head back to class!' came Esttia's voice from inside the school reception.

'Okay, mother,' chorused Inock and Andre.

The boys got up from the steps and headed back into the school for their afternoon lesson. Lalita disappeared into the market crowds looking for something to do until Inock and Andre would be free to spend time with her later that day.

'So, how are you boys finding work at the venator lookout?'

It was nearing the end of the school day and Esttia had just walked into Inock's and Andre's classroom, interrupting Ms Strict's long lecture on the recurrence of the number three in witches' spells: 'Chanting three times … stirring potions three times … three witches … three heroes.'

'It's going really well, mother,' said Inock. 'We are learning a lot about the venators. Not to mention how things work in the lookout.'

'What about you, Andre, dear, how are you finding it all?' asked Esttia.

'It's going really well, actually,' answered Andre. 'It has taught me plenty about the world of work and what is to be expected of me from an employer. I have to be really responsible and not be late and careless where work is concerned.'

'Oh, I am truly pleased to hear that, boys!' Esttia said clapping. 'It's turning out exactly like I had hoped. I am very proud of you two. Do keep up the good work and always remember to be respectful of all the people in the lookout, not just the venators … I know how scary they can be.'

'We will,' said Andre and Inock together.

Then looking at Ms Strict, Esttia said, 'Sorry to disturb you, Ms Strict. Please, do carry on with your lesson.'

'Well, I do not like to be strict, but these young pupils' education should not be interrupted!' Ms Strict said in her harsh little voice, adjusting her crescent-shaped spectacles. 'Now, I will proceed with the lesson, if that is all right with you, Mrs Tehan?'

'So sorry to have been a bother, Ms Strict,' Esttia said before backing out of the room, and bowing slightly, making Inock and Andre snigger quietly.

The lesson continued.

Inock went alone to Rukia's potions shop in the northern end of the market to buy the potions ingredients that Saturday, after volunteering at the venator lookout; Andre had simply refused to be involved at all. 'What you are doing is dangerous, Inock! Don't mess with this stuff!' Andre had warned as Inock got ready to leave the house.

Inock was stood in the small shop lined with glass cabinets and shelves full of colourful potions that came in bottles of all shapes and sizes; there was a counter at the opposite end of the shop entrance with two black girls behind it chatting away, one being Rukia who was in her twenties with her hair wrapped in a dark-coloured scarf and the other was Rikelle. There were no customers in the shop at that time except for Inock.

Inock approached the counter.

'Hello, Rukia. Hello, Rikelle.'

'Hello, Inock, what can we do for you today?' Rikelle asked brightly. 'I told you you'd be back.' She was in a pink dress with a pretty flower pattern and sandals.

Inock leaned in close.

'I want to buy some potions ingredients from you,' he said.

'But we don't sell potions ingredients, Inock, we only sell potions,' Rikelle said with a confused expression. 'I thought you knew that.'

But Rukia quickly shushed her sister.

'Shut up, Rik,' Rukia said. 'I'm sure Inock and I can come to an arrangement. What ingredients do you want, Inock?'

Inock handed over a list of forty-eight ingredients to the older girl.

'We have all of these in the back, I'll give them to you but it won't be cheap, one,' Rukia said after scanning the list.

'But, Rukia-!' Rikelle tried to say but Rukia winked at her, and put a finger to her lips.

'We'll sort him out,' Rukia said. 'But it has to stay between us, Rik. You cannot tell mother!'

At first Rikelle looked perplexed, then like she was about to complain, then she shrugged.

'Okay, but sometimes you can be so weird, sis,' Rikelle said.

Rukia beamed at her sister then turned back to Inock.

'Two hundred and fifty ryza for everything,' she said.

'*What?*' Inock was dumbfounded. He had expected it to cost no more than fifty ryza altogether. 'That's a rip!' he said, flapping an arm angrily.

'I know, one, but that's business,' Rukia said with a wide grin. 'Shall I get them for you then?'

Inock indeed thought he was being swindled but couldn't be bothered to hunt around the market for all those ingredients. And besides, he felt he shouldn't back out with Rikelle right there listening.

'Okay, Rukia, get the ingredients but I am not happy!' Inock said resignedly.

Rukia merely let off a minute laugh and went into the back to find the ingredients on the list.

Rikelle leaned closer to Inock and looked him straight in the eyes.

'So, what do you want all that for?' she asked.

'I'm going to make my own potion,' Inock told her conspiratorially. 'Actually, I got the idea from that book you gave me. I'm going to make a potion that lets me copy other demons' powers even when they're not near me.'

'Really? Sounds exciting!' Rikelle giggled and whispered back. 'But it will not be easy, you know. That kind of potion sounds tricky!'

'I can do it, Rikelle,' Inock said, trying to sound confident. 'And anyway, I've got some help.'

'From who?'

'Friends.'

'Cool … can I help too?'

At hearing this, Inock beamed, and in a hushed voice said, 'Yeah, that sounds great! I'm going to do it tonight in my father's school.'

'Ooh, sounds fun and forbidden. I really want to help now!' Rikelle said. 'What time?'

'Around nine o'clock after dinner. Meet me outside my father's school then.'

'Okay, I'll be there!'

Rukia returned with two bags heavy with the ingredients and passed them to Inock over the counter.

Inock paid, though grudgingly, and left the shop, Rukia calling, 'Nice doing business with you, one, we should do it again soon!'

'Yeah, I'm really sure we should!' Inock replied sarcastically. (It took him ages to save up that much money.)

That evening after dinner and the rest of the family had gone to bed, Inock sneaked downstairs fully dressed, holding the potions ingredients he bought earlier that day and

collected supplies from his mother's potions making kit; he took glass phials, a large copper pot, a wooden stirrer, matches, a tripod, kitchen foil and charcoal he purchased separately; his mother usually used the cooker to brew potions, you see. He then collected the keys to his father's school and left the house.

It was a somewhat chilly night; dark clouds completely obscured the moon, leaving the night black but for the yellow glow emitting from the market lamps, and there was light rain.

Inock found Rikelle and Lalita waiting outside his father's school.

'Great, you made it!' Lalita said, rubbing her hands together in excitement. 'This is going to be so much fun!'

'Hey, Inock,' Rikelle greeted, smiling.

'Hey, you two, are you ready?' Inock asked, glancing around the vicinity for venators and was glad to see there were none nearby.

'Of course, Inock, let's do it!' said Lalita. 'I just wish this annoying rain would go away.'

'Yes, let's do it, let's brew us a potion!' said Rikelle quite enthusiastically.

Inock unlocked the school door and led the way through the small school and upstairs to his and Andre's classroom.

Inock thought the classroom had a completely different, less intimidating feel to it without Ms Strict in it. He got right to it; he spread kitchen foil on the floor, placed some charcoal on it and lit a fire. After the charcoal heat really got going, he placed the copper pot on the tripod over the charcoal, then had Rikelle read him the instructions from the potions book on what ingredients to add and when, while Lalita stirred; he had chopped and prepared the ingredients earlier that day.

The business was underway!

'I cannot wait for you to drink it, Inock!' Lalita said as they worked.

'Me too,' said Inock, adding sliced Rendan root to the bubbling potion. 'I just hope we get it right!'

'Inock, if you're successful, you will have to sell the recipe to my mother,' said Rikelle. 'It would be worth an absolute fortune! Mother would just love to have this sort of potion in her shop.'

'I would give it to you for free, Rikelle,' Inock said, beaming at the girl. 'That's if I'm successful.'

The last ingredient was added just over an hour later, then they had to wait a further hour while it all stewed, Lalita stirring the concoction from time to time, the three of them chatting about one thing or another, the bubbling pot contents giving off a pungent smell.

'Right, I think it's ready,' Rikelle finally told the others, referring to the book. 'It has finally got the right shade of green to it. Inock, put some in a phial and drink away.'

Inock did just that; he carefully poured the potion in a phial and drank. He waited a minute or two, while Rikelle and Lalita watched him with great anticipation.

'I don't feel any different,' Inock said.

'Try firing off a bolt,' Lalita suggested.

'No, that doesn't make sense, Lalita, you're still nearby.'

'Oh. Sorry. I didn't think.'

Then Inock got an idea.

'Why don't I go into father's orbiis alone and see if I can fire one off there?' he suggested.

'Good plan, Inock!' Lalita said.

'What's the orbiis?' Rikelle asked them.

'It's a secret room father uses to train demons,' Inock told Rikelle. 'If I go deep into it, I should be far enough from Lalita. I can try firing off a bolt there. I'll be right back.'

Inock left the room and headed downstairs. Minutes later, he was running across the silver orbiis, headed for the chamber centre. Once there he attempted to emulate Lalita's powers by firing off an energy bolt, but nothing happened— no bolt, not even one!

Inock attempted the motion many times but nothing whatsoever happened. He then tried conjuring an energy ball but that too didn't work. And then he attempted creating an energy shield but to no luck.

Disappointed, Inock exited the stunning orbiis and went back upstairs to the girls and gave them the bad news.

'And you tried more than once?' Lalita asked, looking crestfallen; they had worked so hard and had been so sure it would work.

'Yes, I did. Maybe it takes a while for the potion to kick in?' Inock said, though looking defeated.

Rikelle flipped through the potions book.

'The book says it should be instant,' she told the others glumly, after reading. 'All three of those potions have an instant effect!'

'*Blood-sucking succubus, it didn't work!*' said Lalita.

'Should we try again?'

'No, I'm tired. I think we should leave it for now and try again another time,' said Inock, depressed.

'How about tomorrow night?' Rikelle asked. 'We can try different things when mixing the potion.'

Inock and Lalita agreed to try again the following night.

The trio left the school soon after.

Outside, Rikelle bade Inock and Lalita goodnight and left them. Lalita left for home not long after that, and Inock went in and straight to bed.

It might work tomorrow! I'm sure it will work, Inock thought, hopeful, as he got under his Dijhon the Nut-smasher duvet.

Over the following five nights Inock, Rikelle and Lalita tried making the potion again, changing one thing or another but still got nowhere with it; Inock went to the orbiis each time and tried firing off electric bolts, conjuring energy balls and creating energy shields, but nothing at all happened. All he got was a funny tingly feeling from drinking the stuff.

That is until the sixth night when Inock and Lalita were working alone and Rozanthia materialised in the classroom next to Inock's head; Rikelle had given up trying and did not join them that night.

'Why don't you double the Kijiga leaves and the Linden powder and let the potion stew for an hour longer, then give it some time to cool down?' Rozanthia suggested to the obviously frustrated pair.

Inock doubled the suggested ingredients while Lalita stirred the pot. Then they gave the potion an hour longer to stew and Inock drank the cooled down result. And when Inock went down to the silver orbiis and attempted to fire off bolts of lightning, his heart swelled to the size of a football when the desired result actually happened; he was able to fire off multiple bolts, and after jumping for joy, tried conjuring an enormous energy ball. That too happened as it should, and he hurled it off into the distance.

Inock was over the moon as he ran upstairs to tell the others the good news.

'It worked! It worked!' Inock cried joyfully to Lalita and Rozanthia. 'It actually worked! Thank you, Rozanthia!'

Both Lalita and Rozanthia broke out in instant applause, jumping and dancing circles around Inock.

'You are brilliant, Rozanthia! Thank you so much for the help!'

'Hey, I helped you too, you know!' Lalita screeched as she danced around the room.

'What should we call it?' Lalita asked after they calmed down.

Inock didn't need to think hard on that one.

'We will call it the Inock's Elixir, of course!' he cried.

The next day, sometime in the late afternoon, Inock was sure to drag Lalita and even Andre down to the Haunted Valley ruins where he practiced some of the many powers his father and brother taught him. He hurled rocks with telekinesis, morphed into a bird and soared the skies with Andre, turned invisible and dared the others to find him, swelled his body to triple its size and wrestled with Andre who was transformed into a hulking gomorah, and summoned gusts of wind that toppled Andre and Lalita. And then for amusement, Inock fired exploding energy balls into the shimmering emerald sky and even transformed himself into a venator.

As they left the ruins, Inock felt he couldn't be happier.

And later that day, Inock raced to Rukia's potions shop to tell Rukia and Rikelle the good news.

'Amazing! How awesome! You have invented a really cool and rare potion, Inock!' Rukia said at the end of Inock's rant of his success. 'Knowing power-enhancing potions you'll probably have to drink it every two weeks or so to keep up the

effect. You must tell me the exact ingredients and preparation process. I could make so much money from this!'

'Very wow! Wonderful news, Inock!' is what Rikelle said. She was grinning from ear to ear, and let me tell you, Inock wasn't at all unhappy to see this.

***

Things were going well for Inock since his success with the Inock's Elixir; school was good, he power-trained at every chance he got, and got to spend lots of time with Rikelle making the Inock's Elixir. But then he got the shock of his life when his father caught him doing something he should not be doing.

It was a Sunday evening and Inock, Andre and Lalita were watching the television in Inock's sitting room (A cartoon revolving around comical talking household furniture), and Inock was using telekinesis to spin a spoon before his eyes, when Tehan walked into the room.

Tehan's eyes narrowed in an instant; the man looked around the room at Andre, then at Lalita, then back at Inock. There was no one else in the room; certainly no Samuel Blackwood or anybody else with the power of telekinesis.

'What's going on, Inock?' Tehan demanded loudly. 'How are you doing that?'

All three of them, Inock, Andre and Lalita jumped, the hovering spoon clattering to the floor.

Inock looked to his father.

'Err … I … Err …'

Tell him the truth, Inock! came Andre's voice into Inock's mind. *Tell him or we'll get into serious trouble!* (Andre had

147

broadcasted into Inock's mind using the *Mind to Mind* connection. The threesome had not yet severed the mental link between them.)

Inock shot Andre an annoyed look before looking back at his father.

'Err … I … Err …' Inock stammered again.

'Tell me the truth now, boy!' Tehan exploded. He could tell Inock was about to lie again. 'How were you making that spoon float? Andre, boy, what's going on? You are usually honest.'

Andre looked at Tehan with a pained expression but said nothing. He didn't quite know what to say to the man. He was simply too scared, and at the same time did not want to get Inock in trouble.

Inock knew he couldn't get out of this one. So, he decided to tell his father the whole truth about the Inock's Elixir, the potions book he acquired from Rikelle, and how and where they invented the potion.

'And you made the elixir all by yourselves?' Tehan asked in utter disbelief at the conclusion of the tale. 'That is quite something! A tremendous discovery! How long did it take you to perfect?' Too stunned by Inock's accomplishment, it seemed his rage had subsided.

'Seven tries.'

'Well, I must say, son, it is a terrible thing what you did sneaking around the place brewing potions. Not to mention that it could all have gone horribly wrong-!'

'Told you,' Andre interjected.

'But I am proud of you for your creativity,' Inock's father continued.

'See, Andre? It's all fine!' said Inock, laughing.

'*What!*' exclaimed Andre in shock, making Inock shoot him a smug look. '*This is insane!*'

'I am glad you have told me the truth, son,' said Tehan. 'But I have to be firm with you; you're grounded for two weeks. You may only leave the house to go to school and to work, and I will not power-train you for that period. Furthermore, you are to stop taking the elixir immediately-!'

'But father-!'

'I am not finished, son! You may not take any more of the elixir until your mother has tested it; she is a potions genius, after all,' Tehan said, strictly. 'If there is any danger in the elixir, she will identify it, and if possible, perfect it for us. You may only take more if she says it is all right and safe. New potions and medicines must be tested, especially if they are for the general public. Do I make myself clear, son?'

'Yes, father.'

Tehan left the room, though he didn't look at all mad, Inock thought … he looked proud.

Chapter Ten

Attack of the Giant Multi-Coloured Bird

Mere days later, Kano knocked on Inock's door with urgency. It was the early evening.

Inock answered the door. He was upstairs packing away his Inock's Elixirs and about to drink one when Kano knocked, and Inock pocketed three of the potions.

Esttia had done extensive tests on the tricky elixir and deemed it safe to drink. 'But be careful not to drink too much of it, son. I'd say one potion every two weeks should do,' she said.

'Hey there, Kano!' Inock said to the older boy with the trendy hairstyle and blue fringe. 'This is a nice surprise! Is everything okay?'

'Yes, everything's fine, Inock,' Kano said back happily. Then his face became more serious. 'Actually, I'm here for a specific reason. Chris and I came to Kasama to liberate more onis from the Kasama venator lookout. We need your help … you and Andre. If you are willing that is. Chris is actually waiting for us at the lookout now. We don't have much time.'

'Oh,' said Inock. And there he thought the boy had just dropped by for a friendly visit.

'Yes,' said Kano. 'So will you come?'

'Yes, I can come, I guess,' said Inock. 'Just hold on a second.' He retreated into the house to the sitting room where Andre was watching the television; a documentary on the famous witches and demons of the world. To Andre he said, 'Hey, Kano wants us to go to the lookout and help liberate some onis. Will you come?'

'Forget it, Inock!' said Andre very seriously. 'I do not want to do such a thing! You can go on your own!'

'Come on, Andre, let's go do it together!'

'No way, Inock! Just go alone! I don't want to be in any trouble with your parents! And I know nothing about the AVC if they ask!'

'Well, if you're sure,' said Inock feeling disappointed. 'But I think you are missing out on a lot of fun, you know!'

'I do not need that kind of fun, Inock, forget it!' barked Andre. 'Have you forgotten that your father recently caught you doing powers you shouldn't? You were lucky the punishment was easy. No way am I coming with you!'

'Okay, fine!' said Inock. He left the sitting room and returned to Kano at the front door.

'Andre doesn't want to come, I'm afraid,' he said. 'It'll be just me, you and Chris.'

'Oh … that's a shame,' said Kano, looking disappointed. 'Maybe he can come next time?'

'I highly doubt that,' said Inock, knowing Andre. 'But it never hurts to ask.'

'That's correct, Inock, very right,' said Kano. 'So, are you ready to go? Shall we leave now? Chris is waiting.'

'Yes, okay,' said Inock. 'Let me put on my shoes.'

He went into the house and hastily put on his trainers, then closing the front door, he and Kano were off.

They half ran to the venator lookout, taking the tree-lined dirt path that went directly to the building from the eastern market gate.

Inock and Kano found Chris, who was morphed into a short venator and in full venator uniform, waiting outside the lookout entrance and they proceeded inside, all getting that tingly feeling you get going through an ethereal entrance. The procedure was similar to last time; Venator Chris went into the animals holding chamber, brought out five onis with him, Inock and Kano followed him to the room with the portal leading into the venator realm, Kano using his powers of premonition all way to help them avoid trouble, they got into the venator realm, met with the conspirator Kallam and left the venator complex, and then walking to Kallam's farm, the five onis following.

Only this time when they got to Kallam's farm Venator Chris insisted they follow the man onto the farm and into the forest behind the farm to liberate the onis. 'We might need to do this on our own someday if for any reason you cannot attend, Kallam,' Venator Chris said.

Kallam agreed.

Inock, Kallam, Venator Chris and Kano walked past Kallam's home, along the man's plantation fields and passed through the barrier separating the farm and the forest. Immediately they were surrounded by tall red trees with thick, exposed roots and branches so wide most of the setting sun's light was blocked out. The forest floor was dry, with black earth and scattered with shrubbery here and there.

As they walked through the woodland, Inock told the group about his latest discovery: The Inock's Elixir and what it meant for his powers.

Then something important occurred to Inock.

'Have you guys seen Maliki lately?' he asked. 'I think he took my Demon's Amulet of Power!'

'We haven't seen him since the last time we saw you, Inock,' Kano said. 'But are you sure you didn't just misplace it?'

'No, I'm sure he took it, or at least another member of the AVC took it!' Inock said very firmly. 'I am very sure of that!' There was no way he was wrong.

'Well, if you're sure you didn't misplace it then you are right to suspect Maliki,' Venator Chris said. 'That boy operates by his own rules, which can be really annoying sometimes.'

'That's true,' Kano seconded with a nod.

'We will need to get much deeper into the forest before we release the onis,' Kallam told the group a little while later. 'If we release them too near the farm they might come back and make an awful mess.'

So, they slowly moved through the soaring trees, and the deeper in they went the darker it got, so Kano conjured a yellow light ball that hovered before them as they moved, lighting their way. Then, roughly half an hour later, Kallam said it was safe to liberate the creatures. From his pocket he took an Onis flute and blew into it; the onis growled and lashed their long scaly tails aggressively, Kallam blew into the flute one more time and the five onis took off deeper into the woodland, barking away.

It was as the group was walking back towards Kallam's farm that Inock heard a familiar roaring; he recognised the sounds to be yniqem.

'What's that noise?' Venator Chris asked nervously.

'Sounds like yniqem,' Kallam answered. 'Which is not good! We should hurry and get out of the forest!'

'Why?'

'Because they're wild and vicious, they'll attack us on sight!' said Kallam. 'I think they've probably already caught our scent!'

So, the group of four took off in a sprint, Kano's fist-sized light ball zooming ahead of them. They could hear the yniqem roars as they ran through the trees. On and on they went for many minutes, dodging low branches and bushes, all the while looking up and about for the creatures hounding them.

Then it all went wrong when they reached a vast clearing.

Five adult yniqem swooped down on the group, breathing wide jets of red flames at them, almost killing them all.

The feathery beasts were massive; the size of mammoths, the dragon-like creatures whipped their long tails at their prey below, roaring.

Inock and the others ran ahead into the trees for cover from the deadly flames and kept going.

'Inock, you're the only one with powers to fight,' Kano wheezed as they ran. 'Chase them away! Chase them off!'

So Inock, looking back at the screeching creatures with their flapping wings so wide, began firing off energy balls, using the trees as cover. He made contact many times, but his energy balls were like tennis balls to the yniqem.

'Try something else!' Venator Chris screamed as he dived sideways into a tree with a loud crunch to avoid the fire

raining down on him. It missed him, but only barely. 'Ouch! I think I broke my shoulder!'

Kallam ran over to Venator Chris, saying, 'Don't give up! Get up!' He yanked him up and they wobbled on, Kallam supporting the boy.

Meanwhile, as he ran, in a panic, Inock tried every power he could think of; he hurled energy balls, telekinetically threw stones and boulders he passed, shot jets of green flames that clashed with the yniqems' awesome fire, sometimes engaging in frightening, long power struggles with the creatures where his fire pushed against theirs, launched enormous, blazing green fireballs, and even shot multiple lightning bolts from his hands. And various other powers he learned. And although the flying beasts were damaged, they still kept up the chase, and Inock was getting tired.

A short while later, Inock got an idea. What if he drank more of the Inock's Elixir? He knew the potion had power-enhancing qualities and he had three phials in his pocket; so, as he ran, he opened all three phials and swallowed all of it.

But what happened next wasn't quite what he wanted or expected. In fact, it was a total nightmare!

Inock got very dizzy and his vision blurred. He kept firing off energy balls and fireballs at the fire-breathing beasts in the sky, but his aim was now so off he made no hits.

And the nightmare got even worse when they ran into yet another clearing and something too horrific happened. A gigantic, multi-coloured bird the size of a house swooped down and yanked Inock off the ground in its huge claws. Inock cried out as the bird flew off, with him struggling in its clutches.

The flying fiend screeched as it flapped its enormous wings, speeding away into the distance, being followed by three of the yniqem Inock fought.

They flew on for some time, the bird whizzing through the sky to evade the numerous torrents of red flames aimed at it.

Inock didn't know how long he was suspended in the bird's claws, for he was severely discombobulated from drinking too much of the Inock's Elixir, but he suddenly found himself plummeting down and crash-landed in a bed of twigs and leaves. Unfortunately, he was not alone.

Inock was surrounded by three smaller versions of the multi-coloured bird, all three squawking madly at the new arrival. They were as big as he was, or even bigger.

Inock rightly assumed he was in some kind of nest as he adjusted himself from an awkward position, his senses still askew. He looked about him and saw the colossal bird that had grabbed him battling the three yniqem in the sky not far from the nest. To his dismay he noticed that the oversized nest was perched on the side of a high cliff. And that in the nest, along with him and the infant birds, were two pink eggs the size of footballs.

Inock hauled himself to his feet and then tried climbing out of the nest, but the three birds with him went berserk and began pecking and scratching and screeching at him until he gave in and curled into a ball for protection.

Meanwhile, the battle between the big bird and the three yniqem raged on; the bird was certainly good at swooping and dodging fire hundreds of feet in the air. It would let off this deafening screech that sent the yniqem plummeting until they recovered from the effects and came back for more.

And just when Inock was thinking he was in more trouble than ever, he was surprised and greatly relieved to hear a familiar voice.

'Inock, are you all right? It's me, Kallam!'

Inock turned round to see Kallam there, leaning over the nest and holding out a hand to him, at the same time beating off the three smaller birds with a large branch.

'Thank Existence you're here!' Inock cried, wholly grateful to see the man. 'I thought they would eat me!'

'I'm glad you're okay, son,' Kallam said. 'The others and I hid in the trees until the remaining yniqem lost interest and flew away. Then I followed that astonishing bird. I'm just glad you're alive!'

Inock took Kallam's hand and was yanked out of the nest, the man still fighting off the infant birds with the branch.

Then Inock was taken aback at hearing Kallam say: 'This is brilliant! We're in its nest! We should each take an egg!'

'*What?*'

'The ekinyo bird is very rare and very valuable, we must take an egg each!' Kallam said before climbing into the nest and took out the two pink eggs, simultaneously fighting off the younglings. He climbed out of the nest and handed one egg to Inock, saying, 'Believe me, you'll thank me for this at a later time!'

Inock and Kallam ran for it, leaving the huge squawking birds behind; not to mention the spectacular, ongoing struggle in the sky between the larger bird and the yniqem.

On the sprint down the mountain—Inock's senses were returning to him now—Kallam loudly said: 'The creature that captured you is a very magical bird; the ekinyo bird, whose eggs hatch into a very special bird that can become a loyal

familiar. It's a fantastic animal that can look after itself completely and can aid and support its owner in countless ways, including spiritual growth!'

Inock and Kallam found Kano and Venator Chris near the clearing where Inock was grabbed by the colourful bird, and together they returned to Kallam's farm unhindered.

Once on the farm, Kallam led the way into his single-storey cottage; a cosy open-plan house with a brown sofa and an armchair for a sitting area, a small kitchen with an ancient though usable electric cooker and dining table with two mismatched old chairs, and a separate section that was the bedroom and bathroom combined, where he attended to Venator Chris's shoulder. It turned out to be just a graze, and Kallam even gave Inock a hot tea to help his recovery. 'Drink this, it will calm your nerves, and help chase away the fogginess,' the man said.

Inock, Venator Chris and Kano left Kallam almost an hour later and returned to their realm without any further problems, Kano using his powers of premonition over and over to guide them.

Back at home, Inock showed the ekinyo egg to his family, and after a good amount of begging as well as omitting the details of where he got it from and what it can do when hatched on Inock's part, both Tehan and Esttia let him keep the strange egg.

'But all the responsibility lies with you, boy. *You* will have to look after it when it hatches,' Esttia concluded by saying, quite strictly.

How lucky, Inock thought. He had expected his parents to put up more of a fight. He happily went upstairs and stashed the egg under his bed.

Inock's lucky streak continued on later that week when he was up in the power-training school making more Inock's Elixir with Rikelle. Inock and Rikelle were working alone that night; Lalita was busy at home and Andre simply refused to get involved, and Inock was watching Rikelle mix ingredients into the copper pot when a funny thought came into his mind. Something he had thought about for a period of time. He normally fancied older girls but he thought Rikelle was very worth it; she was extremely pretty, sophisticated and very friendly.

'I bet your boyfriend isn't too happy that you're spending so much time with me,' Inock said. 'Did you tell him about what we are doing together?'

Rikelle laughed.

'I don't have a boyfriend, Inock,' she said, looking away from the pot and up at Inock who was stood over her; she was smiling brightly and parted loose strands of hair from her face behind an ear as she said this.

'I thought you might have a boyfriend,' Inock said, meanwhile thanking Existence she was single after all.

'Well, I don't,' Rikelle said, smiling at him again.

'Do you want a boyfriend?' Inock dared to ask. He was ever so nervous about what he was attempting.

'I would, yes, that would be really nice,' Rikelle said with a giggle.

Inock knew what he wanted to say next, but he was really quite nervous. So when he next spoke, it all came out in a great rush and as a bit of a yell.

'*I want to be your boyfriend!*'

Rikelle giggled again.

'We should go on a date, see how it goes,' she said, smiling at him. 'I like spending time with you, Inock. You are a nice friend and you make me laugh.'

'Awesome!' Inock squeaked, his face stretched in a very pleased grin and turning pink. He was simply over the moon the very pretty girl had agreed to go on a date with him.

Inock never had a real girlfriend before. The closest he ever got was when he kissed one of the market girls he often played with; he was about ten years old. That attempt did not go swimmingly either; after Inock kissed the girl called Lucy and looked away from embarrassment, she scowled then slapped him hard in the face! Lucy laughed at him before running away. From then on, Inock fancied older girls. He figured maybe they would not slap him. Inock never really thought about girls again until he was around thirteen years old, and he met Rikelle. Since that, Inock thought about Rikelle a lot; he always believed she was really nice and pretty and mature. Moreover, he liked that she was exotic and different.

'Cool,' said Rikelle. 'How about two o'clock tomorrow? We can meet in the market.'

'Two o'clock is perfect, it's a date!' answered Inock.

And so it was decided. The pair would rendezvous the following afternoon.

The next day, Inock met Rikelle outside the power-training school; it was a pleasant dry and warm afternoon; the sky was a sparkling green, though scattered with a cloud here and there.

The couple spent an hour or so walking around the market. During that time, both feeling rather shy and awkward, they didn't discuss much. They mostly observed

market dwellers, the eclectic mix of animals and children running and playing noisily around the stalls. That is until Inock bought them both something to eat; fish and vegetable wraps from a fast-food stall.

'Mmm, thank you, Inock,' said Rikelle chewing. They were stood by the food stall. 'This is really very good! And it's fish and vegetables so it's not too fattening, you know.'

'Yes, I really like the food from this stall,' said Inock, his mouth full. 'I come here all the time when I fancy a tasty snack.' ('Thank you,' said the male stall vendor.)

'Well, you chose right, Inock!' said Rikelle, smiling at him. 'Their food is very good. Shall I buy us something to drink with the food?'

'No, don't worry about it, Rikelle,' said Inock. 'I will buy the drinks.'

'Are you sure, Inock? I really don't mind buying them.'

'No really, I insist,' said Inock turning to the stall vendor. 'I'll get us each one of their icy blue drinks; they call it a Suppy. It's crushed ice. They come in different flavours and they're very good and refreshing! Can I have two blue Suppies please?' he asked the stall attendant wearing a white vest and dark shorts.

Inock reached into his shorts pocket and took out a handful of coins. Counting it, he handed the money across the counter to the man.

The vendor got busy pouring the drinks from a large and whirring electric contraption inside the stall. He set the drinks on the counter, placing a colourful straw in each. Inock took the two plastic cups, and handing one to Rikelle, who seemed to really be enjoying her wrap, took it and sipped through the straw.

'Oooh! It tastes amazing!' Rikelle said. 'You were right, Inock! This is a very cool stall! This drink is very ideal for Kasama weather. It's always too hot!'

A man and woman approached the stall and made an order. Then two teenagers came—two boys, and stood by the stall waiting to place an order.

'It's getting busy here,' Inock said. 'Shall we walk in the market some more?'

'Yeah, great, Inock, let's,' said Rikelle, very happily.

They left the food stall and commenced walking through the concrete maze.

'So, you said you eat there all the time?' Rikelle asked before taking another bite of her wrap.

'Yes, I do. Mother's cooking is very good, but sometimes I crave something different, you know?'

'Yes, I understand completely,' said Rikelle. 'My mother and sister are very good cooks too, but sometimes I feel like eating something I made myself. And now that I know about your favourite food place I'll come there too.'

'That's really cool, Rikelle!' said Inock, smiling and chewing away. He thought the date was going very well. Rikelle seemed exceptionally cool and pleased. 'I very much enjoy food in Kasama. And I can show you more stalls with nice food if you want.'

'That would be totally amazing, Inock,' said Rikelle enthusiastically. 'I really like the food local to Kasama too. My favourite is the fish stew with cabbage; I really like that dish combined with mashed green bananas and chapatis.'

'Wow! I really like that meal too!' said Inock, elated. 'It is definitely one of my favourites!'

'Cool,' said Rikelle. 'We have something else in common then! This could really work.'

'I'm totally happy too,' said Inock grinning at her.

After both finishing their wraps, they were feeling a lot less awkward and shy so they talked a lot more. The couple discussed Inock's powers which thrilled Inock immensely, especially when the girl said he was probably the most powerful demon she knew, they talked about the Inock's Elixir, what it was like for people their age to live and work in Kasama, their families where Rikelle mentioned she sometimes got into arguments with her sister, and whatever else that popped into their young minds.

About three quarters into the meeting the couple stopped at a games stall and both had a go on a game where you shot moving red shadow bats with pellets from a plastic gun.

Not much longer later, Inock and Rikelle ran into James, the Oracle's friend. The male witch was accompanied by his wife and two daughters; the young girls, who looked no older than thirteen, were dancing around James, singing an annoyingly catchy rhyme:

Succubus, succubus, blood-suckers will drain you!
Succubus, succubus, blood-suckers will take you!
Succubus, succubus, leave us be!
Succubus, succubus, blood-suckers don't drain me!
Succubus, succubus, blood-suckers don't take me!

The family appeared to be out shopping for the day, James struggling with numerous shopping bags, and after quick hellos and an exchange of pleasantries, James and his family left Inock and Rikelle to it.

'Come, everyone. We shouldn't disturb the young couple on their romantic date,' the male witch said, which made Inock blush abundantly. Rikelle simply giggled to herself.

Inock and Rikelle spent the remainder of the rendezvous in the outside part of a cafe, sipping guava juice and munching on sweet pastries, and because of James's embarrassing comments, awkwardly talking about this that or the other.

As they left the cafe, Rikelle had something to say.

'I'm really glad you agreed for me to help you with the Inock's Elixir that day at my mother's shop, Inock.'

'I'm glad I asked you too, Rikelle,' Inock replied.

'That day is very special to me; imagine if I did not help you with the elixir. Then you would never ask me to be your girlfriend and we wouldn't be on this romantic date now.'

'I always liked you, Rikelle. I think I would have asked you anyway, eventually,' Inock said, even though he knew wholly that she was right.

'That's nice,' said Rikelle dreamily. 'I always liked you too but didn't know how to show you. I like that you are funny and cool.'

At the end of the date, Inock escorted Rikelle to her family's potions shop in the northern end of the market where Rikelle, grinning widely, told him she had a wonderful time and would like to do it again soon.

Inock was so nervous at that point that he awkwardly offered her a hand to shake, saying, 'Yeah cool, me too.'

Rikelle shook his hand with a confused expression before proceeding up the white steps to the shop, still looking flummoxed.

Inock walked away with his chest swelled to double its normal size. He thought the whole thing went exceedingly well.

Later that evening, and in the days that followed, Inock had to endure snide remarks from Lalita about his going out with Rikelle.

Chapter Eleven

Birth of the Five Immortals

Inock, Lalita and Andre were at Dwayne's and Barnarbo's farm once more. The Oracle had sent them there to deliver another fireproof potion.

'You know, I think we need to know the enemy a little better. Barnarbo, what do you say?' Lalita said, as Inock handed Barnarbo the potion by the adult yniqem stables. It was stiflingly hot in that area; the dragon-like creatures sporadically breathed out and belched frightening red flames and fireballs.

'What enemy?' asked Andre.

'Immotshap, of course,' returned Lalita. 'We don't know that much about the guy and I feel the more we know the better our chances. What do you think, Barnarbo?'

'If it's information you want then you've come to the right place,' said Barnarbo. 'I am looking into Immotshap myself and have learned some valuable information from visions. Dwayne, you don't mind if I show them, do you? We've got some time.'

'Yes, go right ahead, Barnarbo, we have time,' said Dwayne, lowering the wooden box he held filled with charcoal and passing a gloved hand through his white hair.

'Great!' said Barnarbo. 'Everybody, follow me.'

Barnarbo took the group to a pond at the back of the yniqem stables, and after reciting a seven-word incantation too fast for the others to understand, and stirring the water with two fingers, said, 'Now look how they all became immortal!'

The pond surface was still, the water clear, with the odd ripple, then a vision appeared.

Inock got excited; it was like being at the cinema, he thought.

The scene was a top-down view of a long and shimmering cathedral-like chamber with a shiny mosaic marble floor and walls. The whole space was lit by many light balls floating just below the high ceiling. There were five people in the centre of the chamber; Mabiyah, as she looked now, the male witch James, Atheva the now Ghost Oracle of the ruins in rectangular-shaped spectacles and looking similar to Mabiyah in appearance though taller and thinner, Demonios with long white hair and a pointy nose, and a fifth man Inock didn't recognise; Immotshap. Immotshap looked to be in his forties or early fifties with long silver hair, a thin face and thin body.

The five men and women were all stood, scantily dressed, each with a bulging pouch hanging from strings around their necks, in front of five man-sized crosses in upright positions, each with a man or woman tied to it, all in their underwear similarly to Mabiyah and the others. But the strange thing to Inock was the people tied to the crosses didn't look unhappy or miserable at all, in fact it was the opposite, they were smiling at the five half naked people stood before them.

'Are you five ready?' Immotshap asked in a deep dreamy voice. He, like the other four appeared to be in some sort of trance.

'Yes, Immotshap, we are,' a man tied to a cross said calmly.

'We thank you for your gift,' Mabiyah said in a tranquil voice.

'And we are happy to offer it, Mabiyah,' one of the tied-up women said. 'As you know, our lives are nearing their ends, and we are more than willing to be a part of this godly experience.'

'Yes, dear Oracle,' another tied up man said. 'When we expire at your hands, you will be forever immortal! That is indeed a gift from the gods themselves!'

'It is our gift to you all,' the second restrained woman said, looking at the five before her and smiling serenely.

Then each of the five witches went over to a table and picked up a silver dagger and a goblet from a large bowl filled with a gleaming, iridescent liquid.

They all returned and placed themselves each in front of a cross and Immotshap, while holding his dagger and goblet heavenward, sang:

I take your life now on this day of Existence.
I value you are a living being in Existence.
All life is precious, I understand that,
but I must take your life here and now as it is.
Full and whole a being you are that.
That I may better my existence, forgive my rudeness.
I love you and all you are and have achieved,
and I thank you for your gift.

I pray for immortality on this day of Existence.

I do pray that it works out well for me and you.

I send you now to another level of existence,

and many know it is better than this suffering.

I choose to end you,

so I may prolong my existence here after you.

It is no selfish act for you have offered for me to

take your life, like no other has.

Though it is a terrible deed,

I pray I will be forgiven for this terrible feat.

And true it is heinous,

but you have chosen, and so have I.

Now I seal the deal.

Your life is mine, fill me up with your vitality.

Your life is mine, fill me up with your vitality.

Your life is mine, forever and always!

Then Immotshap asked the man on the cross before him: 'Do you offer it willingly?'

'I offer my life willingly. It is yours, now and forever!' The man recited.

'Then so be it!' said Immotshap.

Immotshap then moved forward and swiped his dagger at the space before the man. The restrained man's head lolled forwards as though he fell into a sleep. Immotshap placed his goblet beneath the man's head, a bright crimson sort of liquid seeping from the victim's head and into the cup.

Once the blood-like substance had stopped streaming, Immotshap took a step back, placed two fingers into the goblet and rubbed the liquid on his forehead; Inock thought the shape looked like some sort of sigil, then on his eyelids,

then his lips, then throat, heart, stomach, crotch and then on the pouch hanging on his neck. He repeated the lengthy chant.

As soon as he was done chanting, Immotshap was rapidly surrounded by iridescent energies drawing from the dead man's body and the goblet in his hands; the energies billowed all about Immotshap's body, lifting him six feet into the air for a full five minutes, filling him up until he floated back down and gently settled to the floor.

Immotshap got to his feet, looking dazed and confused.

'How do you feel?' Atheva asked, moving to the male witch.

'I think I can feel it,' Immotshap said calmly, with a smile. 'I feel … I feel … better … powerful … energised … MORE ALIVE!'

Mabiyah approached Immotshap and conjured a lit candle with a big bright blue flame out of thin air.

'Here, take this candle, burn your hand. Let us see what will happen,' she said.

Immotshap did as Mabiyah asked and indeed his hand got badly burned for a full ten seconds, but then it quickly healed over, there was not even a scar or smudge. All five witches beamed at one another; it was done.

The vision on the pond surface faded on Barnarbo's command.

'All five of them did it,' Barnarbo said to his stunned audience. 'Each one of the five witches killed a person and gained immortality. So as you can imagine, Immotshap will be no easy foe for whoever takes him on!'

Inock wondered how the Oracle he knew and loved so much would ever get involved in such ghastly rituals. He realised he really didn't know her at all.

And Barnarbo wasn't quite done with the visions; he chose to show his audience more; but this time it was a vision of the two dark witches who escaped limbo: Barla and Anandre.

With another seven-word incantation from Barnarbo, the pond showed visions of the two witches travelling far and wide and in many secret meetings with other powerfuls discussing Immotshap and bringing him back to power. The meetings took part in many places, including abandoned buildings big and small, tombs and private dwellings. And the man and woman appeared to be searching for something that was lost a very long time ago, though Inock and the others did not quite know what.

The final part of the vision was what stuck in Inock's mind the most: Barla and Anandre were in a spacious but cosy parlour with comfy sofas and expensive rugs, shelves laden with ancient artefacts and books, and paintings all along the walls. The room was lit by candles placed tactfully around the space.

'It is good to meet you at last, Kumba,' Anandre was saying to a man who looked to be in his thirties with a short ponytail and was fairly handsome. Like Barla stood next to him, Anandre was dressed in stylish black robes with a red belt at the waist, the soft glow of the candlelight making noticeable his stubble.

'It is pleasant to meet you also,' Kumba, in traditional robes of black, greeted back, shaking Anandre's hand.

There was another man in the room; black, also in his thirties and in robes similar to Kumba's. He was sat on a soft velvet chair several paces away, watching the visitors.

'I think you know why we are here,' Barla said to Kumba.

'Oh, we know why you're here!' the black man said harshly from his corner.

Barla shot him a stern look before turning back to Kumba.

'We have been watching,' Kumba said more gently than his companion.

'And so what do you have to say?' Barla asked Kumba.

'I think you know the answer to that!' the black man chimed in again from where he sat.

'Give them a chance, Avang,' Kumba said to him.

'Ours is a worthy cause … and your organisation only recruits the best. Well, who better than the immortal Immotshap?' Anandre said with determination.

'Have you even found him yet?' Avang sniggered from his corner. 'Oh yes, we've all heard of the terrible tyrant Immotshap the Immortal!'

'No, not yet exactly, but we are close, we are working on it.'

'I'm afraid we cannot join your cause,' Kumba said gently. '*The Collective* are adopting a different way of doing things. No aggression. No oppression. No subjugation.'

'The powerless masses and weaker powerfuls must be ruled!' argued Barla, arms waving in urgency. 'Surely you realise this!'

'The answer is still no, Barla!' said Kumba a little more spiritedly. 'We know all about Immotshap … he was a tyrant … merciless in his ways … a murderer … he betrayed many that followed him … killed many innocents … we are not willing!'

'And let's not forget the little fact that he simply wants to overpower and abuse the powerless masses!' said Avang from

his corner. '*The Collective* do not handle themselves that way anymore!'

'He may be strict and severe in his methods, but Immotshap is still the best leader for our goals!' barked Anandre. 'You cannot deny us! We will be victorious! Choose to join us, we will win!'

'You will not! You do not even have a leader as yet!'

'Surely you realise someone has to take control of this world and its mindless hordes,' Anandre argued. 'With your organisation's resources we cannot fail!'

'We will do it our way!' Kumba fired back. 'Your leader made a terrible name for himself and we simply cannot associate!'

'*Is that your final answer, child?*' Barla asked threateningly. 'I have lived very long you know! We cannot have you as opposition. *The Collective* is either with us or against us! I understand how it must look, but I've come to learn that Immotshap is best choice to lead all powerfuls in this sad age!'

'I'm afraid it is!' Avang said getting up.

'Then you leave us no choice!'

Without another word said, Barla drew a dagger out of thin air and lunged at Kumba, but Avang was fast. The man waved a hand and a shield of energy, reddish in colour, materialised between Kumba and Barla; Barla struck the shield and fell back, cursing.

Avang moved so fast, he was at Kumba's side in flash.

'You dare to challenge *The Collective*?' Avang roared.

'Oh give up! We all know *The Collective* has weakened as of late!' Barla yelled back, recovering.

'Well, I may not be a member of *The Collective* as yet, but I will show you what I alone can do!' Avang fumed then pointed a hand at Barla and Anandre and let roar a series of thick and short, red energy spears. The effect was something to behold.

The shield Barla summoned up for defence could barely take the attack, the powerful energy spears were rather frightful. And Avang just kept firing, seemingly inexhaustible, causing Barla and Anandre to walk backwards, Barla struggling to maintain her shield.

'He's too powerful, Barla!' Anandre cried. 'We cannot keep this up! We must leave!'

Inock laughed to himself when he saw Barla and Anandre turn and run out of the room.

A fierce chase broke out!

Avang and Kumba chased Barla and her companion into a very long corridor overlooking a balcony. The right side of the corridor was a series of sliding, glass doors that stretched on into the distance, sunlight flooding in through them. And to the left were numerous doors leading further into the building; the foursome had just ran out one of these doors.

Anandre was in the lead down the corridor.

Avang was still firing red energy spears at the two witches as he ran, the witches placing clever shields behind their backs as they fled. Kumba was in the rear, his expression murderous.

'You think you can just let yourselves into *The Collective* just like that?' Avang yelled fearsomely, keeping up pace.

'Give it up! You are losers! Your collective is ruined!' Barla cackled as she ran. 'Trying to recruit teenagers! Did

174

Samuel Blackwood even say yes? You were once powerful but now you are finished!'

Kumba and Avang chased the two witches the entire length of the overly long corridor, down a spiralling stairwell, Avang now firing off reddish energy balls as well as energy spears at the fleeing pair, the energy balls bouncing off the curved walls.

They ran for quite some time screaming insults and curses at each other … Until Anandre found the back doors to the fort, pushed them open and within seconds, they were all outside.

Right away, Inock noticed they were outside a humongous fort that stood tall and sturdy on a hilltop. The fort itself was a mammoth square block with four massive round pillars for corners. There was a large pond halfway between the fort and the back gate which Anandre and Barla sprinted towards.

'Your dark ways can never prevail! It never works!' Kumba yelled as he ran. 'We powerfuls in positions of power must act appropriately! And if you don't learn that then you must be stopped! FINISH THE EVIL THINGS OFF, AVANG!'

'WE WILL NEVER SURRENDER!' Anandre bellowed, his voice echoing in the open space. A red energy ball zipped past his ear and flew into the distance.

'The dark ways never last!' Kumba screamed. 'Trust me, I know! It will never work out! You cannot prevail!'

'We must teleport out of this place, Anandre!' Barla called out. 'We cannot win! They are good!'

And so the pair did just that as they ran. They both turned into shadows that quickly dissipated and they were gone.

The image on the pond surface faded once more.

'As you can see, the two witches have been busy recruiting,' Barnarbo told his captivated audience. 'And they are working very hard to locate Immotshap. Also, as you may have noticed, they are searching for something ancient … something I don't quite know what it is yet, though I know it is somehow connected to freeing Immotshap!'

'He sounds atrocious!' said Dwayne gravely. 'Wherever he is I hope he never returns.'

'Us too,' said Inock. Andre and Lalita nodded in agreement.

'I feel the same,' said Barnarbo.

On the ride back to the market, Inock, Andre and Lalita had a lengthy discussion. How could Mabiyah be involved in such wicked rituals? How were they going to recover the Demon's Amulet? And could they take down Immotshap should he rise to power? The evil witch would have an army of powerfuls were he to return!

'Yes, I know it looks bad, but you must realise those people gave their lives willingly,' Andre reminded Inock.

'Inock, I think they were going to die anyway,' Lalita inserted. 'Isn't that what that woman on the cross said?'

'I suppose,' Inock said.

'I think what we should really be worried about is getting back that amulet,' Lalita said next, moving out of the way for a man speeding in the opposite direction atop a gante.

'Should we just go to their lair and look for it?'

'No, I doubt we would find it just lying around the lair. Both Kano and Chris said Maliki must be the one who took it,' explained Inock. 'It's him we need to find.'

'Yes, but how? The guy can teleport himself at will! He could be anywhere.'

'I just hope we never have to face Immotshap like we had to fight that dark witch Dentas,' Andre said worriedly. 'Immotshap sounds horrendous!'

'Indeed he does.'

Chapter Twelve
The Mourning Alien Teens

It was the beginning of July and Inock was back in Unatia, at the conclusion of another AVC meeting. Inock was in a really good mood because he and Andre had a full four weeks off school. Though, he wasn't too happy that the summer holidays were not as long as they were in the previous school years.

Inock cornered Kano and Chris to ask them about the elusive boy Maliki and where he might be hiding. It was actually the only reason he decided to show up for the meeting at all since they lost his Demon's Amulet of Power. Otherwise, he might not have come.

'We haven't seen Maliki since the last time you saw him too, Inock, we told you,' Kano explained gently. 'Maybe you could ask his brother Lonathan, the mortuus.'

I should mention, in Inock's realm, sometimes when non-identical twins were born to a demon, the twin that came out first got all the power and the twin that came out last was completely powerless; the mortuus.

When Inock asked where he could find Lonathan, Kano gave him an address in the city.

Inock left the abandoned theatre on the double and took a green and black taxi to the address.

The taxi ride was only ten minutes, but Inock was so anxious to get to the bottom of the matter that it felt longer. The driver stopped on a quiet street; Inock thanked and paid the man then got out of the car and went up to and knocked on the black door.

A boy of about nineteen with similar features to Maliki and a sad face answered the door.

'Hello, can I help you?' the boy asked in a dull, lifeless voice.

'Yes, I think you might be able to,' Inock said. 'I'm looking for Maliki. Are you Lonathan?'

'Yes, I am, but I haven't seen Maliki for a long time. What do you want with him? What's he done?'

'Oh, it's nothing. He just took something of mine and I really need it back.'

'Who are you?'

'My name is Inock. I met Maliki through the AVC.' Then more quietly: 'The Anti-Venator Clan. You know them?'

'Oh … them!' Lonathan did not sound too pleased at hearing about the AVC. It seemed he had a grudge with them.

Inock was desperate.

'Could you help me find him please?' he asked. 'The thing he took from me is really important to me!'

Lonathan seemed to consider Inock's plea for a moment or two; then his face cleared, and he said, 'Next time I see him I'll ask him about—what was it he took?'

'It's a Demon's Amulet of Power. Just tell him, he'll know what it is.'

'Oh … well, I'm not really involved in those things, but I'll ask him anyway when I see him.'

Thinking, Inock decided to give the boy his address in Kasama Market so he could find him should he hear from Maliki; he was very desperate after all.

As Inock walked away from the door, Lonathan had one final thing to say to him.

'Maliki is dangerous and is not to be trusted!' the boy called out. 'He is bad! And those AVC freaks don't help either!'

Then he slammed the door shut.

***

Lalita's teasing Inock about going out with Rikelle was ceaseless. The girl just would not let it go, which got Inock really annoyed on many occasions. Inock had to put up with many conversations that went in this manner:

'So, are you in looove with her?' Lalita asked, making kissing noises. Inock, Andre and Lalita were all sat in Inock's sitting room watching the television.

'No, I am not in love, Lalita! Stop saying that!' Inock fired back.

'But you must be in looove with Rikelle, you went on a date with her,' Lalita said, mockingly.

'Stop saying I'm in love, Lalita! I don't understand why you're being like this!'

'I think she is jealous, buddy,' said Andre. 'She's in love with you and she doesn't know how to tell you.'

'Oh shut up, Andre! Nobody asked for your opinion!'

'Whatever you say, Lalita. I'm not the one teasing Inock about his date with Rikelle all the time!'

'Yeah, well, he went on a date with the girl. He faaancies her, he loooves her,' Lalita went on.

'Oh shut up, Lalita! Stop talking like this!' Inock said, fuming. 'We have more important matters to be discussing, like getting back the Demon's Amulet of Power instead of you jabbering on about me and Rikelle!'

'He is right you know,' Andre put in. 'We need to get that thing back and destroy it to stop Immotshap being super powerful if those awful dark witches find him. I'm just glad your father didn't notice it's missing.'

'Fine, Inock, I'll let it go, but we all know you looove her.'

They watched the television in silence after that; a cartoon where three best friends were constantly sucked into the television shows they were watching and had to survive countless horrors until they escaped back home, though Inock knew this wasn't the last he would hear on the matter of dating Rikelle.

After Ms Strict raised the issue of the missing ring one too many times in class, Inock and Andre finally decided to travel to Ettaka Village to investigate the matter on a Sunday afternoon.

'How are you getting on with the investigation, boys? I really must recover that ring to get some closure,' the teacher would say.

'Yes, miss … we … err … we're working on it …' Inock once answered.

'It will be resolved anytime now, miss,' said Andre.

The two boys were stood in a small cabinet-lined office; the graveyard caretaker sat in a rickety wooden chair behind

a table covered completely in piles upon piles of dusty files; he faced them.

The boys explained to the grey-haired man who they were and why they were there.

'I'll tell you, it's those stupid teens,' the man said with a rasping voice, apparently ignoring the fact that he was conversing with two teenagers. 'I see them hanging around here all the time! Then one night, a boy was loitering alone; the strangest one of them all. I saw him around here many times and I knew he was an odd little succubus. The little alien freak! They're all freaks with their strange words! I mean, what was he doing spending so much time in a graveyard, I ask you. You can only mourn for so long. Then I saw him hanging around late one night as I did the rounds. And the next day in the morning, I found the grave in question broken into!'

'Why would a teenager do this?' Andre asked.

'How should I know! You're all aliens to me; revolting teenagers!' the old man said bitterly. 'So dangerous and unpredictable! Violent little ones! No manners! Volatile tempers! You might as well all be aliens for all I know!'

'What did he look like … sir?'

'Smug!'

'*Smug?* Is that all you can think to say?' Inock asked, almost losing his temper.

'And stupid-looking, like the rest of them! All of you!'

'We're not all the same, you old man!' Inock roared.

'Thank you for your time!' Andre said through gritted teeth before grabbing Inock's arm and hastily marching him out of the dingy office. He looked close to losing it too.

The ride home was a silent and miserable one; but both Inock and Andre were thinking the same thing: Why would a teenager rob a grave for some old ring? How valuable could the ring be for the boy to commit such a heinous crime? Ms Strict would certainly be disappointed with their outcome, Inock thought.

Something strange was happening with the ekinyo egg Inock stole from the venator realm; it was humming and giving off a faint vibration, which got Inock all excited.

'I bet it's about to hatch, buddy!' cried Andre, doing a little dance. It was the evening and the boys were getting ready for bed when they noticed the almost inaudible humming.

'Oh, I certainly hope so!' Inock squealed, lifting the pink egg from his old toys box where he kept it. 'Kallam said the hatchling would be very special. I can't *wait* to see how special!'

And the happy times carried on for Inock. He was spending a lot of time with Rikelle lately; especially when the pair were brewing the Inock's Elixir alone. They went on two more official dates since their first one, spending them in cafes around the market and Inock was having the time of his life with the girl. No matter how much Lalita teased him about the thing.

For their fourth date Inock had a surprise for Rikelle.

Rikelle knocked on the Tehans' door on a Sunday afternoon as planned; Inock had said he wanted to surprise her.

'I'm here and ready for our date, Inock,' the girl said at seeing Inock. 'Ooh, you were all mysterious. I bet it's going to be a really good one!'

She looked very excited and grinning. She wore a pretty flowery dress and sandals.

Inock collected a pre-packed backpack and suggested Rikelle follow him. It was a very warm and lovely sunny day. Inock led the way out of the market; they walked until they reached the field leading into Gante Forest.

Inock led Rikelle about halfway into the field and took off his backpack. He took a red blanket from the bag and laid it down on the tall grass; then he took two bottles of juice and two sandwiches from the bag, set them down on the blanket, before politely asking Rikelle to sit. Rikelle smiled a pretty smile and obliged.

'I am having fun already, Inock,' she said. 'It's a very nice time.'

The pair ate the chicken sandwiches while sipping the juice and talked for hours about whatever came to mind until the sun set, bathing them both with a warm reddish glow as they watched the skies.

Rikelle was smiling and beaming throughout. And Inock was certainly happy.

'Inock, how much do you like me?' Rikelle asked as they gazed up at the red sky.

'A lot, Rikelle. I like you a great deal. I always have.'

'That's good. I really like you too but I was worried you didn't like me as much. It's good to hear you like me the same.'

'I do, Rikelle,' Inock said feeling content. 'But I don't think your sister Rukia likes me all that much.'

'What makes you say that?' Rikelle asked, turning her gaze from the mesmerising sky and to Inock.

'Because she always overcharges me for everything!'

'Oh, Inock, she overcharges everybody,' replied Rikelle, laughing. 'She likes you, I promise.'

'That's good to hear … I thought it was just me.'

'No, it is not just you, Inock,' Rikelle concluded, smiling at him.

'So, what is it like working with your sister anyway?' Inock asked after a little while.

'It's okay. Rukia is actually really cool once you get to know her. But what I really want to know is, is it true you work for that old witch the Oracle of Kasama Market?'

'Yes, it is. I do jobs for her,' said Inock. And he was very happy and proud to say it.

'*Existence*, what's that like? Is she as strange as they all say she is?' Rikelle asked.

'Well, she can be odd sometimes, what with her knowing everything about everything, but she pays really well. I like her a lot.'

'Well, I suppose someone has to like her,' Rikelle said next. 'People say she is very bizarre and weird to be around.'

'She's not that odd,' Inock said a little defensively. 'She is actually really nice, Rikelle. I've gotten to know you and I think you would really like her.'

'Okay, Inock … I just hope she doesn't keep you away from me too long with her jobs,' Rikelle said. 'I like hanging out with you very much. And thank you for this date; it's really, really cool!'

'I like spending time with you too, Rikelle.'

After that, the pair simply watched the glorious skies, and just when it was getting dark, they left the grass field. The day ended on a great high for the couple. Inock walked Rikelle to

her family shop and he went home feeling happier than a venator who just caught a demon doing something naughty.

And then Lalita's jealousy seemed to reach new heights one evening when Inock, Rikelle and Lalita were brewing more Inock's Elixir.

Rikelle accidentally dropped a glass phial on the floor; it smashed, spilling its contents all over and that seemed to be the last straw for Lalita.

'What do you think you're doing, you idiot?' Lalita shouted.

'*What?*'

'Lalita, calm down!' Inock said in a gentle but firm voice.

'No way! She's an idiot!' Lalita screeched. 'Why's she here anyway? She is not one of us! She's a powerless!'

'Oh, Existence, Lalita!' Inock said, devastated; he felt so badly hurt to hear Lalita say this. 'Please, calm down!'

'I do not like her! She is stealing you away from me, Inock!' Lalita cried, burying her head in her hands.

'Stealing him away from you? Are you mad?' Rikelle said in utter disbelief. 'You're his best friend! I can never change that! No matter how much I like him!'

'What's wrong with you, Lalita?' Inock asked, confused. 'This isn't like you. Why are you acting like this?'

'You know what? It's okay. DON'T WORRY ABOUT ME, INOCK!' Lalita screamed so loud all the venators in the market might have heard her. 'I will go! Never mind me!' She left the room.

Inock and Rikelle heard the school door slide open then close. Lalita was gone.

'What did I do?' Rikelle asked. 'It was just a simple accident.'

'I don't know, she just lost it! It is not like her at all.'

Then Inock got an idea. He chose to use the *Mind to Mind* link to summon Lalita back to the school. (The three friends still hadn't severed the connection.)

Thinking intently of Lalita and her name loudly in his mind, he sent: *Lalita, please come back! Please, Lalita, come back! Don't be angry anymore!*

Instantly he got back: *LEAVE ME ALONE, INOCK! I HATE YOU!*

So Inock gave up on the girl.

And then Inock finally got some news on the Maliki front. It was Tuesday evening and there was a knock at the Tehans' door. When Andre answered the door, he called to Inock to come and see.

Lonathan was stood there, depressed face and all, which soon lit up somewhat, when the boy said, 'I know where he is!'

'Where is he?' Inock asked. (He knew Lonathan referred to Maliki.) Andre went back to the sitting room looking ever so suspicious of the two boys and huffing and puffing.

'He's going to the Kasama venator lookout!' Lonathan said enthusiastically. 'I asked him why he was going there and he refused tell me. So I followed him without him seeing!' He certainly looked excited. It seemed to be the only fun he'd had in a long time.

'All right, let's go find him,' Inock said closing the door behind him.

So Inock and Lonathan raced to the Kasama venator lookout and were lucky enough to actually spot Maliki enter the grand building alone.

187

'He is up to something!' Lonathan said. They were stood at the compound perimeter. 'And I know it's something bad … he has been very secretive lately! More than usual. Should we go in after him?'

Inock was thinking fast and hard. What was Maliki up to? He was curious.

'Yes, let's follow him in, see what he's up to,' he said to Lonathan.

So, the pair ran into the lookout after Maliki and quietly followed the boy. Maliki moved through the lookout undisturbed. Inock and Lonathan followed him into the basement to the room with the gateway leading to the venator realm. The pair saw Maliki enter the chamber but when they moved from the niche they hid in and attempted to enter after Maliki, their path was blocked by an angry-looking venator.

'You cannot enter here!' the venator yelled at the boys. 'What are you doing down here anyway?'

'Sorry, we got lost,' Inock lied before him and Lonathan ran out of the basement and out of the lookout.

Before he left for Unatia, Lonathan promised to try and recover the Demon's Amulet of Power for Inock.

'I know how my brother can be. He's crazy! He let his powers go to his head!' Lonathan said. The boy called out more: 'He thinks he is entitled, that he can do whatever he wants and to whomever he wants!'

Chapter Thirteen
The Other Andre

It was at the conclusion of August that the strange business all started, on a Wednesday morning when Andre left the classroom to go to the toilet. Ms Strict was at the front, writing equations on the board that the boys were supposed to copy down and work out, the teacher's finger zooming through the air, making the chalk magically write on the blackboard.

Andre returned and sat down with a wide grin on his face; then oddly, the classroom door opened again and a second Andre walked into the room.

The Andre sat next to Inock guffawed then vanished in a flash of white light.

'Wha—? Who was that?' Andre asked, looking confused, pointing to the now empty seat.

'What d'you mean?' Inock asked looking just as puzzled. 'I thought it was you! I wondered why you were so happy and grinning to yourself when you sat down.'

'Boys, do get back to work please!' Ms Strict said sternly in her sharp little voice.

'But Ms Strict, didn't you see that? It was another me!'

'What are you blabbering about, young one? Sit down and get back to work!'

Then it happened again and again and again; once when Inock, Villad and Andre were power-training in Gante Forest, once when Inock and Andre were on a mission for the Oracle delivering a magical talking note to a blind witch, then at home one evening during dinner. Andre got up from the dinner table then returned seconds later with a weird grin on his face. And when the real Andre walked back into the kitchen, the false Andre laughed and vanished in a flash.

'Who was that?' Torend asked, his fork of mashed sweet potato halfway to his mouth.

'Are you boys up to something? Inock, was that another power you picked up, boy?' Esttia asked in an accusing tone.

'No, mother, it wasn't me. But it has been happening a lot. He just pretends he's Andre then when the real Andre comes back, he laughs and disappears!'

'Who do you think it is?'

'We don't know,' Inock said, worriedly. It was all very strange … rather bizarre.

'Andre, son, do you have a twin we don't yet know about?' Tehan asked.

'No, sir.'

'Well, whoever it is, I just hope he doesn't cause us any trouble,' said Esttia.

Inock went on another date with Rikelle. The couple were sat outside a fast-food shop in the southern section of the market, on a particularly lovely and pleasant evening, ravishing burgers and sipping passion fruit juice. Most other tables in the outside part of the shop were filled with people eating and chatting. The place was bestowed with magically floating and glowing flowers that were repeatedly played with by the patrons.

Rikelle was discussing her family as they ate:

'And she keeps telling mother every little thing I get up to!' the girl said before taking a bite of her burger. 'What am I supposed to do about that? It's so annoying, Inock you have no idea.'

'Well, actually, I understand what you're saying,' replied Inock. 'Torend won't let me do the things I want to do too!'

'Yes, but I doubt he's as annoying as my sister, Inock,' said Rikelle seriously. She pushed away a glimmering flower that hovered by her head. 'Like last week when I bought myself two new dresses and a pair of shoes from this lovely little shop in the market … Rukia told mother and mother insisted I return all of it. That we can't afford it!'

'Oh.'

'Yes, Inock, it's that bad. I mean, what's the point in having a family business and helping out at the shop if I can't even spend my allowance as I want! And don't even get me started on mother! She is so controlling! She's really, really strict, stricter than all my friends' mothers. She is always so serious all the time!'

'I get that too,' said Inock, sipping from his glass and then flicking away a hovering flower that obstructed his view. 'My parents are very strict too. They tell me off all the time for doing things other people our age do. All the stinking time!'

'Well, I guess everybody's parents are strict,' Rikelle said. 'And I suppose mother is only the way she is because she cares for me and is just being a good mother. But still, it's so annoying!'

'I agree,' said Inock understanding fully what the girl meant. He plucked a bright red petal from a floating flower

and played with it. 'But still,' he continued, 'I think Andre could be a little more fun sometimes.'

'Oh, Andre's fine,' said Rikelle with a dismissive hand gesture. 'I really like that he is mature and responsible.'

'I guess,' said Inock before tossing the flower petal. He took another bite of his burger.

Next, Rikelle put down her half-eaten burger.

'So how are your parents, Inock?' she asked.

Inock found this a bit of an odd question.

'They're fine,' he answered, swallowing. 'Why do you ask?'

'No reason, just wondered … And how about your brothers? How are they?'

Again, Inock thought the question a bit random.

'They're fine too,' he responded anyway. 'Why do you ask? Is something wrong?'

Rikelle hesitated before saying, 'No, nothing's wrong, Inock. Stop being paranoid.'

Inock chewed on his burger in silence while Rikelle played with hers.

'And what about all your friends?' Rikelle asked finally. 'Are they all fine?'

'Friends? What friends?'

'Anyone else, Inock! Think!'

'Like who?'

'How about that Lalita? … She okay? You been hanging out with her much?'

'Same as usual, I guess. Why do you ask?' Inock said, his mouth half-full. He was certainly enjoying his burger. (Lalita had found Inock and Andre in the market about a week after her outburst at Rikelle and said hello, acting like nothing bad

happened between them. Inock chose to ignore her previous anger and just carried on as normal.)

'How much time is "same as usual"?' Rikelle asked, appearing to be getting testy.

'I don't know, Rikelle, just same as usual,' Inock said with a shrug. 'Why do you ask? I don't get it.'

'Oh, no reason … just curious. You don't get it,' Rikelle said, not looking at Inock. She played with her burger for a little while more, not making eye contact with Inock, while Inock chewed on merrily. Then she got up suddenly and said, 'Inock, I have to go now. You don't get it.'

'Why?' asked Inock. 'We only just got started.'

'Because I need to, Inock … You don't get it … I'll see you.' Then she walked off.

Inock wondered why she took off so abruptly; he couldn't figure it out though he could sense something was amiss. And now other patrons in the cafe were staring at him, wondering what he could have done to upset the girl.

Days after his date with Rikelle, Inock went seeking advice on what went wrong from the only other girl around his age he knew; Lalita.

'So why do you think she acted that way, Lalita?' Inock asked as they watched the television in Inock's sitting room. It was just the two of them. Andre was outside running an errand for Esttia.

But Lalita simply crossed her arms and said: 'I have nothing to say to you on the matter, Inock!'

'Oh please, Lalita, please, please, please! You must know what she meant by *I don't get it*,' Inock said back. 'I've told you everything she said to me on the date! What do you think she meant? Why did she walk off like that?'

'I have nothing to say to you about the matter, Inock!' Lalita said, arms still folded.

'Okay then,' said Inock. 'If you won't talk to me about that then tell me this. Why did you get so angry at Rikelle that night up in the classroom? She just had a simple accident! I think we should talk about this, you know. You screamed at her and me!'

'I did nothing wrong, Inock!' Lalita snapped at him. 'I acted how I wanted to act!'

'Yes, but why did you scream at Rikelle? You should probably apologise to her, don't you think?'

'I did nothing wrong, Inock!' Lalita shouted in his face. 'I will not apologise to that girl! And she's right, you don't get a thing at all!'

Inock let it go after that.

In relation to the vanishing Andre clone, things got clearer, though not very a week or so later.

As Inock, Andre and Lalita were power-training in the Haunted Valley ruins, an extremely handsome black boy of about seventeen walked up to the trio.

Inock was levitating a large boulder ten feet in the air with telekinesis, with Lalita shooting multiple energy bolts at it, and Andre was in the form of a gomorah and was smashing bricks when the boy showed up.

'Hello there, you three. Power-training again?' the boy said casually. He wore black shorts, a vest and sandals and was smiling at them.

Andre morphed back into himself.

'Who are you?' Lalita asked.

'I am Kross, we've met.'

He held out a hand to Inock.

'Have we?' Inock asked, dropping the boulder he levitated and shaking the boy's hand. He stared at him trying to bring to memory who he was, but nothing came.

'Yes, we have,' replied the boy, grinning. 'I am the one who's been turning into Andre. Remember in your classroom?'

Inock was instantly furious.

'*Why have you been doing that?*' he hissed.

'Are you in love with Andre or something?' Lalita asked with a snigger. Inock had told her all about the vanishing Andre.

'What do you want with us?' Andre asked, not sounding at all happy either.

'There is something I want you to learn, Andre,' the boy said, sounding serious. 'I want you to learn who you are and where you come from; your true origin.'

'What are you talking about?' asked Andre. 'I know where I come from! My family died! I don't want to think about it!'

'I don't think you do,' Kross said earnestly. 'Like me, Andre here is a god from another realm. I just thought he ought to know.'

'*What!*' Inock, Andre and Lalita all said in unison, in disbelief.

'Yes, it is true. Myself and Andre are both sons of Alloh! A great and mighty god.'

'Why are you saying these things?' Andre asked, looking sceptical.

'It is all waiting for you, Andre,' the strange boy said. 'You always knew you were different. If you realise it, what I'm saying will all make sense.' Then he laughed and just

before he vanished off in a flash of white light with a wide grin, said, 'You should think about that for a while.'

'That was strange,' Andre said after Kross was gone.

'Very. Andre a god? Ha!' Lalita cackled aloud.

'That boy is really annoying!' said Inock. 'I hope he doesn't come back.'

'Do you think he was telling the truth?' Andre asked the others.

'Do you feel like a god?' Lalita asked him.

'No.'

'Do you feel different to everybody else?'

'No.'

'Then he was just playing with our minds. He is just another powerful!'

'Okay.'

And without further discussion the threesome shook the strange experience from their minds and carried on training their powers.

But was Kross telling the truth? Or was he just another mischievous powerful?

***

Inock and Andre were at Dwayne's farm once again, and were both looking down into a barrel of clear water.

You see, curious, the boys had asked Barnarbo how the Oracle and the other immortals had learned how to become immortal; ('Did they devise the ritual themselves?') and Barnarbo, having seen it in a vision already, chose to show them the whole deal.

'It was not easy getting this vision, you know,' Barnarbo said, stood before the boys. 'You will find out why when you see where they got the knowledge to immortality. Those gods aren't something to toy with!'

'*Gods?*' Andre screeched in disbelief. '*Actual gods?*'

'Yes, young Andre, gods. Now watch the water and you will see.'

A vision gradually appeared on the water surface.

It was the middle of the afternoon and Mabiyah, the male witch James, Demonios and Immotshap with silver hair were stood in an open grassy field; they were all dressed in tidy but colourful clothes that would have looked out of place in Kasama; white tunics with green collars, gold belts and gold slippers. All four had their arms raised to the skies and were all chanting vehemently, all saying the same long incantation.

When the four finally stopped chanting, the sky high above them began to shimmer with a transparent sort of energy and Inock and Andre were amazed to see a great city slowly materialise high above the scarce clouds in the sparkling emerald sky.

All four witches then uttered a few words more and were suddenly soaring high in the air; they sped like bullets towards the sky city, and at reaching it all landed gently in a brilliant street amongst towering crystal buildings.

The street the four had landed in was lightly populated with people dressed in bright and awesome colours similar to those the four witches wore.

'We have no time to waste,' James said. 'They will already know we're here. We should hurry and get what we came for. Nothing more.'

'Yes, no time to dillydally,' said Mabiyah. 'And needless to say, we must stick to the plan. We only take what we discussed, nothing more...Do not be tempted to take more or else you will never stop and will be discovered!'

And so, the foursome proceeded down the shiny street, straight to business.

They moved hastily through the city's streets passing people and buildings that were more breath-taking than the last; beautiful people of all colours adorned in gold and crystals and the streets appeared as though they had never known litter or deterioration.

Inock was surprised to see people teleporting in or out of the streets the witches passed and there were also people flying serenely here and there. Mostly everyone looked quite happy and content.

The witches reached a great white building surrounded by ever-so-tall red trees with golden leaves and bright green flowers. The building had a silver and gold sign above the main entrance that read: *PLACE OF KNOWLEDGE.*

The group proceeded up the marble steps and entered the library.

The inside of the building was amazingly massive! Something magical, Inock was wowed to see it was more than triple the size it appeared to be from the outside. The open-plan space looked like a library with tall and wide bookshelves and hundreds of tables with people sat at them, reading or staring at paper-thin monitors.

Immotshap led the way along an aisle and down a long set of steps then took two turns. Minutes later, they stopped at the entrance of what appeared to be a basement chamber; a long empty room. Immotshap placed a hand in the space where the

door would be, closed his eyes, and then moving the hand in circular motions, while at the same time chanting in a strange language … two desperate minutes passed and a bluish energy barrier appeared in the doorway then fast dissipated.

His eyes snapping open, Immotshap said, 'It is done! It was blocked but it is now clear.'

The four entered the low-ceilinged chamber.

'Mabiyah, it is time,' Demonios said, looking at the Oracle. 'Be quick, they'll be here soon.'

'I know, I know, young one,' Mabiyah said then she reached into her tunic pocket and took out a piece of paper. From this she read six words and Inock was stunned to see the walls of the room slowly transform into shelves lined with silver and golden books.

'Time to start the search,' Immotshap said. 'We must be fast!'

So, the four witches began searching through the shelves, checking book titles.

'I insist we find that tome!' said Immotshap as they searched on. 'What we stand to gain will grant us more time than we could have hoped for; we can live long and learn a great many things!'

'I feel the same, Immotshap,' said James, replacing on a shelf an elaborate silver book. 'We will be unstoppable and can possess all the time we need to amass immense knowledge!'

'I MUST HAVE IT ALL!' vociferated Immotshap. 'WE WILL RULE!'

'It will truly be the greatest of achievements!' said Demonios fervently. 'We must succeed! We will succeed!'

'Quiet, you three!' hissed Mabiyah, who was floating just below the low ceiling, looking at a particularly hefty golden book. 'We do not want to be discovered! We are intruders after all.'

Many minutes passed.

'Over here, I found it!' James called out. 'I finally found it!' He held a chunky silver book.

'Wonderful! This is astronomical!' cried Immotshap, dashing over to him. 'Thank Existence you found it before the guards arrived! Though, perhaps now we can search for-!'

'*We take nothing more or we risk being discovered!*' Mabiyah hissed, stopping the greed.

But before another word was uttered, a man's voice rang out, 'Down here! They're down here!'

And within seconds three men in gold and white tunics and boots and all holding white staffs appeared through the doorway into the long chamber.

'Intruders! Halt!' one of the men bellowed.

The three guards charged.

'No one breaks into the realm of the gods and lives!' another man yelled as he ran.

'Filth! Scum! Kill them all!'

The three guards aimed their staffs at the witches and white beams of energy erupted forth. Immotshap defended himself and his peers with a quickly said spell: a shield that deflected the powerful beams, the stray energy exploding books and shelves.

The guards fired and fired but Immotshap's shield held.

While James pocketed the silver book he located, Immotshap did something else; with a wave of a hand and a few words uttered, Mabiyah, James, Demonios and

Immotshap switched places with the guards. Now the intruders were closer to the chamber entrance while the three guards were not.

Then it was Mabiyah's turn to act; with a swift wave of a hand, the three guards, who were charging, froze mid-step; Mabiyah had cast a spell to suspend the guards like statues.

And the four witches wasted no time; they ran for it; back upstairs and through the library, startling many people and causing an uproar. Once outside, they were hounded by even more brilliantly dressed guards, some flying high above.

A violent chase broke out where the countless guards fired devastating beams of power and electricity from their staffs at the foursome, and each witch would create a shield or deflect the attack.

People ran screaming; men, women and children as the deflected beams and various other projectiles bombarded buildings, causing debris and dust to rain down.

'INTRUDERS MUST BE DESTROYED! CONTAMINATION CANNOT BE ALLOWED!' was what could be heard over and over as the four witches escaped the wrath of the gods. And 'HOW DID THEY BREAK THROUGH THE VEIL? IMPOSSIBLE THIEVES!'

Immotshap, James, Mabiyah and Demonios all ran, firing off jets of wild green flames and throwing massive exploding fireballs at their pursuers. Furthermore, they aimed crackling energy bolts and sharp, piercing bluish energy spikes!

Immotshap in particular stood out to Inock. His raging fireballs were the largest and the most devastating, his face fierce and set in great determination, his silver hair flying. As Inock watched, the male witch killed three flying guards with well-aimed fireballs and electric bolts and snapped another's

neck with some form of telekinesis, sending the remaining guards in crazy fits of rage.

'MURDERERS! KILL THEM!'
'THEY MUST NOT ESCAPE!'
'INVADERS MUST DIE!'

'ALMOST THERE! KEEP GOING!' Immotshap called to the others as he sprinted, killing another sentry.

People were running in all directions in an attempt to escape the chaos, crying and screaming their heads off.

'We must return to the edge of the city!' James called out.

'We might not make it home at this rate!' cried Demonios.

A mammoth chunk of a falling building fell in the witches' path and they had to run around it, Mabiyah bringing up the rear. To Inock, she appeared to be the slowest.

'Why are they chased by the guards?' Inock heard a scared-looking bystander ask another.

'They must be criminals!' a man answered. 'What an odd occurrence. We have not heard of wrongdoers in many years!'

'ALMOST THERE, EVERYONE!' James yelled, launching an electric fireball that just missed one of the pursuing flying guards. 'KEEP GOING! IT WILL BE WORTH IT SHOULD WE SUCCEED!'

'INVADERS MUST DIE!'
'INTRUDERS MUST BE DESTROYED! CONTAMINATION CANNOT BE ALLOWED!'

Eventually, the witches reached the edge of the floating city, and pushing confused civilians out of their way, all four

leapt off the end, Demonios taking a direct hit in the back. And they plummeted down, down and down, back to their world.

The godly guards did not follow any further.

The vision on the water surface faded at Barnarbo's command.

'A plethora of knowledge and the only book they took was one on immortality!' Barnarbo said to Inock and Andre, arms flapping up in frustration. 'As you saw, that realm is well protected … so it took some doing on my part to see into that place and what happened there that day.'

'*Wow!* A world filled with gods?' wondered Inock, rubbing his moist chin.

'Yes, gods, child,' Barnarbo told them.

'That city looked amazing! Like a fantastic dream! The people were so golden! And *oh* the buildings!'

'I know,' said Barnarbo.

'Do they let people like us go up there?'

'No. Never!'

'Never?'

'Never. And I think you saw why. They live completely differently to us. Their world is far more peaceful and immensely and immeasurably more advanced,' explained Barnarbo.

'Shame we're not allowed up there!' said Andre. 'About the stolen knowledge; with so much increased time and life, maybe even an eternity, you really can achieve a lot and gain almost infinite knowledge, among other things!'

'I know, young one. None the less, I hope that quenched your curiosity as to how the five learned the secrets to

immortality.'

'It did, Barnarbo. Thank you.'

Chapter Fourteen
The God Alloh!

Inock and Andre spotted Maliki speed out of Kasama Market atop gante when they were riding in after a mission for the Oracle.

'Existence, there he is! Let's follow him and see where he goes!' Inock said quickly.

The two boys turned around and followed Maliki—at a distance—to Embuyaga Village.

Ten minutes into the village, Maliki met with a familiar face; the dark witch Barla of all people, in a semi-dark alleyway.

Inock and Andre waited around a corner and listened to the witch and Maliki talk in hushed tones.

Barla seemed to be pleading with Maliki, who did not sound pleased about something.

'Why did you ask me to meet you here?' Maliki barked.

'We're all being watched, this was the best place to meet, Maliki! I cast a spell on the area; it was the easiest place to hide!'

'Whatever! Look, you people are taking too long!'

'We're doing all we can!'

'You still haven't found it! I have waited for this for so long!'

'We're getting close, just make sure you are prepared to do what you'll be required to do when the time comes!'

Maliki made a clucking noise before going on to say, 'Yeah, that's if your people ever find it.'

'I told you, we've almost got it! Just one last piece and your job will be up—hold on, I sense something.'

Inock and Andre didn't hear the witch Barla come round the corner; she caught them eavesdropping and quite unawares and what happened next was total calamity!

Barla conjured ropes that in a flash tied around Inock and Andre, but Andre swiftly morphed into a green two-tailed squirrel and ran free. Then Andre turned into an onis; his favourite animal, and repeatedly lashed at Barla with his two slithering tails, wrapping them around her. Onis Andre squeezed Barla tight until she could take no more; suddenly she fast conjured up a blade and slashed both his tails off before telekinetically hurling him into a wall.

Andre fell unconscious as it seemed.

At that point, Inock had freed himself and smashed Barla into a wall with telekinesis then fired an energy ball at her, which Maliki—just appeared round the corner—quickly cancelled out with powerful, sizzling energy bolts.

'Do you like my witchy bolts?' Maliki gloated. 'Barla's been teaching me magic. She taught me how to conjure them up and energy balls too!'

'YOU ARE ON THE WRONG SIDE!' Inock yelled before firing energy bolts of his own at Maliki.

Maliki countered with more frightening electric bolts and they were locked in a deadly power struggle.

But to Inock's dismay, Barla ran up and added to Maliki's fire with greater energy bolts!

Inock gave it his all but he quickly realised it wasn't enough; the evil pair won out; the energy-connecting-point moved towards him and almost touched his fingers, the power and energy of the struggle billowing up all around him, sparks striking all over; if the magical power touched his body, he would be killed!

Being smart, Inock decided to dive sideways out of the line of fire, the power connection breaking.

'You evil witch!' Inock screamed from the ground. '*What do you want for our world?*'

'Nothing a child can handle!' Barla said with a sneer. 'It is time we witches took control!'

'But Maliki can't be much older than me!'

'Well, he gets it better! He is no child!' Barla breathed, advancing on Inock, her fingers sparking with bluish bolts.

'Maliki said you dark witches embrace more and are not afraid of consequences,' said Inock. 'These things are not tampered with for a good reason! Countless realms would fall into chaos!'

'That is not for you to worry about!' hissed Barla. 'Soon you will be dead!'

***

Andre found himself at the edge of a green cliff. The sun was high up in the sky though not as high as he thought it should be, feeding the surrounding areas afar with love and energy. Way down below at the base of the cliff were golden figures, some on their backs soaking in the golden ball's rays,

and some were sat chatting amongst themselves. They all appeared to be naked but glistening and perfect, needing no clothing. And Andre could see what appeared to be children laughing and playing. He next looked in the distance to see more golden beings flying in air, and others just hovering and talking.

Andre could sense the rays of the sun wash over him, enveloping him in a feeling that made him feel wholly content. He wanted nothing more from Existence but to just lie there and take in the sun's love. Forever and nothing more.

'Alluring, isn't it?' came a man's voice from behind Andre. It was a beautiful melodic voice that could send you into a dizzying trance.

Andre turned around to see a golden man approach him. He was magnificent, but not the sort of beauty Andre knew from his world; it was far more wholesome and complete … not just what could be seen by the eyes; Andre could surely sense it.

'Who are you? Where am I?' Andre asked the strange being. His voice came out though did not seem from his mouth but from his mind … and when the man spoke, Andre understood him in his mind and not just by the words said out loud. It was a sort of pure and simple comprehension; like telepathy!

'I am Alloh! You father. Although you have a mortal father, your true spirit father is me. And as to your second question; you are in another place from where you usually are, a higher level of existence to the one you are used to,' the golden man said. 'And you are welcome here, Andre. I know you and you know me, though you are not fully aware. I am one of many gods.'

'Why am I here? I was attacked … I was fighting … now I'm here,' Andre said, ever so confused.

'That is correct … I was watching … you are now here … and I would like you to stay here,' said Alloh. 'This is your heritage as a god … you are welcome to stay.'

Andre thought for a while as the golden god waited for his response.

'Must I stay?' he asked. 'I like my world and my life. (Andre certainly remembered his home, though it was difficult.) I have a good family and friends. I am well and content.'

'Indeed, I have watched you live that way for a time now, Andre. I would rather you stayed here. But if you would prefer to stay where you are, I will wait,' the golden man said, though looking happier than disappointed. 'It is all waiting for you, my son. Kross told you that much. If you accept you may come and exist with us. It is a kinder world. One filled with pure, unpolluted love and understanding … it is undeniable. We are your kin.'

It took a little while for Andre to figure out what the god meant, but it finally came to him; Kross—the teenage boy who told Andre he was a god's son and that Andre was a god himself.

Andre had to fight with all his mind and will, for the blissful comfort he was experiencing was exceedingly tempting; the pure, undeniable love and untainted joys he felt just then. He was conflicted. He could sense that as long as he stayed in that place, he would want nothing more than to simply be there and revel in the love and sense of completion and non-wanting-ness.

But he said, 'I will go back. It is not easy but I like what I have. I love my family and friends. And though it is a harsh world filled with many minefields, I am well. I will exist there for a while longer.' Alloh was nodding in agreement. 'I like the Tehans, they're loving and kind to me.'

Then something more occurred to Andre; he breathed in deeply then decided to get something off his chest seeing as he was conversing with a god.

'There are some things that have been on my mind, Alloh,' he began. 'People talk about enlightenment ... I know you can live a simple human life and be happy, and those that are not happy enough seek more ... What is enlightenment and transcending?'

Alloh smiled a deep smile at Andre.

'You will be just fine, child,' the god said. 'Though I will say this, some may argue that you might alter the way you live as a human so that you may reach different heights of thinking and perception; you can change your life to gain what you desire. If you want enlightenment, read the right books, explore, experience, observe. And this is quite important: think, reflect and see what you find, live accordingly in relation to what you desire to achieve. Just because you are a human and suffer human nature does not mean you have to be an animal. Though it may be hard, you can transcend simply by changing the way you live, behave and think.'

Andre was nodding, so the god continued.

'If you are looking to change yourself for the better, consider your lifestyle; the lifestyle you've grown accustomed to. What elements of it need revising and changing... You might consider examining your beliefs and

actions with particular focus on certain areas: religiously, psychologically, economically, attitudinally.'

'Thank you, Alloh,' said Andre.

'And Andre,' said Alloh next. 'Though I love you more than you may ever realise and thus need you to stay with us, I will allow for you to return.'

Then Andre noticed something; he looked at his hands then at his arms, and then his feet and realised he too was golden, naked but shimmering and perfect.

Just then, seven doll-sized beings with white, glowing angel wings all dressed in white appeared at Andre's side. They had long white hair and their skin was a pea green colour.

'Ah, I see the helpers are here,' Alloh said.

And just then something clicked in Andre's mind; the small green creatures; he saw similar beings years ago when the Death Kikomo tried to suck the life out of him in the Kasama Powerless-only School and they helped him survive.

'What are these?' Andre asked. 'I remember them … though only vaguely.'

'We are guardians, Andre,' one of the green creatures spoke in a small but deep man's voice. 'We have been looking after you. Especially when you needed us the most. But be wary of devils…beings similar to us.'

'Weird… Thank you,' was all Andre could say.

'Yes. We have kept careful eyes on you, young Andre,' said another of the green beings.

'Umm, thank you,' Andre said again. He gazed at what was meant to be the sun and felt he was surrounded by far more love than he could ever comprehend.

'You are welcome, child, though no thank you is ever necessary,' a doll-sized creature said. 'Our reward is in your success at life and your wellbeing. You are doing well.'

'Umm, thank you.'

'You're welcome, child.'

'May we carry on looking after you, child? We heard you refused to stay here with us,' another doll-sized creature said, a woman's voice this time.

'Umm, I think that's fine,' answered Andre.

'Good, certainly we like you considerably.'

'What about the rest of the world?' Andre asked his audience.

'It is a sorry but well-progressing world. It will be fine,' Alloh answered him.

'It is I suppose…'

'Andre it is time for you to return to your realm,' Alloh said next. 'But before you go, I must insist on informing you, son, you are always welcome. You can never do wrong.'

'Thank you…father.' Andre surely felt awkward saying that. He had no idea how to handle himself just then.

'However, before you depart, young one, there is something I choose to inform you of. There is another child of mine in your realm at this very moment; a boy with similar skin colour to yours. Musalla is his name. Find him. Let him know he too is a god. I love him dearly.'

Andre chuckled at hearing this. He knew Musa well. He met the older boy through Samuel Blackwood. Musa was nice if not a bit sarcastic.

Then suddenly Andre could hear Inock's voice calling his name; it sounded all strange and echoed.

'Goodbye for now, Andre,' Alloh said. 'I will watch you from time to time.'

***

When Andre came to, Barla and Maliki were gone and Inock was crouching over him, still calling his name. Andre was now morphed back into his human self.

Inock told Andre that after he was knocked unconscious, strong winds soon came and literally blew Barla and Maliki into the sky and far, far away.

'I wonder if the wind was Alloh's doing,' Andre mumbled to himself. He remembered everything.

'Who's Alloh?'

'Never mind…nothing.'

'Can you believe that loser Maliki is working with the dark witches? What do you think they're close to finding?' Inock asked, helping Andre up.

'I don't know … Immotshap?'

'Hmm, maybe,' said Inock. 'And what job do you think they need Maliki to do?'

'I don't know but it does not sound good, Inock,' Andre said, massaging the back of his head. 'Maliki has turned out to be worse than we thought; he is disingenuous and really bad! Oh, why is it raining now?' he finished as, indeed, it had just started to rain.

The boys located their gante and hopped into the saddles.

'Yes, it looks that way,' Inock said after a moment's thought, answering about Maliki being bad. 'Can you ride?'

'Yeah, I should be fine,' Andre told him, still rubbing his head. 'I'm sore, though. And this rain doesn't help!'

The pair began the journey home, feeling defeated, though Andre was smiling to himself; now enlightened he couldn't be happier.

Inock's Ekinyo egg finally did what it was bound to do. It hatched!

Inock and Andre were in their bedroom doing homework at the only table in the room when a ding went off, seemingly in both their minds. They next heard a loud cracking sound, and when Inock looked to his old toys box on the floor, he saw that the ekinyo egg had cracked at the top.

The boys gathered around the egg and watched as the rest of it cracked and split open before a chubby, gooey, multi-coloured bird emerged from the shells, its orange beak protruding. The creature resembled a baby eagle but with blue, yellow, green and red feathers.

'*Existence!* It's just hatched!' cried Andre.

'Finally!' cheered Inock. He lifted up and cupped the fat bird in his hands. He held it out to Andre. 'Kiss it! It's cute!' he said giggling.

'What? No way!'

'Oh go on!'

'No way!'

'Oh go no!'

'Oh fine!' And so, Andre kissed the bird before saying, 'Go get it some food, Inock. I'm sure it's hungry.'

'Do we need to feed it already? Existence, what do we feed it?' Inock squealed dancing about with the bird in his hands.

'Whatever you like—actually, no, not anything … maybe bird food?'

'What's bird food?' asked Inock.

'I don't know … seeds? Biscuits?'

'All right, I'll go get some biscuits and nuts!' Inock said before handing the hatchling to Andre and leaving the room.

He returned momentarily with biscuits, which he went onto feeding the pudgy animal, on the bottom bunk—Andre's bunk. It squeaked and chirped adorably as it gobbled everything down.

'Should we tell the others of the arrival?'

'No, it's late. No need to wake them.'

Andre cleared out the toys box, stuffing all the toys under the bed.

'It will live in here. We can look after it, Inock, together,' he said at the end of the chore. 'What should we name it? Is it a boy or a girl?'

'It looks like a boy bird to me, so how about Thomas?'

'No, that's too long,' Andre said thoughtfully. 'How about Tony?'

'Tony sounds good … Tony it is then. Hey Tony! Chirp, chirp, chirp, Tony,' Inock said making faces at the baby bird. He lowered it in the toys box and they watched it skip and dance about for some time, pecking at the remains of the biscuits.

… Inock and Andre each got into bed, leaving the light switched on for the infant bird.

'I am so glad it finally hatched, Andre!' said Inock after many minutes of silence. 'But what do you think mother and father will say when they see it? I know they said it was okay for me to have it, but somehow I get the feeling they won't like it. Remember what happened to Stump the onis?'

'I remember Stump,' said Andre from the bottom bunk. 'That was a big disaster! But I think Tony is okay. He's small,

whereas Stump was massive. And anyway, you asked them this time and they said yes, so they can't stop you from keeping it.'

'I suppose,' said Inock. 'I bet Torend will be jealous I have him though.'

Andre laughed.

'I sincerely doubt that!' he said. 'Torend's too busy to be jealous of you.'

'I guess,' said Inock. 'Would you want one for yourself, Andre?'

'Not really. I can turn into any animal I like so getting a pet would be a bit redundant.'

'So you are a pet?'

'No, of course not, Inock! Shut it! I just think since I can change into any animal I like, getting a pet would be rather pointless.'

'I guess,' said Inock, yawning. He was starting to feel sleepy.

'And you have to be responsible to have pets. I am too young for that. You will have to look after Tony all the time, you know.'

'I'm sure it won't be that hard,' replied Inock.

'Well, let's just wait and see, brother. Do you think Rikelle will like it?'

'I don't know,' answered Inock. 'Maybe. She is a bit of a mystery, Rikelle. Her and Lalita do not seem to get on. It's really annoying!'

'You just need to figure it out, Inock,' advised Andre. 'Girls are not easy, you see.'

'I guess not,' Inock said back.

They were both soon asleep, the colourful bird squeaking and singing away into the night.

In their sleep, both brothers had peaceful and picturesque colour-filled dreams.

Chapter Fifteen
Rescuing the Dark Witch

The Oracle summoned Inock, Lalita and Andre once again to her chambers.

The three friends were in Inock's sitting room watching the television, (A cartoon of a teenage witch whose family owned an island with other citizens living there, and the young witch got into many comical and sometimes perilous situations managing the many properties on the island owned by his over-demanding family.) when a gomorah knocked on the front door.

Andre answered the door and too petrified of the creature, he screamed. After he was done screaming and yelling, the gomorah spoke in Mabiyah's voice.

'Young one, I need to see you, young Inock and young Lalita in my chambers, immediately. Come now!'

It vanished in a flash of white light, baring its yellow teeth.

The trio went to the Oracle right away.

When they got to Mabiyah's chamber she wasn't alone; James the male witch, in his knee-length coat, was sat at the small table with her.

James smiled at seeing them all there.

218

'Ah, young ones, you have arrived at last,' the Oracle said, smiling.

'Hello, Oracle,' the three greeted in unison.

'Hello there, guys,' James greeted Inock, Andre and Lalita. 'Good to see you again.'

'Hello, James,' Inock and the other two said back.

'So, how is your girlfriend?' James asked, looking at Inock. 'The one I saw you with in the market that time.'

While Lalita huffed and frowned at the question, Inock said, 'She's fine, James.'

'She certainly was very pretty.'

'Thank you, James.'

'Yes … now, getting to business,' said the Oracle. 'I have summoned you all here today for a particularly important job. We need to liberate Dentasa!' (The Oracle liked to use the full version of the name Dentas.)

'*What?*' was a chorus of three disbelieving voices; Inock's, Andre's and Lalita's.

'Yes, young ones, we do. She knows the secret to defeating-!'

'No way, Oracle, that witch tried to kill us!' Lalita cut the Oracle off by saying. Dentas was a witch that Inock, Andre and Lalita got arrested many months before. Though previously dark and sinister, the witch was fighting to leave the dark ways behind.

'I'm afraid it must be done, young one!' Mabiyah said firmly, small fists clenching.

'No way, Oracle!' Lalita protested once more. 'She was evil and tried to kill us!'

'It is essential!' the Oracle told Lalita, stamping a fist on the table. 'She will aid us in Immotshap's defeat when he

returns. And besides, you three invaded the woman. She was merely defending herself!'

'Oracle, surely there is another way?' Andre said.

'There is not, young one … it must be this way. Dentasa is crucial to stopping Immotshap. That evil will be upon us soon enough.'

'Okay. As you wish, Oracle,' responded Andre.

'Fine, I suppose!' Lalita muttered under her breath. Then more loudly, 'But if she tries to kill me, don't blame me if I kill her first!'

'She will not, Lalita,' James told her benignly.

'Fine!'

'Excellent,' said Mabiyah. 'Now, Dentasa knows the secret to defeating Immotshap; more specifically, how to undo his immortality. As you three know, Immotshap underwent a ritual to make himself immortal—that's right, young ones, I am aware that dear Barnarbo showed you how it was done. Each one of us brought a secret ingredient to the ritual that the others didn't know. And I am sure Dentasa knows Immotshap's secret ingredient, which I believe is the key to undoing him. If we can learn what this is we may better be able to find it and destroy it!'

Like a light bulb had switched on inside his head, Inock surmised that must be what was contained within the pouches hanging from the witches' necks when they performed the ritual to make them immortal!

'How does Dentas know Immotshap's secret ingredient?' Inock asked.

'Believe me, she knows,' the Oracle said with a knowing smile.

'Therefore, we must rescue her from the venators,' James concluded. 'Immotshap must be stopped before he rises to power again! He forcibly assumed the position of leader amongst the immortals. A position he did not rightly deserve!'

'Where are the venators keeping Dentas, Oracle?' Andre asked.

'In a powerfuls-only prison. You can get to the prison through the Kasama venator lookout. But I must warn you, my powers do not allow me sight into the prison, so when you enter it, you will have to use your own initiative to set Dentasa free. But don't fret,' the Oracle quickly added at seeing the three's horrified faces. 'Young James will accompany you.'

'Thank Existence!' said Lalita. 'I thought you wanted us to free that evil woman all alone without help!'

'I would be remiss to risk your safety that way, young Lalita,' said Mabiyah gently.

The Oracle then proceeded to give the three teenagers and James specific instructions to the prison and asked them to go immediately.

'We'll go now, Oracle.'

The foursome walked to the venator lookout, entered the mammoth building and went down into the basement. Once there, with a spell, James turned them all invisible and they proceeded through an ethereal door into a chamber swarming with venators and onis.

It was a circular chamber with balconies all along the curved walls and a great circular gateway in the centre of the room.

As planned James cast a blanket sleeping spell on all the venators and onis in the room.

James then went over to a console, keyed in a passcode given to him by the Oracle, the portal in the centre of the room activated, the previously empty space inside the gateway turning into greyish ripples and the four of them proceeded through.

On the other side, the group found themselves in a chamber similar to the one they just left behind.

But soon they all became visible.

The two venators in the room charged right at them, blowing into Onis flutes commanding the four onis in the space to attack.

Both Inock and Lalita fired off weak energy bolts at the two men knocking them unconscious.

Andre morphed into a gomorah and with his giant gomorah fists pummelled two onis into the floor until they collapsed.

James disabled the other two onis into a sleep with a swift chant, Andre turning back into himself.

'Great work, everyone! Now come on, let's find a way out,' said James. 'The Oracle was informed the prisoners are kept outside of this complex. We need to go outside.' He said the spell to make them all invisible, but it didn't seem to work. 'Just a minute, everyone. My powers seem to be playing up.' He said the spell again and they were all invisible.

They exited the chamber through the only ethereal entrance available, which was situated along a balcony and ended up in a corridor lit by miniature light balls.

It took the group over ten minutes to navigate through the numerous corridors and chambers … they eventually made it out of the venator building.

But the world they found themselves in was completely alien; Inock got a bad feeling from the whole place in an instant. They were in a city of black tower blocks with no sun in the sky, just darkness broken by lamp posts all along the black streets.

'Is this another realm?' Andre asked.

'Sort of … it's a pocket dimension, a prison for powerfuls,' James said.

Gazing about, Inock noticed flying creatures that resembled onis circling the many blocks. Like onis, the beasts had long crocodile jaws, two very long slithering tails and wide batwings that flapped slowly. Some of the ghastly creatures were perched on top of the buildings, their glowing red eyes scanning the streets below.

James's invisibility spell seemed to fail again; they were suddenly visible.

'Existence! I can see you, Inock,' said Lalita. 'And you, Andre.'

'Oh dear,' said James. 'My powers are not working like they should! Regardless, the Oracle said Dentasa is kept in tower 56. But first…' He said the spell to make them all invisible again but nothing happened.

'What's wrong?' Inock asked. 'I can still see you all.'

James tried the spell again but still it didn't work.

Then he said, 'I think I know what's wrong … Mabiyah warned me about this.'

'What is it?'

'This whole dimension is built to fight powerfuls. Our powers don't work so well while we're in it. Dear me, this will not be easy … follow me.'

'I hope we don't get killed or something!' said Lalita worriedly.

'Let us make haste,' said James. He did not look very sure.

He took off down a street and the others followed. They moved through the semi-dark streets hiding in shadows so as to not be spotted by the flying beasts, patrolling venators and numerous onis in the grim streets.

When they finally located tower 56, which had the number 56 at the top of it, James tried the invisibility spell again and Inock noticed he did so with greater concentration, and luckily, it worked on the third try.

Invisible, Inock, Andre, Lalita and James tiptoed past the venators at the building entrance, Inock whispered the door unlocking spell Rozanthia taught him: '*Door Recludo,*' and they entered stealthily.

Once inside, they were in a vast black hallway.

'We don't have to search the entire block for her,' James told the others. 'I have a tricky but useful spell that will locate Dentasa for us.' He said twelve strange words and a small whitish ball of light appeared before them all. The ball began moving down the hallway and they sprinted after it.

About halfway down the wide corridor the white ball of light vanished into the ceiling.

'*Blood-sucking succubus!* We need to get upstairs quick!' James said.

So, they located a stairwell and ran up, looking in the hallway of each level until finally, all short of breath, they saw the ball of light floating along the tenth floor corridor. They chased the magical thing to door number 113, which had a black energy barrier before it.

James said three words and they were all visible again.

When Inock went to cast his *Door Recludo* spell on the door, James stopped him and said this barrier would take more than just a basic unlocking spell.

'Besides,' James said, 'the door is bound to be alarmed. I know a way around that.'

So, the older witch did his magic; a lengthy chant along with complex hand motions, and minutes later, the black barrier to the prison vanished and they entered.

The inside looked like any other flat but with black walls and no windows whatsoever. They were in semi-darkness, a nasty blackish glow emanating from the very walls, which prompted James to cast an illumination spell; he managed to create a tiny feeble light on the fifth attempt.

There was a dark toilet, what appeared to be a grisly kitchen, and a bedroom and a sitting room all on one floor.

The rescue group moved into the sitting room where they came across a single brown sofa along a wall with an old grimy rug in the middle of the space; Dentas was crouched on the dirty rug, her hands wrapped tightly around her head. She wore what Inock assumed used to be a beautiful black gown; it was tattered and caked in dirt. The witch was quietly sobbing, mumbling inaudibly, her usually long wavy black hair a ball of mess.

'Dentasa? Is that you?' James whispered. 'It is me, James. We've come to get you out!'

Dentas stopped sobbing and looked up. The witch frowned when her eyes fell on Inock, then her frown deepened when she saw Andre, then even more so when she saw Lalita. But she managed a feeble smile when her eyes slid to James stood there, smiling back.

'Is this real?' Dentas asked from the floor. Her voice was small.

'Yes, it is, Dentasa,' James said gently, still smiling.

'Not another trick?'

'No. Not a trick, dear one.'

Dentas got to her feet slowly and embraced James in a fierce hug, her once stunning face regaining some of its beauty.

'What are you doing here?' she cried, taking a better look at James and the others. 'How did you get in? What are you doing with these children? I remember them! They got me into this awful mess!'

'We're all here to break you out, Dentasa. Mabiyah the Oracle sent us!'

'Thank Existence! I tried and tried to escape but the very walls are designed to siphon a witch's power and magic. It is impossible to get out! This whole realm feeds on us! They use the power stolen to reinforce the stinking prison, it's an inescapable loop!'

'I know, Dentasa. I can sense it!' replied James, rubbing his stubbly chin. 'This is why we must be fast! All our powers are being drained even as we speak. We must get out this instant!'

James led the way out of the depressing flat and it was as they hastened down the hallway that they ran into trouble.

Two venators appeared through a doorway at the far end of the corridor accompanied by four onis.

The two men yelled and screamed for the intruders to surrender before breaking into a run towards the group.

Inock and the others ran for it, and reaching the end of the corridor, they burst through the door and poured into the stairwell.

As they ran downward, James suggested they split into two groups to lead the venators away; he urged that Inock take Dentas and head for the gateway to their home realm while the others led the venators and onis the wrong way.

'Inock, you're second strongest since Dentasa cannot fight,' James said as they jumped two steps at a time. 'She's too drained! You will need to look after her. Once you go through the portal her powers should begin to return to her. We need to be quick since every moment we spend in this sickening dimension our powers are being sucked out of us! We'll meet you in our own realm.'

At reaching the exit to the block, Inock burst through the doors speedily followed by Dentas.

The two venators outside were about to run after the pair when James and the rest also ran through the entrance. One venator chose to chase James, Andre and Lalita and another went after Inock and Dentas.

'GET THEM!' shouted one of the venators.

'DON'T LET THEM GET AWAY!' said the other.

Too anxious to worry about the others, Inock grabbed Dentas by the arm and ran down the gloomy street with her in tow. They made it two blocks when suddenly an Onis flute rang out! Venators poured out of every street, followed by double the onis and to Inock's dismay, hordes of the horrific flying onis creatures swooped down from the skies and they too joined the chase, screeching as they dived, their claws sharp and ready to rip Inock and Dentas to shreds.

Inock wondered if they would make it out alive.

Inock let go of Dentas's hand and began firing off energy balls and green fireballs at the flying monstrosities and onis that got close to him and the witch; he just hoped he would remember the way back to the gateway.

'Kill them! Criminals can never escape!' yelled a venator, his eyes focused on inock.

'destroy them!' called out another.

'the demonic filth must never go free!' roared yet another.

Inock let loose many powers as he ran. He used telekinesis to hurl venators into walls, energy bolts to stun onis and lightning strikes and gusts of winds at the flying creatures. He even hurled a few energy balls, many of which were diced to shreds by the venators' magical whips. He got so into attacking his pursuers that Dentas took the lead and he lost track of her for a full minute … until he turned a corner after a well-aimed blazing, green fireball at one of the flying beasts and caught sight of her.

Before he caught up to Dentas, Inock turned around and with great effort summoned a mighty wind that sent many venators and both types of onis creatures flying across the black sky.

There was only one resilient venator left in the chase now with no visible onis, though many of the flying monstrosities could still be seen high in the black sky, circling.

The lone venator unhooked his venator's whip and lashed at Inock, catching him at the foot. Inock went flying and the man repeated the motion, wrapping the whip around Inock's chest as he landed face first on the hard ground.

Instantly, Inock could feel the magical whip siphon his energies. (Venators' whips would sap all your energy as soon as they touched you; which included magical energy and

power.) He screamed out in terror and the venator laughed boisterously.

'Thought you could break out, did you? *There is no escape for you demon scum!*'

But before you could say, 'whizzing fireball,' the venator went flying. Something had just knocked into him and when Inock looked he saw Dentas stood where the man had been. The witch had charged very hard into the man like a raging bull.

Inock freed himself from the disgusting whip then hurled the venator, as he was getting up, into a wall with telekinesis, rendering him unconscious.

'Thanks a lot, Dentas,' Inock cried, grabbing Dentas by the arm and resuming the run. 'He had me there. I could feel all my strength and power going out of me!'

'Yes, I know the feeling. It's those nasty whips of theirs!'

As they approached the building with the gateway inside, with great effort, Inock made both himself and Dentas invisible and they ran in.

They moved through the complex and into the portal room undisturbed.

But there was just one problem; there was a venator and two onis in the room and the onis sniffed Inock and Dentas out as soon as they entered.

An onis charged at the invisible pair, knocking Dentas off the balcony, Dentas becoming visible. The witch screamed.

Inock was quick. He jumped off the balcony, and using telekinesis grabbed Dentas before she hit the floor, then floated gently down. Then swift as lightning, he fiercely fired

energy bolts at the venator, knocking him out, and then at the two onis, which also collapsed.

'Thank you, Inock!' breathed Dentas. 'You are very well-trained!'

But they still had a problem: Inock didn't know the passcode to the gateway! He fumbled with a console, keying in a set of random codes but nothing happened. He was in a great panic, his heart racing. He knew venators could charge into the room at any second!

Inock turned to Dentas and was about to ask the frightened woman for help with the thing when James, Andre and Lalita came running into the place.

'No time to waste. They're coming!' James said rapidly. He sped at the console, punched in the passcode and all five of them ran through the drumming and reverberating portal.

Back in their realm, in the gateway chamber, the group found the room swarming with venators and onis. James cast an invisibility spell on all five of them, before yelling: 'Everyone, get to the Oracle's!'

The numerous onis in the room attempted to sniff out the intruders. Blind to the others' locations, Inock started aiming violent energy bolts as he ran for the room exit. He intended to do as James ordered and run to Mabiyah's. And there was more fire and destructive projectiles from the others, making the whole room flash over and over with fire and magical energy.

Venators and onis were being thrown all over, screaming and yelling and snarling; those venators who were still standing cracked their whips at seemingly empty space, debris clattering to the floor and lights flickering. The noise of it was like a world war!

An onis' long jaws missed Inock by inches as he ran out of the room. He didn't stop running until he reached the base of the Oracle's steps, surprisingly unharmed.

The others all turned up one by one over the next few minutes; first James and Dentas, then Lalita, and lastly Andre in bird form.

Inside her chambers, with the rescue party and Dentas all calmed and visible again, the Oracle congratulated them for their success.

Then Lalita got straight to it. She asked Dentas about Immotshap's secret ingredient.

'But Mabiyah already knows the answer to that,' Dentas responded.

Without a single word more said, Lalita marched out of the room in a huff. And after collecting payment for the job, Inock and Andre followed her out.

'She used us!' Lalita roared as she marched through the sunny market. 'She knew the secret but she made us rescue that witch anyway!'

'I can sort of understand why,' Andre inserted. 'She warned us not to get involved with Dentas, but we did not listen. We got the woman arrested anyway. And besides, Dentas is her sister, remember? She couldn't let her suffer like that!'

'Still, she used us!'

'Things turned out okay, didn't they?' Inock supplied. 'The Oracle said Dentas will go to live with Esmatilda in the ruins.' (Esmatilda was a stunningly beautiful witch who lived in the Haunted Valley ruins.)

'Yeah, I know. But she still used us, Inock!'

Inock and Andre certainly were busy in the days that followed. With school, Ms Strict was really piling on the assignments and Inock wondered if this wasn't due to the fact that they did not yet recover her missing ring, they had power-training, Inock's dating Rikelle, dealing with family life and the boys looking after Tony, the ekinyo bird, who wasn't as lively these days as it was in the beginning and was now the size of a large eagle, with a full set of colourful feathers. Inock couldn't work out what was wrong with the bird. But things soon took a turn to the lighter side when they went on a mission for the Oracle to Lalita's village to deliver an envelope and a jewel-encrusted golden key.

As Inock handed over the key and envelope to the recipient—a man with green feathers for hair, a familiar lemur-like creature but with two red tails leapt into sight and snatched the golden key before taking off; a sixonas cat.

Inock and Andre knew where the animal was headed, of course. After begging the key's recipient to wait, the boys followed the creature to Lalita's home, leaving the man blinking in surprise, hand still held out.

'Did it do it again?' Lalita asked, coming outside after Laden. They were at the rear of the house.

'Yes, it did. Now hand over the key!' Andre barked, holding out a hand.

Grinning and apologising unconvincingly Laden gave him the golden key. He held Sixon in his arms.

'You need to stop training that thing to steal, Laden!' Lalita scolded her brother.

'Whatever, little sis. It's just a bit of fun!' Laden said, stroking the animal's back. 'No harm done, right Sixon? I love sixonas cats!'

'You're such a waste of space, Laden!' spat Lalita. 'A typical explorer with no compass!'

'What's that?' asked Andre.

'He isn't happy about many things so he causes trouble aimlessly!' explained Lalita.

'Sounds about right,' said Andre. He frowned at the older boy.

Inock and Andre delivered the key and envelope to the bird-man, then returned to Lalita's home where she suggested they practice the *Imperiuo Fenestram* spell.

The trio had gotten rather good with the spell. In a glass bowl of clear water, they saw and heard Laden, sat in the sitting room, congratulate Sixon for a job well done before the vision faded to another location; a bird's eye view of Tharah's farm. (Tharah was a beautiful girl not much older than them and she was a good friend of Inock's. She looked Indian and lived on a farm with many animals.)

The beautiful Tharah was singing to her many assorted cubs in their round pen.

'What's happened? Why did it change?' Lalita wondered, brow creased in frustration.

'Sorry, I was thinking about Tony and Tharah just popped into my mind,' said Inock.

'Well, at least the image is a lot clearer this time,' put in Andre.

Inock got an idea; he decided it was time he visited Tharah on her farm; he was dying to show off Tony the ekinyo bird to her. He knew she was good with animals, maybe she could figure out why the bird was so low-spirited lately, not to mention he hadn't seen Stump his tailless onis cub in weeks.

He put it to the others and they both agreed it was a brilliant idea.

So Inock, Lalita and Andre left Lalita's home and rode to Kasama Market, collected the ekinyo bird and then raced to the Luiss farm in Gante Village.

The farm itself was an expansive and stunning place with green and brown fields along with tall colourful trees, and a large farmhouse.

On the farm, by the cubs' pen—four gante cubs, an unusual three-tailed onis cub, a gampe cub and a tailless onis cub, Tharah telepathically communicated with the ekinyo bird. Tharah was a Dogan; a type of demon that could speak with animals telepathically, though Dogans sometimes said the words out loud. All Dogans had glowing blue eyes that looked like full moons.

'The bird is depressed because you refuse to let it out so it may fly free. It just told me so,' Tharah told Inock, Andre and Lalita after the long psychic communication with the colourful bird.

'I could have told you that!' Lalita said to the boys, arms crossed. Like the others, she sat on a cube of hay. 'You two are dumb! Of course it's sad, birds need to fly to be free.'

'From what Tony told me,' Tharah went on to divulge, 'it can be like a spirit guide to its owner, giving them restful sleep and a general calmness within. Tony can also bring good luck and be a loyal companion. These are things it somehow knows, being special and all. He really desires to do all these things for you, Inock. It likes you very much.'

Inock made a mental note to leave his bedroom window open more often so Tony could fly outside and return whenever it wanted.

Then taking the bird from Tharah, looking into its eyes, Inock said, 'Tony, I love you too, boy. You can be my best friend and we can look after each other!'

'Boys are so silly!' Lalita said, giggling.

'Oh shut up, Lalita!' said Inock.

'You shut up!' she fired back, though looking amused.

***

Inock and Andre noticed something odd while working at the venator lookout. The pair were returning to the Records Department after lunch when they spotted Maliki in the lookout, acting suspicious; the older boy was hurrying down a corridor and looked as though he did not want to be seen; so the brothers decided to follow him, both morphed into large green flies.

They stalked Maliki into the basement and into the chamber with the portal that led to the venator realm. Once in there Maliki went through the gateway and the boys went after him as flies. In the red sky realm, Maliki left the building with the gateway and went outside, where he walked to a beach and boarded a big ship with multiple sails.

Inock took Andre's lead and changed into a black raven mid-flight. The two large birds perched on a ship railing near Maliki. They sailed on calm waters for just over an hour, to a small island where Maliki alighted, along with several other people and the young demon hurried through a forest and to a fort obscured by thick and soaring trees.

There were tens of venators stood guard every twelve or so feet outside the black fort; not to mention their countless onis and the flying onis beasts Inock fought in the powerfuls-

only prison perched at every tower and dotted all over the ruby sky.

Outside the fort, Maliki teleported out of sight; the boys didn't know where to, but they assumed it must have been into the fort itself.

Inock and Andre landed at the base of a tall black tree and morphed into themselves to discuss their next move.

'He teleported into the fort, didn't he?' Andre asked.

'He must have. Where else is there to go on this island…there is nothing else in sight!'

'Should we follow him in, d'you think?' said Andre.

'No, it's too well guarded. We don't know what we would walk into. We might come across something really dangerous! And besides, we need to get back to the records room. We're already very late returning from lunch!'

But as he said that, Inock got an idea. He asked Andre to follow him before morphing into a bird.

The pair flew across the red sky, Inock leading the way. He landed outside the house on Kallam's farm before transforming back into himself; Andre quickly followed suit.

'What are we doing here, Inock?' Andre questioned.

'I want to talk with Kallam. We must find out what's in that fort.'

'Oh … good idea! But we should hurry and get back to our realm, they'll be looking for us.'

Inock knocked on the cottage door and it soon opened.

Kallam blinked at seeing the two boys there.

'Hello, Inock,' Kallam said. 'Sorry, was I meant to meet you and the AVC? Did I forget something?'

'Sorry, Kallam,' Inock began. 'No, we didn't have a meeting today. We won't keep you. I just wanted to ask you

something.' And he told the man about the hidden fort in the forest.

'That fort is a holding place for bad things,' Kallam said, his eyes narrowed in thought. 'Though I don't know why your friend would be sneaking into there. It's dangerous and is filled with the worst contraptions and mechanics you can find.'

Kallam then asked Inock how his ekinyo egg was doing, saying his had already hatched.

Inock gladly informed the black man his had hatched too and was getting bigger and bigger by the day.

'Ekinyo birds are really handy to have around,' Kallam mentioned. 'It will help and assist you in ways you won't even know about. They can even expand to very large sizes. Ekinyo truly are magical creatures!'

The boys returned to their realm shortly after that.

Chapter Sixteen
Secret Meetings

It was a hot but overcast afternoon and Inock was atop gante, riding to Muzimu Village to meet with the immortal witch James.

Inock had been hanging out in the market with Andre and other market children when suddenly in his mind he heard: *Inock, do not be afraid. It is I, James, the Oracle's friend. You may think back to me.*

James, is it really you? Inock thought back. He walked away from the five teenagers and Andre. He lingered behind a magic wands stall. *How are you doing this? I hope I'm not going insane and I'm imagining all this!*

You are not going mad, Inock, sent back James. *I am a well-accomplished witch; psychic conversing is a gift I picked up. And do not worry, I'm not reading your mind. Only what you think back to me ... Inock, I have a request.*

What's the request?

I would like you to visit me at my home, broadcasted James. *There are matters I would like to discuss with you.*

All right. Do you want me to come now?

Excellent. Now would be most welcome, young one, replied James. *My home is near the centre of Muzimu Village. It is a large mansion—white. You cannot miss it.*

All right, thanks. I will ride there now.

As he hurried to the market stables, Inock thought that was a very bizarre thing James did talking into his mind so randomly. He had found the mental intrusion surprising and, admittedly somewhat unnerving.

… Inock was at a well-manicured front yard in no time and rang the doorbell to the stately home. James answered the door.

'Inock! Great, you came. Come in, come in! Do you need hydration; it's terribly hot, isn't it!'

The grand house was even more impressive on the inside with giant vases containing small flowering trees. There were luxurious soft chairs here and there, plush sofas, expensive paintings and sculptures, not to mention the numerous bookshelves throughout the place and deluxe television as big as Inock's in the reception room.

James led the way into a private room with comfortable seating. Inock was amazed, looking around at all the expensive room furnishings.

And then; Inock sat on a cream sofa sipping lychee juice, James sat nearby.

'So how are you, Inock?' James began.

'I'm okay. And you, James?'

'Yes, I am well too … How is your lovely girlfriend?'

'She's fine, James. Is that why you called me?'

James chuckled then after a sip of his juice got to it.

'No. That is not why I summoned you, Inock,' he said. 'But why skip the pleasantries… When you have lived as long

239

as I have you learn to appreciate the little things in life. Seriously though, Inock, I've summoned you here to share a bit of information with you. I am hoping you might shed some light on the matter.'

'What is it?'

'Well, it is odd; I've been watching and following many of the dark witches associated with Barla and Anandre, and they all led me to venator lookouts. They almost always vanish around the lookouts!'

'Do you know why?' Inock asked, taking another sip of his juice.

'No, I don't yet know why,' the male witch said. 'I thought I should tell you this since you and your friends set your hearts on preventing Immotshap from rising to power. I am after the same thing. The Oracle informed me we have the same goals, you see.'

'Oh … okay … yeah, we do. We want to stop him too. He sounds terrible!'

'Yes, well I thought maybe you could make something of the information. But something has been disturbing my sanity about the whole business; is it a trap set to throw us off? Perhaps a trap to have me arrested by the venators knowing I was following them? Have you and your friends come across anything like this?'

Thinking the two incidents might be connected, Inock shared with James about Maliki sneaking into the venator realm and the fort the boy teleported into.

'I don't think those two matters are connected, young one,' the immortal witch answered. 'Your friend Maliki probably has his personal reasons for sneaking into the venator realm and into the fort you mentioned. Perhaps he is

a thief and desired to steal some form of technological gizmo from there. The witches are up to something grand, I just know it!'

'I just hope Immotshap never returns!' Inock said next. 'The whole business is too strange and terrible! He would murder everyone and everything!'

'I understand entirely how you feel, young one,' said James. 'Immotshap was a cruel man. He was diabolical! And he was rather temperamental; at times he would seem perfectly agreeable and then he was moody and standoffish the next. And he *loved* to use people! He would seduce women and collude with powerful people; those he felt he needed he kept a falsely sweet relationship with. And those he didn't need he treated like scum!'

'*Existence*, he is wretched!' said Inock. 'I would never do those things!'

'Well, that is the world we live in, young one. Some people can be rather cruel and dismal. And having lived longer than your ordinary man I can tell you there are many of that kind.'

'That's not good at all!' said Inock, just disgusted at the sound of such individuals.

'But do not let me depress you, Inock. You are still young. You will meet many worthy people in your life … Speaking of which, how is your lovely girlfriend actually doing these days?'

Wondering why the male witch was so interested in his love life and Rikelle, Inock answered, 'She's fine, James.'

'That's very good to hear, young one,' he said after taking a sip from his glass, his eyes on Inock. 'You must cherish the relationships you build in your life. And remember, the

friendships you cultivate when young can be the most valuable. There is nothing better in this world than an old friend, believe me. Especially when you have lived as long as I have.'

Inock understood most of what the ancient witch was saying, but still he wondered if maybe James fancied Rikelle. He chortled thinking how odd that would be, what with the man probably being hundreds and hundreds of years older than them.

The private meeting came to an end when James's wife and two daughters came into the room, the wife carrying a platter of sliced fruits and the children insisted on playing with their father. Inock enjoyed the fruit offered to him before leaving the dwelling.

Back on Dwayne's yniqem farm, there to deliver a fireproof potion, Inock and Andre found Lalita there. Lalita explained to the brothers she went there to seek Barnarbo's help with a spell from her mother's spell book: The *Invocate Fenestram* spell, a spell that would allow her to look at visions of the past. The ekinyo bird had followed Inock to the lively farm. Ever since Tharah told them what the mystical bird needed, Inock started taking it outside and on errands and adventures with him. And it had gotten rather huge!

Barnarbo said there was something he desired to share with the boys and Lalita.

'I have spent considerable time looking into it, trying to find their weaknesses, but something doesn't add up,' Barnarbo told Inock, Andre, Lalita and Dwayne. They stood around a barrel of clear water by a large shed, and Barnarbo had just chanted a spell to activate a vision, stirring the water. 'It seems no one really liked Immotshap, not even the other

immortals. Through visions I have discovered that many people hated the evil filth; he was such a cruel powerful who used intimidation and tricks to rule those below him. Countless individuals wanted to see him destroyed. So why do those witches want him back? You just watch and see.'

The surface of the water gradually turned into a bird's eye view of three figures in a plush sitting room talking; one was Mabiyah who was sat on a cream sofa. Sitting next to her was Atheva, the now Ghost Oracle in her rectangular-shaped spectacles. And finally, there was James who stood by a chair.

'He is not our leader!' James was saying vehemently, arms waving in anger. 'He does not deserve to be in charge of the immortals. The filth tarnished everything…bastardised the vision!'

'James is right, Mabiyah,' Atheva said in a sharp voice. 'He is not worthy of the leader role. A position might I remind you, he automatically assumed! And I think we are all well aware he envies you, Mabiyah. He fears your potential.'

'I know, I know,' Mabiyah said in her small voice. 'And he cannot stay in charge for much longer, this is true.'

'But what can we do? He's a tyrant killing left right and centre! He is single-handedly earning all five of us a bad name,' said James, with desperation.

'I have been considering we might find a way to disable him … stop him and his cruel ways,' said Mabiyah.

'Do you know his secret ingredient yet, Mabiyah?' James asked. 'If anyone can find out what that is it's you. Perhaps we could nullify his immortality and be rid of the evil thing!'

Mabiyah smiled a knowing smile.

'I do,' the old witch said. 'I've recently *seen*…'

'You do? Why didn't you say? What is it?'

The vision on the water faded at Barnarbo's doing and Inock couldn't believe he stopped it just then; they were about to discover the very thing that could help them defeat Immotshap!

'What was his secret ingredient?' Andre asked, before Inock or Lalita could.

'It's some kind of jewel,' Barnarbo told them. 'They don't say much more about it after that.'

Inock swapped worried looks with Andre and Lalita; he wondered if the jewel was the Demon's Amulet of Power he once possessed.

'As you can see, the other immortals detested Immotshap and Immotshap certainly hated Mabiyah for her potential,' Barnarbo said. 'He hated and resented her for how powerful she was and could become.'

'Let me show you more,' Barnarbo next said along with the incantation, and on the water surface appeared an image of five men and women in a forest at night, speaking in hushed tones. One of them, Inock quickly noticed was Barla. All five were dressed in stylish black robes and were given light by a small light ball hovering meagre yards above them.

'This cannot go on any longer!' Barla said.

'That's what you keep saying, but what do you suppose we do about him? Immotshap's immortal!' a man said to the group in a gruff voice. He had long grey hair tied loosely at the nape.

'I am certain even one of them can be killed!' another man proposed. 'Or at least imprisoned so he cannot rule us any further! Perhaps if we set him up to be captured by the authorities?'

'No, they're all severely powerful! *He's* too powerful! The authorities would never survive the attack!' Barla said in response. 'Being a superbly skilled witch myself I've lived very long and will live significantly longer. I cannot abide under Immotshap's rule for that time!'

'So what, then? We cannot and should not surrender just like that! He is our leader but he's a terrible one! Look what he did to poor Defanda. He killed her merely for speaking out of turn!'

'We'll find a way,' Barla said. 'We simply must! I will not rest until I learn the secret to defeating them!'

She could not have looked fiercer and more determined.

'One way or another, the terrible tyrant Immotshap the immortal must be stopped!' another man said, this one Indian-looking.

Once again, the vision faded at Barnarbo's command.

'Now do you see? Not many people liked Immotshap,' the handsome witch said. 'Not even his closest followers, so I don't know why they are desperate to bring him back! And those five were supposed to be some of his most trusted disciples. And as you witnessed, one of them was the witch Barla.'

'I thought she wanted him back?' Inock wondered out loud.

'I don't get it either,' said Andre.

'The whole thing is confusing!' spoke up Lalita.

'A great mystery,' said Barnarbo.

Dwayne nodded in agreement.

'It is a very tricky business,' Dwayne said. He looked just as puzzled as the others.

Inock and Andre discussed the issue at length on the ride home. Lalita had stayed with Barnarbo so he might help her with the *Invocate Fenestram* spell; Inock had shown no interest in that spell since it sounded so complex when Lalita told him how it worked.

And then the two brothers returned to Unatia, to the AVC lair to speak with the group about Maliki. They wanted to find out more about the older boy, along with recovering the Demon's Amulet he stole and what he was up to by meeting with dark witches and sneaking into the venator realm alone. It was the beginning of November.

Inock and Andre were standing in the main theatre conversing with Kano, Chris and Erin just telling the trio what they saw Maliki do in the venator realm and about the attack in Embuyaga Village.

'We have no clue why he would sneak into the venator realm alone,' the girl Erin said. Her black hair was pulled back in a ponytail. 'But whatever it is it can't be good. And I'm truly sorry he attacked you in Embuyaga Village, Inock. We really must exclude him from the AVC!'

'We haven't seen him in a long time,' Kano with the trendy hairstyle and blue fringe said. 'Sorry he attacked you, Inock. I guess we were all very wrong about him.'

'Yeah, he doesn't really follow our rules, so we don't get much help from him,' said Chris with the close-shaven hair. 'Did you get a chance to speak with his brother yet?'

'Yes, I did,' answered Inock. 'Me and Lonathan actually followed him together and we saw him sneak into the venator realm.'

'And you have no idea what he's up to?' Andre asked.

Kano and Chris exchanged a look that told Inock they knew more than they were letting on.

'We think he is searching for power and is working with dark witches to get it,' said Chris.

'What kind of power? How?'

The two older boys exchanged yet another look before Chris said, 'We don't know. But since you're here, why don't you two accompany us on an onis liberating mission? Inock, I think you're the strongest one here and we can always use the backup.'

Well, that certainly boosted Inock's confidence. How could he refuse?

'Yes, it's all right, I'll help,' Inock said quite happily.

Kano turned on Andre.

'What about you? Will you come?' he asked.

Andre looked conflicted. He had never been on an onis liberating mission before.

'Come on, Andre, it's easy,' Inock urged his brother. 'These lot really know what they're doing. We won't get caught!'

'I don't know, it just sounds wrong,' Andre said.

'Please, Andre. It would mean a lot to us … to me,' said Erin, laying a hand on Andre's shoulder and smiling.

'All right, I will go but I'm really not sure about all this,' said Andre.

And so, they were off to the Unatia venator lookout; it was Inock, Andre, Chris and Kano who went this time, not to mention the ekinyo bird flying about Inock's head.

The mission went perfectly until the group entered the chamber with the gateway that would lead them into the venator realm, five onis following behind them.

Venator Chris and Kano had just gone through the rippling portal when three venators and six onis entered the room.

'Hey! What are you two doing in here?' one of the venators yelled.

'What are they doing with those onis?'

'Where're you taking them?' asked the third venator loudly.

It was too late for Inock and Andre to run through the gateway.

The situation turned sour!

One of the venators blew into his Onis flute and all the onis in the chamber turned on the two boys, lashing their long scaly tails at them; even the onis they were meant to liberate.

'Andre, run!' Inock bellowed before he smashed three onis into a wall with telekinesis; they didn't get back up.

Inock turned invisible.

Andre froze.

The venators cracked their whips and ran at Andre and so did all the remaining onis. They were just feet from Andre when the ekinyo bird acted.

It all happened very fast.

The multi-coloured bird expanded to five times its size, swooped down and clawed at the onis and venators; the onis lashed their tails at the bird, wrapping them around its neck, Andre still frozen behind it.

Then Inock almost burst into wild laughter when he saw the bird teleport itself out of the onis' grasps, reappear high above them all, then let off a shrill screech, knocking unconscious everyone and everything but Andre.

Andre was left untouched.

Inock turned visible, sprinted over to Andre, grabbed him by the arm and ran with him out of the chamber and back to Kasama.

'Sorry, Inock. I froze!' Andre managed to say as they ran for it. 'I've never been up against venators before. I just didn't know what to do!'

Inock decided not to go on any more onis freeing missions. It was far too much trouble, he thought.

Inock and Rikelle were once again on a date in the market, to Inock's great delight.

The girl had knocked on Inock's door and it was Andre who answered. When Inock came to the door, Andre retreated back into the house.

'Oh good, Inock, you're home,' Rikelle said. 'I thought you might not be.'

'Oh hey, Rikelle,' greeted Inock. 'Are you okay? Is everything all right? How are you feeling now?'

'I'm well, Inock. I'm sorry about the last time we met,' she answered. 'I was thinking … do you want to spend some time together?'

'When?'

'Now, you silly boy,' said Rikelle, smiling. 'I'm sorry about…' Her voice faded. And then: 'I would like it if we spent some more time together. We can go to one of my favourite cafes in the market. It can be a date.'

'Wow! That sounds great!' replied Inock, with a smile. 'Let me put on shoes.'

Now the pair were sat in the outside section of a cafe in the northern end of the market, both munching on sweet pastries and sipping lychee juice while discussing the Inock's Elixir and how well it was working for Inock. The cafe wasn't

busy, only two other tables had people at them; two couples talking quietly.

'And you're sure there are no side effects?' Rikelle asked. It was a warm and humid afternoon, the market loud with the usual Kasama Market sounds. 'We barely knew what we were doing when we brewed it! Such a great discovery for demons with powers like yours.'

'I'm telling you, I've suffered none. My mother tested it. Well, except for that time in the venator... well, when I drank too much of it.' Inock did not tell his girlfriend about the venators' true origins, or that he actually went to their realm. He never wanted to get her involved in all that madness.

'Well, you are lucky, Inock. We really didn't know what we were doing when we invented it,' said Rikelle and then taking a sip of her drink. 'And you hear all sorts of stories of demons and witches overdosing on power-enhancing potions. My sister tells me about that sort of thing all the time. We got lucky, lucky, lucky!'

'Well, my mother tested it; she said it's fine,' Inock said. Then he grinned cheekily and added, 'And I think my father might try it out himself ... if he's not already using it.'

Rikelle snickered at the comment.

'By the way, Inock,' the girl said next, 'I went back to your favourite food stall and ordered a beans and avocado wrap. It was really nice.'

'Cool. I am glad you like the stall, Rikelle. But to be honest, I've never heard of that wrap. Maybe I might try it out sometime. Is it really good?'

'Very good, Inock!' said Rikelle nodding vigorously, her long hair swishing as she did. 'In fact, it is so good I cannot believe you've never tried it. The beans were very nice with

the sauce the man put in the wrap. And oh, the avocado was very sweet!'

'Then I have to try it out,' said Inock, rising.

'Not now, Inock!' said Rikelle quickly. 'We're on a date, you silly boy.'

'Oh yeah, I guess that's true,' said Inock, sitting back down and blushing.

'Just try it the next time you go there.'

'I will.'

Then Rikelle did something unexpected; she raised a hand to the air and said three strange words. Suddenly, glowing red flowers appeared around all the tables in the cafe, making the patrons clap with cheer. Rikelle said five words more and miniature, different coloured blobs of light came into being all around. The other customers gasped, pointing.

'I learned those spells for you, Inock,' Rikelle said, lowering her arm. 'I made the flowers and the lights. Do you like it?'

'Wow! I love it!' breathed Inock, looking up and all over.

Rikelle beamed.

'Let that Lalita say I'm a powerless now! She would swallow her words!'

'It's really cool, Rikelle,' said Inock. He grinned at her. 'I wish I knew a spell like that.'

'I could teach you sometime,' Rikelle told him. 'Although, then it wouldn't be so special. It's our secret spell. Just the two of us.'

'Thank you, Rikelle,' said Inock. 'I'm having a good time!'

'So … are you happy with us, Inock?' Rikelle said next.

'You mean our relationship?'

251

'Yes, of course I mean our relationship, Inock!'

'Yes, I'm very happy with you, Rikelle,' said Inock in answer. 'I'm surprised you even need to ask.'

'That's good to hear. How is your Last School going anyway? I'm doing really well myself. I get good marks.'

'It's going great,' said Inock. 'Ms Strict is a really cool teacher. I like that she is a witch. And I really enjoy the World History classes.'

'Good. So how is that girl that's always with you anyway?'

'Who? What girl?'

'You know who I mean, Inock. Do not pretend!'

'You don't mean Lalita, do you?' asked Inock. 'She is not *some girl!* You know her.' He sipped from his glass and took another bite of his pastry, though feeling slightly uncomfortable for what was being discussed at present.

'After the other day? I don't think I like her at all!'

'Come on, Rikelle. She was just upset!'

'Upset? *She completely lost it!*'

'But she's usually okay, Rikelle,' Inock argued.

'She wants to split us up, Inock! I heard what she said: *Stealing you away from her?* Is she mad? She's too intrusive!'

'It's just Lalita being Lalita,' Inock said pleadingly. 'She is opinionated.'

'Well, if you think it's all okay then maybe you should be with her right now!' Rikelle said angrily and she got up and walked away, leaving Inock ever so baffled.

Why was Rikelle so angry? It was only Lalita. Inock was left at sea about the whole thing. And now people at the other tables were all staring at him for Rikelle had been that loud

before her departure. Inock got up, leaving his food unfinished and he too left the area.

Two days later, Inock and Andre had an engagement that took Inock's mind off Rikelle and their argument a little; he racked his brain trying to work out what had gone wrong with the relationship for the whole two days.

The engagement was an admissions meeting at Unatia University that would determine if the two boys got into the university and where on campus they would live.

The brothers met with the admissions team separately. During his meeting with the panel of three; two men and a woman, Inock was asked many questions. The questions included: what he expected and wanted from a university experience; what he intended to do after graduation; how he lived at the moment and with whom, and if he was confident that he could take care of himself on his own. Inock answered the inquiries as best he could, mentioning his family on several occasions, that he just wanted to study more after Last School, and that he would like to maybe go into law enforcement as a career or be a power-trainer like his famous father and brother. Also that he could indeed look after himself well and even knew how to prepare and cook several dishes.

At the end of both their meetings both boys walked away feeling they did rather well. Furthermore, Inock and Andre were informed they would receive a letter each that would tell them if they got a position at the university, considering their grades met the university's standards.

Chapter Seventeen
The Light Ball Spell

'Miss, why do you think your family's ring was stolen from the grave? It's all so baffling.'

Inock was in class, sat next to Andre; the two boys were answering essay type Law questions from a textbook when something had occurred to Inock; who would break into a grave to steal a ring and why? So, he chose to ask his teacher a bit more on the matter thinking it might help them decipher why it was stolen in the first place.

Ms Strict was sat at her table at the opposite end of the room, marking the boys' coursework. She looked up, her hair bun bobbing comically as she did.

'Well, boys,' Ms Strict began, 'it was a very famous ring owned by a powerful demon. My grandfather got it from said demon who told him it was a ring of great power, that it was very special and was to be treated as such. Perhaps that is why it was stolen. Though how the culprit knew it was buried with him is beyond me.'

'Do you have any idea who might have stolen it?' asked Andre, who was ignoring his work and listening to Inock and the teacher.

'That's what I needed you boys to find out, now isn't it,' Ms Strict said, brandishing a red pen at the boys. 'Now, back to work this instant.'

That afternoon, Inock, Andre and Lalita spent their lunchtime speculating about the stolen ring, who might have stolen it and why. As usual, they were sat on the school steps, after having enjoyed tuna and pasta salads prepared by Esttia and Lalita had a burger she bought in the market.

'Do you think the thief knew that the ring had great power?' Inock asked the other two.

'Maybe they did not steal it for that reason,' Andre suggested. 'Perhaps they broke into any old grave just to see what they could find.'

'Or maybe the thief was just a loser who likes to break into graves. Maybe they didn't even know there would be a powerful ring in the grave,' Lalita said, smoothing her pigtails. 'It was just a weird teenager, I think.'

'But if they knew it was a ring of great power and that it was in that grave, I bet they stole it for a purpose,' Inock put in.

'Or perhaps they knew and just wanted to sell it?' Andre wondered, gazing up at the green sky, his eyes half closed. It was a very relaxed, lazy sort of day.

'All right,' said Inock. 'But I get the feeling the ring is somehow connected to the Demon's Amulet of Power. I mean think about it; they both have great power.'

'That is right, Inock!' Lalita said energetically, showing a bit more interest in the conversation. 'They are both objects of great power! What do you think it all means?'

'I don't know what it all means,' said Inock. 'But I want to find out for myself what it is all about!'

'We might consider that they were made by the same demon...' Andre proposed.

'I suppose that's something to think about,' said Inock. 'Maybe they were. I really want to find out more!'

That evening, as he lay in bed trying to doze off, something occurred to Inock; perhaps it was Maliki who stole Ms Strict's ring. Didn't the AVC say Maliki was searching for power? Both the ring and the Demon's Amulet of Power were very powerful magical objects ... and the graveyard caretaker had said he suspected it was a teenager who broke into the grave.

Inock decided to return to the graveyard the following day and ask the man to describe the teenage boy he saw; conceivably it really was Maliki.

The next day, in the caretaker's office, the old man confirmed Inock's suspicions; the boy the man suspected to have broken into the grave, the one he saw hanging around the site the night before the grave was broken into sounded very similar in appearance to Maliki. The caretaker revealed: He looked to be in his late teens, had neat black hair and wore black jeans.

Inock could not help wondering: What did Maliki want with two objects of great power? Was he trying to make himself more powerful? Somehow Inock suspected the boy was up to much more than that. That Maliki was up to something very bad indeed.

***

Inock and Andre were atop gante headed to Agua Village, a village north of Kasama Market, somewhere not far from

Dwayne's and Barnarbo's farm. It was the early evening and the boys were on a job for the Oracle; to deliver a sealed envelope to a man in the village, and were discussing Rikelle and Lalita as they maintained a light trot.

'And I told her it was just Lalita being Lalita,' Inock was saying. 'What do you think got her so upset?'

'It sounds a lot like Lalita was being bossy again,' said Andre. 'You know how she is.'

'Yes, but Rikelle should understand that Lalita and I are just friends. She got mad over nothing!' Inock said feeling ever so confused.

'Yeah, but she is a girl. They see things differently. From what you told me it sounds like Lalita did not want you two to be together and I think that's what Rikelle picked up on; she feels threatened.'

'Ha. By Lalita? She is just a friend!'

'Yes, Inock, but I don't think Rikelle sees it that way … especially after that argument they had.'

'Oh, I see…so I just have to tell Rikelle that she shouldn't be jealous?'

It was Andre's turn to laugh.

'No, Inock! You cannot say that to your girlfriend! Rikelle would lose it if you implied she's jealous. I think you could just tell her not to worry, that you are not interested in Lalita that way. I think that might calm her down.'

'All right, I'll try that,' Inock replied, feeling hopeful. It seemed like good advice.

The brothers found the old man the Oracle described to them outside his home; he stood next to a giant sunflower, supporting his weight on a walking stick, and after hopping off their gante Inock handed him the envelope.

257

'This is from the Oracle of Kasama Market; Mabiyah.'

'This might work,' the old man muttered with a chuckle, after opening and reading the envelope's contents. Then turning to Inock and Andre, who were mounting their gante: 'Might I offer you boys a small job? I will pay you well, of course.'

The brothers swapped a curious look before sliding off their gante saddles and walking back to the old man.

'What's the job?' Inock asked, hands in shorts pockets.

'I need you to steal back a spell book that was recently stolen from me.' When Inock and Andre swapped worried looks the man quickly added, 'I promise you, it won't be dangerous and the book really does belong to me. I put a tracking charm on it and know exactly where it is. I will pay you immensely for the job, of course.'

'Where is it?'

'And why do you not get it yourself?'

'These old bones of mine won't allow, I'm afraid,' the man answered, gesturing to his body. 'The book is being kept in an abandoned mansion on the edge of the village. The mansion is now a hideout place for rowdy teenagers. They stole the book from me! So, will you do this for an old man? Do not forget I'll pay you very well.' He smiled at the two boys, revealing green teeth.

Inock thought about the offer before saying, 'Okay, we'll get the book for you.' It sounded like the payment would be astronomical and he could not say no to that.

'Sure, sounds like a worthy job,' Andre said. 'You seem honest, old man.'

'Great! Wonderful news!' cried the old man switching his walking stick to the other hand. He then went on to give the

boys directions to the mansion and a full description of the spell book so they would know it if they found it.

Inock and Andre left the man and rode to the three-storey mansion promptly. It was dark now, their way illuminated by tall lamp posts.

They sneaked into the mansion through a downstairs window that was slightly open. They quietly searched the downstairs section of the decaying house: the kitchen, dining room, parlour, storage rooms and toilets but failed to find the book. The boys moved onto the next level up but still found nothing resembling a spell book.

After a long time of searching the third floor, in a bedroom the brothers eventually found a book similar to the one the old man described.

'Do you think this is it?' Andre asked, letting go of the mattress he was holding up; it fell with a thud, sending dust clouds all over the very messy room. He held a book.

'Shhh! We don't want to be found, Andre!' Inock said in a whisper. He walked over from the wardrobe he was searching and looked at the book. It was a very large book bound in black leather with artful gold writing on the front.

Inock took the book from Andre and flipped through the pages. It certainly looked very much like a spell book; filled with spells and incantations, rituals, stories and diagrams to boot.

'Yes, this must be it,' Inock said in a strained voice. 'Come, let's get out of here before we are discovered.'

They tiptoed out of the room, and it was as they gingerly made their way down the stairs when they heard male voices behind them: 'Hey, who are you?' and 'What are you two doing in our house?'

Both Inock and Andre turned round to see two boys who looked to be in their late teens, both in leather jackets with trendy and tidy hair.

'Run!' Inock yelled before him and Andre sprinted down the curving stairs.

Within seconds energy balls were whizzing through the air, barely missing the fleeing brothers and hitting the curved walls.

Panicked, Inock and Andre started jumping four steps at a time, the older boys hot on their trail, yelling at them to stop.

It was when an energy ball singed a section off his hair that Inock began placing tall and wide energy shields behind him as he ran.

Then something brilliant, scary and unexpected happened.

One of the older boys expanded his body to the size of a giant and jumped over the banister to in front of Inock and Andre, stopping them in their tracks. He was over twelve feet tall and five feet wide. Inock thought now he and Andre were in some serious trouble.

The giant boy expanded his fists to an even greater size and began swinging at Inock and Andre.

Andre was fast; before the temporary giant reached them, he transformed himself into a gomorah whose size rivalled that of the giant's; the two clashed, swapping mighty blows.

Meanwhile, the remaining teenager fired energy bolts at Inock. Inock fought back with energy bolts of his own to match; the two were locked in a fierce power struggle for a while, stray bits of energy and lightning cracking the walls.

The giant and the gomorah pummelled each other while Inock and the energy manipulator destroyed their surrounds

with stray energy and power from their colliding energy balls and energy bolts.

Then gomorah Andre delivered a well-placed blow to the giant's stomach, making him scream out and double over in pain. The gomorah next lifted up the giant and hurled him at his demon companion, sending them both flying over the banister.

Inock and Andre took their chance to run for it, Andre transforming back into himself as he ran.

The brothers made it outside unhindered, hopped onto their gante and rode off with the spell book, laughing to themselves.

It was quite late by the time Inock and Andre rode away from the mansion, so they decided to take the spell book home with them and return to Agua Village the following day. They would deliver the magical book to its rightful owner then.

At home, after a late dinner and after their mother had a go at them both for being late for the meal, lying in bed, Inock had a quick peek at the spell book, picking up on the old man's thoughts, private rituals and beliefs; it was quite the thing to read, and all rather interesting to Inock. In the book, the man had written about his very personal magical discoveries, self-invented rituals and very private and unique thoughts in relation to his worldview.

Eventually, Inock found a spell he believed might come in handy.

The spell instructions and other details were handwritten on a page titled: *The Light Ball Spell.*

Most other spells Inock looked at seemed too personal and too complex but this one seemed easy enough.

Inock read the spell instructions and tried it out; he attempted to conjure up a ball of light but got nowhere with it. He figured it was down to tiredness and decided it wouldn't hurt to ask the book owner how to properly work the spell.

The following day, Inock returned to Agua Village alone and knocked on the old man's door.

At the door, the witch gave Inock three hundred ryza as payment for recovering his spell book.

Inock realised this was the perfect chance to ask the man about the *Light Ball* spell. So he asked.

'She predicted right...' the old witch said, smiling to himself. 'Oh that Oracle.' He chuckled. 'You have really helped me out so follow me. I will do you a favour. I am going to grant your request and show you how to work the spell.'

The witch led Inock around the house and into his back garden.

Stood in a garden of countless tall and vibrant banana trees as well as giant sunflowers, the man began the lesson.

He held out a hand, palm facing up, a look of mild concentration came across his face, he uttered, '*Produs Lumen!*' and a fist-sized ball of light appeared there.

Inock was too mesmerised by the thing; he thought it looked like a small sun, its glow combating that of the afternoon sun high in the sky.

'It is a simple enough spell,' said the old witch. 'Summon magical power to the space you want the light ball to appear and will it to transform into pure light. The incantation is mostly for beginners; it aids the creation of light if you say it out loud, but with enough experience you will not have to say it to achieve the desired result.'

Inock was nodding slowly in comprehension.

The old man continued to explain: 'But before you reach that level; sometimes you might need to say the incantation more than once if you're just starting out. The most important part of the execution is summoning the power and willing it into nothing but light. Do you understand all this?'

Inock had a decent idea of spellcasting by now, having already executed several spells successfully. Additionally, he possessed a satisfactory understanding of magic and power.

So, to the old man he said, 'Yes, I think I understand.'

'Okay then, young man, go ahead and try it,' the witch said. His light ball was still alive between them.

So Inock held out a hand, palm facing up, willed and imagined power gathering there above his palm and willed it to transform into light. He kept stealing glances at the old man's large light ball. It took him several repeats of the incantation: *'Produs Lumen!'* and a great deal of concentration, but eventually he conjured a sort of light that lasted for three full seconds; it was no bigger than a dot but was a light none the less.

Inock tried and tried again, all the while repeating the incantation, *'Produs Lumen!'* the old man continuously encouraging him on.

Inock managed to create a nut-sized ball of light; it lasted a full ten seconds before it vanished.

'Yes! I did it!' Inock cried. 'That wasn't too hard at all!'

'Congratulations, young man! You got it swiftly! I am surprised and rather impressed!' said the old man to Inock. He grinned, showing once more his green teeth. 'Of course, you'll need to practice it many times more before you can make the light ball last.' He looked at his own ball of light and explained further: 'To regulate the light intensity simply will

more power to the light ball and will it to brighten. The more power you add the brighter and bigger it can be.' His light ball grew in brightness as he said this. 'And to dim the light, simply with your mind, will it to diminish until it reaches the desired intensity.' His light ball decreased in size and brightness. 'And to kill the light completely, concentrate and will it out of existence until it dissipates and vanishes entirely. Understand?'

'Yes, I think I do,' said Inock memorising all he was taught.

'Go ahead and try it again, young man,' the old witch ordered.

So Inock had another go at conjuring a light ball. It worked yet again, this one bigger than the last and this time it lasted a full thirty seconds before it died out, Inock giggling away as he stared at it.

'Well done, young one!' cheered the old man. 'You learn fast! Remember all I've told you, in fact write it all down the first chance you get, lest you forget. And remember; practice, practice, practice! You simply have to train and practice to perfect your control over the ball of light. That is all you need to know.'

The lesson was over.

Inock left the old man alone as the witch entered his house through the front door, and rode his gante back home. He was extremely pleased that he had learned a new spell. Inock simply couldn't wait to tell Andre, Rozanthia and Lalita all about it.

***

Inock was nervous. It was six o'clock in the evening and he was watching the television with his whole family and Lalita, the programme being one of Andre's favourites: a documentary about water and its mystical effects; but something was on Inock's mind. His spellwork was progressing well, his efforts on the *Light Ball* spell coming along nicely. He was getting better and better with the *Imperiuo Fenestram* spell every time he practiced with Lalita, though Andre had lost all interest in that particular spell. Lalita was also regularly practicing the *Invocate Fenestram* spell which would allow them to look at visions of the past. Their *Mind to Mind* mental connection was always strong whenever they communicated telepathically. Inock's other demon powers were advancing pleasantly, and he was doing well with schoolwork. But one thing; Inock had not seen Rikelle in a considerable period of time; the girl did not try to find him since their altercation at the cafe and he certainly felt he should give her a while to calm down.

But the thing that really had Inock anxious was that a whole week had gone by and the ekinyo bird did not return home. And to make matters worse, Inock was having restless sleep. Inock wondered if the magical bird got lost or was perhaps eaten by wild animals. Where was the thing?

Then, something wonderful happened. Later that night, as the Tehans slept, Inock had a very bizarre and strange dream that eased his mind—or what he thought was a dream; the ekinyo bird appeared to him and spoke to him in what appeared to be his bedroom only more colourful, telling him it was perfectly all right and would return to him. Furthermore, Tony explained he was aware Inock missed him

profoundly, that they have such a special connection he would always return to Inock.

Chapter Eighteen
New Valley Village

Something amazingly magical happened; something beyond spectacular, even for Inock's world.

It was Saturday evening and Inock and Lalita were walking to the Haunted Valley ruins; Inock had promised to teach Lalita the *Light Ball* spell in the ruins; the ekinyo bird was in miniature form and was perched on Inock's shoulder. The mysterious bird had returned to Inock three days earlier as he was in class and settled itself on his shoulder, to Ms Strict's great annoyance. 'Get out! Shoo! Shoo! Shoo, you silly bird!' said the teacher, in her harsh little voice, wagging a long ruler at the animal. But the bird did not leave, just blinking at her, so the old witch just gave up, Inock giggling.

But when Inock and Lalita got to the ruins, they discovered something impossible, something entirely unexpected; the ruined village was ruins no more! All the houses were intact, shiny and new, trees lined the village streets, tall artistic structures were dotted here and there and people walked about the place, many chatting happily to themselves. What was going on?

Inock wondered if he was dreaming. But when the two friends reached Esmatilda's cottage (A little white cottage

with flowerbeds going all around it and purple flowers growing neatly around the small, white windows and door frame.) and knocked on her door, and asked the beautiful witch what happened there, Esmatilda corrected them, saying it was definitely no dream. Esmatilda was a witch who lived in hiding until months previously when Inock and his friends cleared her name of a crime she was tricked into committing.

'They came about a week ago,' the witch explained to Inock and Lalita as they sat in her cosy sitting room, which was simply three white armchairs in a semicircle, a wooden coffee table in the middle of the space with a clean flower-patterned tablecloth. They were sipping passion fruit juice. 'Men, women and children from all over the world and most are witches! They were all secretive at first; then they put into motion a grand spell that completely revived our village in a span of just two days! Everything is as it once was. Even the trees look the same! It's magic beyond magic!'

'Why did they do it? Why did they revive the village?' Lalita asked, still looking wholly stunned.

'I don't understand it either,' said Esmatilda. 'But a lot of them just keep saying things like: Immotshap will return soon. That they did all of this for him. I haven't figured out why though; Immotshap has been missing for years and years and he was truly terrible, a great evil! And to be honest I think he's dead.'

'Are they nice people, Esmatilda?' Inock asked excitedly.

'They seem okay, very secretive though. And I'll tell you something more; they can never replace the original folks that lived in this village before, no one ever can!'

'It's really special!' exclaimed Inock. 'To think that such grand and powerful magic exists!'

'It is brilliant. Very amazing!' Lalita sang, unable to contain herself. 'The magic and power it must have taken to recreate the entire village! Unbelievable!'

'Yes, though they want a tyrant for a leader, those witches and demons really did something remarkable here,' Esmatilda said, indeed sounding very impressed. 'They now call it New Valley Village. Do you know it used to be called Valley Village? A very apt name they came up with.'

'And they're all waiting for Immotshap to return?' Inock asked.

'Well, yes, that is what they all say but they have a temporary leader, a young boy called Adem. He is loved and worshipped by the villagers, which I find quite odd. He is a descendant of Immotshap, you see. They treat that boy like royalty; he is a young but powerful witch.'

… On the walk to Gante Forest—Inock and Lalita had decided it was best to just go and train their magic there and leave the witches to their revived village, the pair had plenty to discuss. The two friends found the whole business of the renewed village bizarre. How could these people want Immotshap back? He was an atrocious and cruel ruler! And what about praising and worshipping this Adem boy; what were they all thinking?

After some negotiation on the matter, Inock and Lalita decided to go back to the village the next day and see if they could take a look at Adem the chosen one.

On returning to New Valley Village the following day, Inock, Lalita and Andre ('This I have to see!' Andre had said when Inock enlightened him to New Valley Village.) they actually managed to get a glimpse of Adem. The young boy, who Inock thought looked about thirteen, was walking and

talking with two people along the village streets. Of all the people in the world, they saw Adem chatting away with Barla and the AVC member Maliki.

Inock, Andre and Lalita tried following the three without being seen, but when Barla, Maliki and Adem turned a corner and the skulking gang followed, they were nowhere to be found. It seemed the two wrongdoers and Adem had vanished!

The three friends' curiosity about Adem wasn't satisfied until the next day, however. Inock, Andre and Lalita and this time the ghost Rozanthia returned to New Valley Village to find the whole place decorated heavily in bright colours and the villagers were in high celebration; there was a very loud and boisterous parade going on.

The trio and Rozanthia followed the noisy parade throughout the village that ended inside the previously named crumbling temple; a humongous building with an angular roof.

The inside of the temple was just as impressive as the outside, with long benches and chairs, stretching balconies also with countless seats, and there was a colossal statue at the far end of the long room of an old, bearded man in robes. The statue's arms were stretched out in front of it, palms facing up. In its left hand was a round grey moon, and in its right hovered a golden sun.

Inock and his friends sat through a service where the preacher lectured the villagers on the greatness and superiority of Immotshap and how and why they should praise Immotshap's descendant Adem.

With all four friends sat in the back, Inock simply could not believe his eyes and ears as Adem was lifted on a

decorated chair and paraded around the cathedral, everyone singing in frenzied ecstasy.

Adem was eventually deposited at the rear of the temple where he exited through a back door.

Inock, Andre and Lalita decided to move along the temple sidepaths, avoiding the crowds and followed Adem through the door.

But when they got into the back room there was no Adem, and strangely there was no other way out of the space. Inock noticed the room was furnished with a large wooden desk, a chair, filing cabinets, a tall lamp and the walls were lined with bookshelves.

'What's going on? Where did he go?' Andre asked the others.

'I don't have a clue,' said Lalita. 'It's weird. He can't have gone far though, there's no other way out of this room apart from the one we just entered through.'

Then Inock got an idea.

'Rozanthia, are you still here?' he asked.

'Yes, I am, Inock.' And Rozanthia materialised right next to Inock, teddy bear and all. 'What's wrong?'

'Did you enter this room before us? Did you see where he went? You can go through walls,' Inock said.

'I'll look around,' Rozanthia told them before vanishing through a wall.

Inock, Lalita and Andre waited patiently for several minutes until Rozanthia returned; she was grinning.

'There are hidden chambers below us and a set of steps leading down behind that wall.' She pointed to the back wall.

'Hidden chambers? How do we get to the stairs?' Lalita asked, her bubbling excitement showing.

'I don't know,' said Rozanthia. 'But there is a lever on the other side which I assume is to open some kind of concealed door.'

'We have to get to those stairs and find the hidden rooms!' Lalita squealed. 'I bet there's some treasures down there!'

So, the group began searching the room for anything that might be hidden or disguised; levers, trick bricks, fake books …

'Aha! I found it!' Lalita screeched when she pressed hard on an exposed brick and a section of the back wall slid open, revealing a spiralling stairwell.

The trio of friends wasted no time and hurried down the steps, Lalita all excited and in the lead, Rozanthia invisible once more.

At the base of the stairs the group found themselves in total darkness. And it was not any normal darkness, Inock sensed. The very lack of light seemed to press on their skin and eardrums. Inock wasted no time and magically conjured a light ball that illuminated the space before them; it appeared they were in an office similar to the one they left upstairs, but it was empty; no Adem. So, the excited group progressed across the room and through a door.

They emerged in a chamber lit so brightly by a football-sized light ball hanging below the ceiling that they all had to shield their eyes. Without hesitation Inock focused on the magical light, willing and forcing it to dim to a level that was bearable.

But this room too was empty; there was no Adem.

The group walked across this room also, went through a door and ended up in a very long and shimmering cathedral-like chamber with a shiny mosaic marble floor and walls. The

whole space was lit by a giant light ball floating just below the high ceiling that made the walls and floor glisten and sparkle.

Inock thought the place seemed very familiar, and when he tried to recall why, a memory came to mind. This was the same chamber Mabiyah the Oracle, the male witch James, Immotshap, Demonios and Atheva had used to conduct their immortality rituals! Inock was dumbfounded. He simply couldn't believe he was in that place and it was ever so beautiful to behold! It simply glistened and shined.

But this chamber was not empty.

The adored young witch Adem was at the far end of the long room, and what's more, there was a young girl lying on the floor before him.

'HEY! YOU ARE NOT ALLOWED DOWN HERE!' Adem called out at spotting the intruders. 'THIS IS A PRIVATE PLACE!'

Even from the distance, Inock heard Adem recite a spell and suddenly Inock, Andre and Lalita found themselves being pushed back by strong gusts of wind. All three of them fell backwards and rolling on the floor, the winds were that strong; but they hastily jumped to their feet, and Inock and Lalita conjured up wide energy shields that protected all three of them from the howling winds.

Adem maintained the spell while the three friends took one difficult step after another towards the boy, their bluish energy shields holding.

It was tough doing but the threesome eventually made it to Adem and the young girl lying on the floor.

Inock suffered a nasty shock.

He was too stunned to see the girl on the shiny floor before Adem was, undoubtedly Rozanthia! Of course he recognised her; her skin was white as snow, her dress was a dazzling white and her long, flowy hair was a brilliant silver colour. Rozanthia was a ghost no more. Furthermore, she appeared older than Inock remembered her; she looked about fourteen years old.

'What did you do to Rozanthia?' Inock roared over the howling winds. 'Stop this spell!'

'We want to talk to you,' Andre called.

Adem uttered a brief incantation and the crazy winds died out.

Inock and Lalita snuffed their energy shields, all three friends breathing a sigh of relief.

'What have you done to poor Rozanthia?' Inock cried, running to Rozanthia's body. He cradled her in his arms and she began to come to.

'I gave her what she wanted!' Adem said confidently to the group before him. 'It's what she asked. She wanted a body, so I granted it.'

'Oh, you're just full of miracles, aren't you?' Lalita said dryly.

'That girl found me down here and asked me to grant her that wish, a body. She told me she used to live in this village a long time ago, and since I am praised and worshipped by all in this village, I granted her the wish! She's awake now; you can ask her yourselves if you don't believe me!'

'I did ask him for this, Inock,' Rozanthia said groggily. 'I wanted to live again!'

'So you see? I was merely being kind!' barked Adem. 'I simply created her a body like she asked!'

'If you are so kind, why did you try to stop us from reaching you with all those obstacles?' Lalita said, pointing an angry finger at the young witch. 'We know you and those witches are up to no good!'

'We all saw you with them!' said Inock.

'What I do with the witches is my business!' snarled Adem. 'I do not desire to explain myself to you all! I am worshipped! I am adored by many! And I was only protecting myself and this sacred temple!'

'You must tell us about Immotshap and what the witches want with him!' Andre spoke up. He looked angry. 'Surely you people don't want him back!'

'I told you i have no desire to explain myself to you all!' Adem roared at his audience. 'I am worshipped! I am a far more accomplished witch than most witches my age; power runs in my family! I am his descendant!'

'Please tell us what you're all up to!' trying a different tactic, Andre begged.

'It is none of your concern! I bet you're not even from this village!' Adem said, furiously. He looked at Rozanthia and gently said, 'Rozanthia, I want to offer you a home in this village, my village. There are plenty of unoccupied houses, you are always welcome.' Then turning his eyes on the others, he snapped, 'The rest of you should leave immediately! You are not welcome!' The worshipped witch then marched out of the glimmering chamber, looking furious.

Inock looked down at Rozanthia with worry on his face. She seemed to be feeling better.

'Rozanthia, are you okay?' Inock asked. 'He didn't hurt you, did he?'

'No, I'm fine, Inock. I'll stay in the village,' Rozanthia replied. 'It is what I've always wanted; to live in my village like before. It's really beautiful here.'

'Is that really what you wanted, Rozy?' Inock asked, softly.

'It is.'

Inock, Andre, Lalita and Rozanthia all left the secret chambers and returned to the temple upstairs. Inock was glad to see Rozanthia was well enough and could walk.

'I cannot believe you have a real live body now, Rozanthia! It's unbelievable!' Inock screeched.

Rozanthia left them all and went to find Adem so he could show her to her new home.

On the way out of New Valley Village, Inock was livid Adem refused to tell them anything useful.

'What can we do? He hasn't done anything wrong,' Andre said. 'It's not like we can have him arrested for being worshipped.'

'We will just have to stop them all and their stupid plans to bring Immotshap to power ourselves then!' Inock said. He just knew the whole business would end badly.

While volunteering at the venator lookout, Inock was surprised to spot the dark witch who escaped death with Barla walking briskly down a hallway. Inock had left the Records Department to use the toilets when he saw the man called Anandre; the male witch wore stylish black robes.

Inock decided to stealthily follow the man, and after several turns was led into a chamber with rows and rows of glass cabinets full of what appeared to be magical artefacts. What's more, at entering the very long room, Inock discovered five venators lying unconscious on the floor and

the evil witch was nowhere to be found, which he found very odd.

Later that day, at the Tehans' residence, when Inock informed Lalita and Andre about the strange occurrence in the lookout, Lalita happily proposed they use a spell she was learning to find out what really happened to the five venators; the *Invocate Fenestram* spell. They were in the sitting room.

Inock agreed and ran to the kitchen to collect a bowl of clear water as Lalita commanded.

Inock gently lowered the glass bowl on the black glass coffee table in the middle of the room, before him and Andre gave Lalita space to work her magic.

And so Lalita placed an index finger into the water and began stirring counterclockwise, while reciting a twenty-word incantation.

Inock and Andre waited patiently, both excited, while Lalita stirred the water and repeated the tricky incantation over and over … then Inock was simply awestruck to see a top-down vision of the lookout chamber with glass cabinets appear on the water surface. Five venators were in the long room; four were inspecting the magical artefacts and the fifth was sat at a desk, busily typing away at a paper-thin, almost invisible computer.

Lalita stopped stirring and stepped back. Inock could see she was grinning from ear to ear.

'There you go, I did it!' the girl declared in a happy and high voice. 'It should show us what happened in that room earlier today. Barnarbo taught me how to do it. That is the chamber, is it not, Inock?'

'Yeah, it is. Well done, Lalita!'

And surely enough, Anandre walked into the room, drew a phial from his robes pocket, opened it, poured a sparkling, bluish dust from the phial onto his palm and then blew the dust at the five venators who right away collapsed to the floor.

To follow, the dark witch moved to a shelf and took a black, metallic wrist brace from it before vanishing into thin air.

Inock laughed out loud when he saw himself enter the curious chamber five seconds later.

'That's me! Cool!' Inock screamed.

The vision dissipated when Lalita gently touched the water surface with an index finger and said two odd words.

'Focus, Inock. He stole something!' Andre said. 'A black bracelet! And I bet you it's magical and a particularly powerful one too!'

'Wow, well done Lalita for conjuring the vision. Really nice work!' said Inock, looking really impressed. 'Blood-sucking succubus, you mastered the spell!'

'My pleasure, Inock. But why do you think that witch stole that particular wrist brace and left everything else?' Lalita asked, her expression thoughtful.

'I don't know,' answered Inock. 'But I get the feeling Andre is right; it is probably an incredibly powerful item. And whatever it is for, it cannot be good!'

***

Inock, Andre, Lalita and Rozanthia were all excited; Farewell Day was almost upon them!

Inock and Andre were on break from school and were working double time at the venator lookout on Esttia's orders. 'I want you boys to get a good idea of what it's really like to

have a regular job,' their mother had said when she insisted they work more hours at the lookout. And the boys didn't mind all that much since Radock the friendly venator entertained them with endless comical and interesting stories about venators while at work, like how some venators were terrified of onis. ('Ha! That has got to be the single most hilarious thing I ever heard!' Inock said at full volume one lunchtime, earning himself an angry stare from a passing venator.)

Rozanthia seemed to be happy living alone in New Valley Village; she visited Inock in the market almost every day. At first Inock found it strange to see Rozanthia as a real live girl on every occasion they were together, but he soon got used to seeing her that way; he enjoyed her company all the same, ghost or not, but he secretly desired and missed her being there with him all the time as a ghost.

On Farewell Eve, Inock and Andre received some really good news. Two letters were slotted into the Tehans' letterbox, and when Torend announced who the letters were addressed to and where it appeared they came from, Inock and Andre ran straight at him from the sitting room where they were watching the television.

Inock ripped open his envelope to indeed find a typewritten document from Unatia University. The letter informed that Inock had been granted a conditional acceptance into the University to study Law, focusing on Powerfuls Affairs; additionally, Inock was granted accommodation on the main university campus, on the condition that his Last School grades were satisfactory.

Stood next to Inock, Andre whooped as he shrilly informed Torend he received similar news.

At hearing the news, Esttia and Tehan were tremendously delighted for the boys; Esttia cooked them all a splendid feast in celebration that evening.

Chapter Nineteen

Farewell Invasion

'IIINOCK! LALITA'S HERE!'

Esttia's loud call awoke Inock from a cosy sleep.

It was finally Farewell Day and Inock was thrilled. This was to be his and Andre's final Farewell living with their parents and Torend.

In Inock's world the final day of each year was highly celebrated; it was called Farewell Day; a time when people all around the world celebrated the year gone and welcomed the new. But Farewell Day was especially momentous to demons and witches since it was one of the few days in the year when they could openly use their powers and not be disturbed by the venators; within reason, of course.

Inock hastily washed and tidied his appearance, got dressed in smart and clean shorts and T-shirt, and raced downstairs with Andre to catch the Farewell *Power Trials* episode.

The house was thoroughly decorated with the Farewell colours; red, orange and green; it had been that way for over a week now. Bright banners wishing all that saw them a Happy Farewell hung throughout the house.

The boys collected their breakfast of nuts, fruits and cereal from the kitchen, wishing their mother, father and Torend in the kitchen a Happy Farewell. Esttia was already cooking up a feast to celebrate the day, the aromas sending Inock's nose in spells of ecstasy.

The brothers found Lalita and Rozanthia already in the sitting room waiting for them while watching the television.

The year's *Power Trials* final took place on a magically created island as well as inside and outside of a colossal fort; it lasted three hours altogether but Inock knew the whole thing took over three months to film. He was never more exhilarated to watch his favourite programme on the massive 3D television.

The final involved a series of challenges faced by two finalists; the energy manipulator Dijhon the Nut-smasher and a challenger called The World Rocker, a demon who could fly.

Inock, Andre, Lalita and Rozanthia all watched the entire show, and all four friends were screaming and jumping about the room at the completion of each trial.

Trial One: The two competitors started off as hovering tiny specks that grew and grew into babies, they got eyes and started to see, then they were teenagers and finally themselves as adults. They were lowered onto the floor; Dijhon wore skin-tight green shorts, shiny gold boots and no shirt, leaving his big muscles exposed; he was bald. The World Rocker was in green jogging trousers and an orange vest, topped off with red boots; he also wore a long red cape. As soon as they touched the floor, both contenders had to race through a long chamber dodging swinging axes and cannon fire; the first to the end of the room and through a door at the end won. The

World Rocker won that round, he soared through many of the obstacles. Inock thought his red cape looked very cool.

Trial Two: The competitors were in a large arena facing each other, each with twenty demons behind him; Dijhon's fighters were all dressed in white combat outfits and World Rocker's were all in black. A bell rang out signalling the start of a battle and the scene went mad; it was a constant clash of white on black. Each competitor's fighters had an array of powers, a grand demon fight, Dijhon and World Rocker also fighting. At the end of the skirmish, Dijhon the Nut-smasher had three fighters standing and The World Rocker had none. Dijhon won that round.

Trial Three: Dijhon and World Rocker were in a forest fighting a giant each. Each contender had ghostly clones of themselves in the forest; each time Dijhon or World Rocker were touched by a ghost clone of themselves they grew in size, becoming near-giants themselves, and if touched by the enemy's ghost clones they shrunk. The first one to defeat their giant won the round. The World Rocker won that round by flying dizzying circles around his giant; the giant crashed on the forest floor, too dizzy and confused and unable to stand any longer.

Trial Four: Dijhon and World Rocker were in a semi-dark chamber, both on hovering platforms with a massive cannon attached to it. Each contender was firing fireballs at his opponent and his clones in the space. World Rocker won the round when he disabled all of Dijhon's clones. Then both demons had to race to the chamber exit without being crushed by falling, blazing boulders.

Trial Five: Dijhon and World Rocker were at the bottom of a tall tower, each on a platform; each platform had a wind-

up lever and another man in a mask stood on the platform holding a big fireball cannon. Dijhon and World Rocker each had to pump up the lever on their platform to make it rise. The first to elevate their platform to the very top of the tower won; but each time Dijhon or World Rocker were struck by a fireball, their platform would fall ten feet. Dijhon got to the top of the tower first and therefore won that round.

Trial Six: Dijhon and World Rocker had to swim through a long, submerged chamber and get to the other side, all the while dodging aggressive sea creatures, both big and small. To make matters more complex they both were fast running out of oxygen and felt unnaturally tired as they were being supernaturally drained of energy throughout the challenge. Dijhon won that round.

Trial Seven: Dijhon and World Rocker were in a vast and really bright chamber dodging flying succubi and red shadow bats as they raced to the top of a golden pyramid.

When Dijhon made it to the top of the dazzling pyramid first, he won the golden trophy. And as soon as he snatched the glowing cup that hovered mid-air, he floated into the air himself, seeming lighter than air and shimmering and shining with a whitish-golden light. Having won more tasks throughout as well as the golden trophy, Dijhon the Nut-smasher won the finals.

Inock was over the moon that Dijhon won the finals; Dijhon was his favourite *Power Trials* contender.

After the *Power Trials* show, Lalita said she needed to go outside and meet with her boyfriend to hang out.

'*Boyfriend?* I didn't know you had a boyfriend!' Inock said in disbelief.

Lalita has a boyfriend? Inock thought privately, shaking his head. It was too insane to consider; she was simply too bossy.

'How long have you been together? Who is it?' Andre asked, looking shocked.

'If you must know, we've been together about a month,' Lalita answered then she seemed to hesitate. She looked away then back at the boys and added, 'Actually, you know who he is.'

Rozanthia gasped, then holding a hand on her mouth.

'Who is it?' the silver-haired girl asked, seeming to glow in a dazzling white dress and sandals.

'It's Kano from the AVC, he's really nice. I went to meet with the AVC on my own and we got talking. We have been on three dates. It was nice.'

'No way! He's way older than you, Lalita!' Inock said.

'Ha! You mean he's not stupid and immature!' retorted Lalita with great sarcasm in her voice.

'If you say so,' said Andre.

'Anyway, do you guys want to come with me to meet him? We can watch the powers show,' Lalita said next, looking a little embarrassed. (Every year on Farewell Day, witches and demons put on a powers display on a large floating stage near the market centre.)

'Let's go, I'm dying to see this year's show!' exclaimed Inock. He got up, quickly followed by Andre.

'Wow, I would love to see it,' said Rozanthia. 'Especially now that I can be around others with bodies and can enjoy the market smells and everything else!'

So Inock, Lalita, Rozanthia and Andre left the house and went out into the market after Esttia allowed them to leave.

As you can imagine, the entire market was a lot busier than usual. The stalls were heavily decorated keeping in mind the Farewell colours, glittering streamers hanging from lamp post to lamp post. The tall tower at the market centre was painted in the Farewell colours, people were teleporting into the market in thick puffs of white smoke and witches and demons were showing off their powers everywhere you looked.

After they met with Kano with the trendy hairstyle and blue fringe as well as Villad the ex-thief, Inock and his friends headed right for the powers display stage, pushing through thick crowds watching the magical show until they got to the front.

Inock just didn't know which act to take in first. Lined up on a wide and immensely long, hovering glass stage were many performers. There was a small boy juggling five large energy balls, fire-eaters who swallowed blue fire then blew it out in rings that expanded as they floated up and other shapes, a boy having a kickabout with an energy ball like it was a football (Lalita said, 'I could do that!'), a red-haired girl who sat on a floating chair reading a book within a swirling ball of water, self-cloning demons, a witch who conjured up multi-coloured clouds and made them swirl in the sky in splendid patterns, a man who kept turning invisible then back to be seen and finally, a man who would grow tree branches out of his arms then turn into a tree completely, and then repeat the trick.

Since he was power-trained more regularly and drinking the Inock's Elixir, Inock could pull off many of the powers displayed and so was not as impressed as he used to be in the past.

After getting their fill of the show, the gang walked around the market buying and munching on a variety of snacks, some only sold on that day like the snack called *Rolex* which was fried egg omelette, chopped cabbage and chopped tomatoes wrapped in a chapatti, while chatting away and taking in the many phenomenal sights they came across. So many people were to be seen using their powers openly; people levitating things; people levitating their very bodies; a boy creating and manipulating water, making it swirl in complicated formations; people morphing into animals; one girl who could transform into ordinary objects such as wardrobes and plates; a man creating and playing with fire and so many more.

It was a merry time until Inock and his friends heard loud bangs accompanied by wild screams coming from somewhere in the market.

'What's going on?'

'What's all that noise?'

'I don't know but we should go and find out what it is! It doesn't sound good,' Andre said, dropping his *Rolex* on the ground. He ran towards the source of the calamity, closely followed by the others.

Faint chanting of 'IMMOTSHAP WILL RISE AGAIN!' could be heard as the group searched for the source of the commotion. The noise seemed to be coming from somewhere near the centre of the market.

Inock and his cohorts followed the ongoing bangs and screams to the powers display stage, to find people were running in all directions, fleeing from whizzing, exploding fireballs and energy balls, not to mention the rampant gante, gampe and numerous other creatures. Bodies were flying

287

everywhere and when Inock looked about he saw the source of the disturbance. It was three young witches; two girls and a boy in their teens, all in stylish robes, using magic and powers to terrorise the market crowds and animals.

'IMMOTSHAP WILL RISE AGAIN!' all three witches kept chanting, over and over as they caused absolute chaos, and cackled away at the disorder they achieved.

'YOU SHOULDN'T BE WHORING YOURSELVES OUT FOR ALL TO SEE! YOU ARE SPECIAL!' the boy witch stopped chanting and yelled, aiming bright sparks at the hovering stage. The performers were all still on the stage, though watching with terrified eyes.

'IMMOTSHAP WILL RISE AGAIN! IMMOTSHAP WILL RISE AGAIN! IMMOTSHAP WILL RISE AGAIN!'

'WHAT ARE YOU DOING, YOU FOOLS? This is a peaceful celebration! You have no right to do this!' a man stood by the stage called out at the three witches, but they either didn't hear him over all the screams or chose to ignore him.

'YOU SHOULDN'T WHORE YOURSELVES OUT! YOU'RE ALL SPECIAL, DON'T YOU KNOW THAT? THESE PEOPLE DO NOT DESERVE US! THEY'RE SCUM TO BE TREATED AS SUCH!' the male witch roared again. He next conjured and launched a blue fireball at the stage, hitting the boy who earlier had a kickabout with an energy ball. The boy fell back and Inock was relieved to see him quickly recover and jump to his feet, and massaging his back though his T-shirt was burnt. It wasn't a lethal blow.

The witch who conjured up multi-coloured clouds on the stage pointed wildly and exploded: 'WE KNOW WE ARE SPECIAL, YOU SCREAMING CRETINS! THAT'S WHY WE'RE SHARING OUR GIFTS WITH THE WORLD! LEAVE AT ONCE! IMMOTSHAP IS GONE FOREVER!'

'IMMOTSHAP WILL RISE AGAIN!' the two female teen witches chanted powerfully, over and over, firing exploding fireballs into the dispersing crowds.

'YOU SHOULD NOT WHORE YOURSELVES OUT TO SCUM!' shrieked the male witch.

'FOOLS! IMMOTSHAP IS DEAD! LEAVE AT ONCE BEFORE THE VENATORS GET YOU!' the clouds conjurer shouted back violently.

'IMMOTSHAP WILL RETURN TO POWER! POWERFULS WILL RULE THE WORLD!' vociferated the male witch. 'THE VENATORS AND POWERLESS MASSES MUST TREMBLE!'

Meanwhile, the girls with him chanted: 'IMMOTSHAP WILL RISE AGAIN!' They still aimed exploding fireballs into people and animals.

Inock, Andre, Lalita, Villad, Rozanthia and Kano, all looking appalled, got involved. They too bellowed at the three witches to disappear, insisting Immotshap will never rule again.

'Go away! Immotshap was cruel and will never return!' shouted Inock, after many minutes of them all yelling and fighting with the witches.

'He will return!' said one of the witches.

'Never!' roared Inock.

'He will return, I promise you!'

'Not if I have anything to do with it!' screamed Lalita.

Most of the spectators fled while the powerfuls on stage and Inock and his friends all screamed violently at the invaders, who persisted on using all manner of powers to terrorise anything in sight; people, animals and even produce and the very stalls exploding.

The boy of the attackers seemed to really enjoy tormenting and causing chaos, at one point even propelling into the air and projecting thunderous energy bolts and enormous, exploding red energy balls down below, sending everything flying in all directions.

Inock thought, of the three invaders he hated the boy the most!

Then finally, to Inock's great relief, though he wouldn't have admitted it to anyone, six venators came marching at the scene, followed by over twelve snarling onis.

Cackling wildly, the male witch fired a zipping energy ball at the venators, which was swiftly dissipated into shreds by a venator's whip, and the venators more furious than ever all blew into Onis flutes, commanding their onis to charge and attack.

As twelve onis went for the witches, one of the girls called out a spell and suddenly four of the onis attacked their kin. It was a grand onis scrimmage; long slithering tails lashing, mad growling, sharp teeth sinking into thick necks. It was quite the spectacle! This went on for a long while, all three witches guffawing at the struggle before them.

The venators could not have looked angrier.

A venator blew into an Onis flute and one onis tore away from the kerfuffle, leapt and wrapped its tails around the male witch, gagging him.

At seeing this, his female companions ran off into the crowds, sniggering and one called out: 'IMMOTSHAP WILL RISE AGAIN! HE WILL RETURN! HE WILL RULE! HE IS THE CONQUEROR!'

Three venators ran after the fleeing witches while the captured one was dragged off.

The whole market seemed to let out a sigh of relief.

The performers on the stage resumed their acts, the powers display organiser reassuring everyone that unlike those three invaders, the performers would never hurt anyone.

In complete disbelief at what they witnessed, Inock and his friends returned to their celebrations, people all around helping one another recover from the madness and the frightened animals being soothed and placated.

'What were they doing, scaring people like that?' Andre asked the others. He still looked wholly stunned. 'It's all so crazy!'

'It is all Immotshap's fault, if you ask me!' Inock said. 'He's not even back yet and already everyone is going crazy over him!'

'Well, let's hope he never returns!' commented Kano.

The others all nodded in agreement, all mumbling assenting comments.

Inock and Andre returned home later in the day for a feast with the rest of the family.

And then, there was a knock at the Tehans' door that evening and Esttia left the rest of the family in the sitting room watching the television to answer the door.

'IIInock, there is a really pretty girl here to see you,' the family soon heard. They were watching a much beloved Farewell movie about a demon who married a very famous

king's daughter then ended up murdering her by accident, only to follow her into the afterlife where he rescued her from unbearable torment, bringing her back to life.

Instantly, or so it seemed to Inock the whole family was interested to see who it was at the door. Torend got up first and went to the door then walking back into the sitting room with a funny grin on his face, and mouthed to Inock, 'She's really pretty!'

Tehan rose next and went to have a look. He returned bearing a grin very similar to Torend's.

Andre just smiled to himself, guessing who it might be.

Inock decided to go to the door and see for himself. He was pleased to see Rikelle smile brightly back at him.

Esttia left them to it and returned to the sitting room with a juicy, smug smile on her face.

Rikelle wished Inock a Happy Farewell before apologising to him for how she left things the last time they met. The girl then went on to ask Inock if he would be her boyfriend again.

'I thought—but I thought—weren't we? I thought we still were together!' was what Inock said.

'Oh, sorry, I thought we broke up,' Rikelle responded awkwardly. 'You haven't visited me, Inock. I did not see you for weeks so I thought…' Her voice trailed off. 'By the way, did you hear about that attack in the market today? I missed it but heard it was very bad.'

'Well, I didn't think we broke up!' said Inock a little angrily. 'I just wanted to give you some space. You were really angry with me, Rikelle. And yeah, I heard about the attack.'

'Sorry about that, it's just that I know that girl Lalita doesn't like me and you hang out with her a lot.'

'We are just friends. Me and Lalita will never be more than friends, please believe me!'

'I know, Inock,' said Rikelle. 'I have thought about it a lot and maybe I overreacted. Sorry.' She brightened up and added, 'So … can we try again?'

Though he thought it weird that she assumed they broke up just like that, Inock still fancied Rikelle.

'Okay, that sounds good to me,' he said with a broad smile and an uplifted heart. Then he clumsily offered her a hand to shake.

She shook it with a wide grin.

Inock invited Rikelle in to watch the television with him and his family, but the girl said she had to go and meet her sister; the couple arranged to meet the following day instead.

Chapter Twenty
Maliki Succeeds

It was the middle of January and Inock was in New Valley Village once again; but this time he was alone.

Inock was moving through the stunning village headed for Rozanthia's home. Rozanthia had summoned Inock telepathically—she really was a very well-accomplished witch—and had insisted he come alone, saying she needed to talk with him privately.

Inock got to Rozanthia's home undisturbed by the witches or demons he passed. The house Rozanthia had described into Inock's mind was a decent-sized, red-bricked bungalow. And when Inock banged the knocker and Rozanthia let him inside, he was even more impressed. It was a proper home, he thought; like grownups owned.

Inock wondered what it would be like to own a home of his own as Rozanthia showed him around. They made small talk as she showed him her large bedroom with a double bed, bathroom with shower, garden and finally the kitchen and sitting room in one.

Inock simply couldn't believe someone as young as Rozanthia owned her own home. Or that someone as young as Adem had the power to grant such luxuries to anyone.

At the end of the house tour Rozanthia asked Inock to sit down on the sofa in the sitting room while she prepared some fresh mango juice.

Rozanthia brought two full glasses over, placing them on the glass coffee table in the sitting room section, along with freshly sliced jackfruit.

'It's really cool here, Rozanthia!' Inock said, sipping his mango juice and playing with his jackfruit slices. 'I cannot believe it's all yours!'

'I know, I've been very blessed,' Rozanthia said, though not as happily as Inock would have expected her to.

'Is something the matter, Rozanthia?' Inock asked. 'You don't seem happy.'

You see, Inock had been friends with Rozanthia since he was about seven years old. It was the middle of the afternoon, the sun was very bright and very hot, with birds squawking and flying high in the sparkling emerald sky; and as he played alone in the Haunted Valley ruins, Inock suddenly heard a girl's voice cheering him on to continue what he was doing; aiming small rocks through the holes in the crumbling temple. The ghost had materialised right in front of Inock, and they spent a very pleasant and merry day together, chatting and laughing away. After that, Rozanthia followed Inock to his home in the market and they became very good friends from then on.

But now Rozanthia didn't seem happy at all.

'I miss being a ghost, Inock,' Rozanthia began. 'I like my life now, but it is all so different. And mostly, I miss being with you all the time, even when you didn't know I was there. I really loved being with you … but now I can't!'

Inock wasn't too surprised to hear all this. He quite missed having Rozanthia there all the time as well.

'I've noticed the difference too; it feels different without you, Rozanthia...not very good,' he said. 'But you have to stay happy. You're alive again! Surely it is better than being dead?'

'I am not so sure, Inock,' Rozanthia said a little glumly. 'I feel alone all the time and there's all these things I have to deal with now; or should I say, deal with again! It gets tough and lonely.'

'But, Rozanthia, you can visit me and my family whenever you want, and Andre's always happy to see you. You two are similar; you're both very responsible! Well, more responsible than me anyway.'

Rozanthia smiled at hearing this. She quite liked Andre.

'And I suppose I do have the witches and other people of this village. They can teach me plenty, even if you think they're all dark,' she said. And then when Inock got a sceptical look on his face she quickly added, 'Though I don't trust them like I trust you, Inock. Don't worry.'

Inock thought for a bit, trying to come up with anything that would cheer up Rozanthia.

'I will visit you more also,' he said. 'Now that I know where you live, I'll visit all the time. I promise, Rozanthia!'

Rozanthia smiled again then she hesitated.

'You know, I've been speaking with Adem ...' she began. 'He said he can change me back to my old self if it's really what I want, then I can spend more time with you.'

Certainly, Inock was shocked to hear this.

'No way, Rozanthia!' Inock cried. 'You don't need to do that! You have a life now! You can make new friends and live

like you want, really experience stuff! You should stay this way! And anyway, I'll see you; you can visit me and I'll visit you.'

'I've missed you, Inock!' Rozanthia exclaimed, doing a little clap and smiling ever more brightly. 'We had fun together, didn't we? I really have missed you and the way we were together! But you are right, I will stay this way. I shouldn't be deluded with thoughts of moving on. I should be happy with the life I have and live it…focus on the positives and not the difficult parts.'

'Great!' hollered Inock. He got up and did a little dance in celebration. 'And do not let that witch Adem convince you otherwise. And I really have missed you too, Rozanthia! We had fun!'

The pair enjoyed their juice and jackfruit and chatted about old times; like the afternoon Inock was chased by carnivorous flies in the Haunted Valley ruins. And another memory where Inock got attacked by a man-eating ogre in a swampland, when he was sent out on a mission for the Oracle. They talked and laughed and remembered … until Inock had to head home.

It was as Inock walked through New Valley Village along a quiet street from Rozanthia's home that he spotted Maliki and Adem walking and talking in whispers; the pair seemed to be arguing about something. Inock quietly followed them and soon realised they were headed towards the once named crumbling temple. Minutes later, Maliki and Adem reached and entered the long temple with an angular roof.

And even without following them in, Inock had an idea where in the temple the secretive pair were headed; to the hidden chambers beneath the big building.

Inock decided to enter the temple and wasn't surprised to find people praying inside. And he was even less surprised and a little angered when the people he passed sounded to be praying to the tyrant Immotshap. He made it to the door leading into the back chamber without being stopped and put an ear to the door. Inock could hear Maliki and Adem quite clearly; the two boys were arguing on the other side of the door.

'I hope you've kept that ring safe, Maliki. We all took a great risk in trusting you with the task!' came Adem's voice.

'Of course I have, sir! Don't you think I know how important it is? I came to you people, remember that!' Maliki said back.

'All right. And how is the amulet?'

'It is well and safe too. Look, I have all three here.' Then after three seconds' pause Inock heard, 'I actually came to tell you Barla just gave me the Brace of Power Anandre stole from the lookout. He just brought it to her minutes ago … finally! He certainly took his time about it. He stole it so long ago.'

'Anandre informed me he wanted to authenticate it, I'm sure it was all in the name of Immotshap,' Adem said.

'They were looking for that thing for too long! I found the Demon's Amulet of Power in less time!'

'You got lucky, Maliki. You merely took it from a child!' Adem argued.

'Well, either way, I'm the one that found it! Your people searched for it for ages and couldn't find it. That moron the power-trainer's son had it all along and probably didn't even know the extent of its power or what it could be used for. And

let's not forget I had to steal the ring from that filthy grave. You lot forced me to!'

'Yes, but you did that with our help! You wouldn't have known where to find the ring if it wasn't for us witches!'

Then Inock heard Maliki say, 'Do not for a second forget that I'm the best man for the job; or should I say, the best demon! You should have more confidence in me, sir! I am going to the venators' realm after here.'

'And you remember the plan well?' Adem asked.

Inock could tell Maliki made a clucking noise with his tongue, even through the door.

'Of course I do, Adem … sir!' Maliki went on to say.

'Tell it to me just to be sure.'

'Fine! I will … sir! I am to go to the venator lookout, enter their realm, go to the hidden fort and teleport into Immotshap's prison, unlock his prison with these three relics of power, finally freeing the adored leader. I am telling you, I'm the best man for the job! You know I'm the only one who can do it right, being a natural teleporter. The witches' teleportation abilities didn't work so well in the alien realm, did they? Answer me that!'

'Yes, you are right of course, Maliki.'

'Those stupid powerful-hating venators won't see me coming! I only came to see you before doing the deed because we planned this together for so long. I should go now.'

'Maliki, wait. Before you go, I have something to give you.'

'What is it … sir?'

'It's something of lord Immotshap's. Something that has been passed down in my family for generations; something crucial; Immotshap's orb of power!'

'Does he need that?' Inock heard Maliki ask.

'Yes, very much so. This orb is really lord Immotshap's treasured power source and the secret to his immortality. Anything else he claimed to be his source of power was a lie to fool his enemies; there were many enemies. It is the true secret to his immortality, my grandfather told me so. Without it he is like any ordinary witch. Without this, our lord is not so powerful. If it were ever destroyed, he becomes mortal. I must stress this: look after it well!'

'All right, sir. I'll deliver the thing to him swiftly,' Inock heard Maliki respond. 'Immotshap will be free! Immotshap will return! Immotshap will rise! Immotshap will rule!'

There was a long silence then Inock heard bricks scraping; he inferred it was Adem opening the entrance into the secret chambers below. Inock also guessed Maliki just teleported away to the venator lookout so he could sneak into the venator realm!

Inock simply could not believe what he heard. He realised Andre was right; Maliki was disingenuous and a worse person than they initially thought! Inock's mind raced trying to come up with what to do next; and he knew he must be unhesitating before the worst happened!

One plan came to Inock; he could rally his friends and together they could stop Maliki before the sinister boy freed the tyrannical witch; after all, Inock and his friends knew the location of Immotshap's prison: the dark fort in the venator realm.

But what about informing the venators of Maliki's plan? Inock thought this over for a while then made up his mind; getting the venators involved was too risky. They would ask too many questions he and his friends couldn't answer.

Remembering that the psychic link of the *Mind to Mind* spell was still active between them, Inock thought of Andre, thought his name in his mind and then broadcasted.

Andre, can you hear me?

Inock! Is that you? Where are you?

Andre, I have something very important to tell you ... Listen!

Inock thought to Andre everything he heard eavesdropping on Maliki and Adem.

What should we do? Andre sent back, after the world-changing tale.

I think we should go and stop him ourselves! Inock thought.

But why can't we just tell the venators their plans?

Because they'll ask how we know about the hidden fort and their realm, Andre. It's too risky! It now makes sense why me and that weird boy Lonathan saw him going into the Kasama lookout and into their realm alone!

Okay, meet me at the Kasama venator lookout now.

What about Lalita? Inock asked. *Will you tell her?*

She would be seen, Inock! But you and I can use my power to turn into flies and sneak into their realm. We can do it just us two. We must! Immotshap must not be freed!

Okay! See you at the lookout, I guess.

Inock exited the temple and ran all the way to the Kasama venator lookout. Andre waited for him outside the epic building and together they entered, found a quiet spot and morphed into large green and yellow flies.

301

The two flies buzzed into the basement and flew through the rippling portal leading into the venator realm; there Inock and his brother transformed into mammoth yniqem, before flying at great speeds across the bright ruby sky to the fort hidden in the forest.

When they neared the black fort, Inock and Andre landed out of sight of the guarding venators, the many onis and the flying onis beasts with eerily glowing red eyes, and together they decided to shrink into flies once more; they zipped unseen straight through a window and into the fort.

The brothers found a quiet spot where they turned human, their shorts and T-shirts unaffected.

The inside of the fort was grimy with exposed, hefty grey bricks, and everything was in semi-darkness. It smelled damp, to Inock.

'This place looks very big,' said Andre. 'I say we split up to search for Maliki!'

'If you think that's best,' Inock said back. 'Contact me if you find him and I'll do the same.' He walked away from his brother, and Andre too took off in the opposite direction.

Inock went peeking into chamber after chamber; most rooms were empty and some doors were locked with quiet whimpering coming from within them, and there were some where the inhabitants yelled out 'I DON'T BELONG HERE!' when they heard Inock's footsteps.

Thinking it was too dark, Inock conjured up a light ball and searched on. Before long, he had to kill the magical light when he heard approaching footsteps accompanied by male voices. Thinking fast, Inock turned into a fly and waited around a corner. Two venators walked past, both with angry stares. Inock changed back into himself and searched on but

in semi-darkness; he knew he had to be more careful, no doubt there were more venators patrolling the prison.

It was when he went lower into the grim fort and through a metal gate in the form of a fly that Inock heard a familiar voice; Maliki's voice!

Inock followed the voice down a wide corridor and soon found himself at the entrance of a sizeable chamber. He quickly contacted Andre telepathically, telling him he located Maliki and where he could be found.

Inock let out a nervous breath, hoping it might ease his trembling and to calm his nerves … He entered the chamber.

Inock was greeted by the strangest sight. There appeared to be nothing in the room but a great ball of greenish energy, and in the very centre of that ball was a man naked except for the small tight shorts he wore, his arms and legs spread out as though he was frozen mid star jump. Immotshap's eyes were closed, and he appeared to be unconscious.

Maliki was at the base of the greenish ball.

'I will free you, lord Immotshap,' Maliki spoke. 'The unlocking is almost complete. You will rule again!'

On closer look at the man in the ball of green energy, Inock realised it was indeed Immotshap. The witch was thinner than he looked in Barnarbo's visions, though his long silver hair seemed the same.

The three relics of power; the Demon's Amulet of Power, Ms Strict's stolen ring and the black Brace of Power were revolving really fast around the great ball of energy with brilliant beams of some sort of magic shooting from the artefacts at the round prison; the whole display gave off loud whooshing and vibrating sounds that shook the very walls. It

appeared, to Inock, the sphere was gradually diminishing as the magic beams from the three relics penetrated it.

Inock knew what was happening; Immotshap's prison was being broken down!

'Stop this, Maliki!' Inock shouted. He was furious with the older boy. Maliki wanted very bad things for their world. 'YOU CANNOT FREE THIS TYRANT!'

Maliki jumped and turned around with shock and surprise on his face, then at seeing who called to him smirked.

'Ha! You're too late! The unlocking is almost complete!'

And it was true, Immotshap's prison was now so diminished his toes and fingers were out of it.

'You cannot do this, Maliki! He is an evil man! He will destroy the world as we know it!' Inock cried desperately.

'This man is the greatest ruler our world has ever seen!' Maliki called back over all the noise. 'Powerfuls all around the world will praise me for freeing him! He will rule! *We* will rule! He will rise! Powerfuls must rise!'

'Believe me, Maliki, I understand what it's like to be a demon in this world with all the venators everywhere, but this man cannot be trusted! He rules badly and even kills!'

'NO! He must be freed! He's been imprisoned here too long! Do you know he was one of the firsts to invade this realm? If he had succeeded, we wouldn't have venators to deal with! The scared fools captured him and the others and locked them all away! But not for much longer! He deserves to be freed!'

'But he is a terrible ruler! You can't trust him! No one can trust such an evil being!' Inock was desperate, he was very close to attacking Maliki if the older boy didn't listen.

'No way, Inock!' loudly replied Maliki over all the whooshing and vibrating noises. Dust and small bits of concrete rained down from the ceiling. 'Once I get his orb of power around his neck the job will be complete! Nothing and no one will stop us! There's nothing you can do! I hate the venators!'

Maliki held the orb of power at eye level; it was a large sparkling diamond shaped like a teardrop, attached to an ornate silver chain.

'WE WILL NOT SURRENDER!' yelled Maliki. 'I WILL NOT SURRENDER!'

Just then Andre came to Inock's side and gasped at what he saw.

The noise suddenly died out and when Inock looked up at the prisoner he trembled.

The unlocking was complete!

Immotshap's body lowered slowly to the stone floor, his eyes opening; the three relics of power were scattered around the space.

Maliki too looked to the prisoner and saw that Immotshap was finally freed. The boy looked back at Inock and Andre and grinned before teleporting to his master's side.

What happened next was very fast.

Inock's heart quickened to lightning speed; he knew it was all over once Maliki got that dreadful orb around the evil witch's neck.

Across the chamber, Maliki did just that; he lowered the mystical necklace on Immotshap.

Inock conjured, aimed and hurled an energy ball at Immotshap.

Maliki lay a hand on Immotshap's shoulder and teleported them both away in an instant, the energy ball crashing into a wall with a thunderous bang. Energy sprinkled all over, leaving scorch marks.

Immotshap was finally free!

'What shall we do now?' Andre asked. He looked very scared, and his legs seemed to shake. 'We were too late, Inock!'

'Our only option now is to destroy Immotshap's orb of power, if we can find him!'

Inock went over and collected the three artefacts of power.

At least Ms Strict will be pleased we found her ring, he thought. However, he was filled with bitterness, rage and great dread.

The two brothers left the prison.

Days went by and Inock and his friends didn't hear any news about Immotshap or dark witches taking over the world. Inock and all of them kept an eye out for Maliki and the witches Barla and Anandre but never saw them anywhere. They returned to New Valley Village many times and walked its streets, hoping to run into Maliki or Adem again but to no luck, no matter how many times Lalita insisted Immotshap must be hidden somewhere in the village.

'He must be down there! It's their main base!' she would say every instance the subject of Immotshap came up.

All the while, Inock blamed himself for Immotshap's escape; he figured if he did not show off the Demon's Amulet of Power to the AVC and all those other people, the witches would never have known where it was and as a result, Maliki couldn't have stolen it.

Even Mabiyah the Oracle had zero news on the matter. The gang even went to Dwayne's yniqem farm and spoke with Barnarbo, but the usually crafty witch had no new information.

'The witches must have Immotshap hidden magically. No one I confided in can locate him! They certainly know their witchcraft,' Barnarbo said.

Inock and Andre also dared visiting Kallam in the venators' realm to ask the man for advice on what to do about Immotshap; but Kallam said nothing more than to report the escape to the venators; which Inock and his friends chose not to do. They simply couldn't risk going to the authorities. And anyway, Inock was sure the venators knew by now Immotshap had escaped them and were searching for the evil.

Inock returned Ms Strict's ring to her, and was at least happy to see her great delight. He eventually replaced the Demon's Amulet of Power back in the display cabinet in the sitting room. Inock knew he was very fortunate that his father did not search the cabinet looking for the magical relic before he returned it. And another thing; the brothers said nothing to the rest of the family on Immotshap and what they really got up to in the year; Inock insisted his parents would be too furious and might never forgive him for engaging in such dangerous things.

Though Inock and Andre were concerned that a terrible witch had been released back into their world and him along with his army of sinister witches were most likely up to no good, they had other concerns on their minds like the upcoming school exams, working at the venator lookout and Inock's power-training with his father.

And then that boy Kross turned up again, to Inock's and Lalita's great irritation.

The strange boy walked up to Inock, Andre, Villad and Lalita as they were sat on the school steps discussing the elusive immortal witch.

'Oh, it's you!' Lalita said, at seeing the boy approach. 'What do you want this time? Come to tell us taller tales about gods?'

Kross ignored her.

'So, you finally spoke to Alloh, brother. I heard that you did,' the boy said, looking directly at Andre.

'Yes, I did,' said Andre seriously.

'And you chose to stay here?' Kross asked.

Then with a glance at Inock added, 'With them?'

'Yes, I chose to stay. I like my life the way it is! Is that a problem?'

'Andre, what's going on?' Inock asked, sounding concerned. 'What are you two talking about?'

'It's all right, Inock,' Andre replied, not taking his eyes off Kross. 'It's nothing. This guy won't bother us anymore. You can go now, Kross. I am fine!'

A look of great sadness came across Kross's face.

'Okay, brother. If that is what you want,' Kross said. 'Though why you would choose to remain in such a … let's say, interesting place, is escaping my understanding. But I will be looking out for you anyway.'

'That's fine,' Andre said, still not taking his eyes off the young god.

'Good to hear,' said Kross.

The mischievous boy teleported away in flashes of white light right before their eyes.

'What was all that about?' Inock asked, looking at Andre. 'What a strange boy!'

'I'll tell you about it someday. Don't worry, buddy,' Andre told him.

Not a fortnight after that exchange Inock and Andre sat their school examinations in the venator lookout along with other privately schooled children.

At the end of the exams weeks, Inock felt as though a huge weight had been lifted. He thought he did well enough in the examinations and Andre seemed to think the same about his own performance.

Inock knew that if he achieved the marks required to get into Unatia University he would be moving from home and doing that raised an issue for him; should he end his relationship with Rikelle before going to live in Unatia? He very much liked the pretty girl, so it was a very tough decision.

Inock raised the issue the next time he saw Rikelle and she insisted they stay together.

'We can make it work. Trust me, Inock. Unatia is really not that far away, especially if we use the venator transporters to travel between Kasama and the city,' Rikelle explained to Inock as they gazed at a dazzling golden sunset down at the Kasama docks. They were on yet another date. 'I can visit you all the time and you can visit me too.'

Then Inock did something that surprised even himself; he turned and kissed Rikelle on the lips then quickly pulled away. He suddenly felt very shy and embarrassed, hoping she would react in a good way.

Rikelle giggled then looked at the sky.

Inock beamed, feeling happier than he had done in a long time. He silently breathed, 'Yes! I did it!'

In the end Inock chose to stay with Rikelle and see how it would all work out.

Chapter Twenty One

Wars in New Valley Village

And then one afternoon, at the beginning of April as Inock, Andre, Lalita and Villad watched *Power Trials* in Inock's sitting room, Tony the ekinyo bird pecking at a bowl of seeds and nuts by Inock, Lalita got a brilliant idea. (It was still the school holidays, so they were relaxed and enjoying themselves.)

'I bet Immotshap's hidden in the secret chambers under the temple! Where else would he be?' Lalita screamed, jumping up in the armchair.

'What are you talking about, Lalita?' Andre asked, looking at Lalita as though she was mentally unstable.

'What d'you think I'm talking about? *The evil witches!* Immotshap! Don't tell me you forgot about him already!' Lalita said, flapping her arms over her head to drive the point. 'Think about it, guys! Where else would he be?'

Andre turned to Inock.

'What do you think, Inock?' Andre asked. 'Do you think he is down there?'

'Of course he is! It's their base!' Lalita cried, her eyes popping. 'He has to be! And all we have to do is find him and

tell the venators his location! I'm sure they'll be more than happy to get him back!'

'Actually, I think she has a point,' said Inock thinking. 'It's the only place in New Valley Village we didn't check.'

'And remember, they think no one knows about the hidden chambers! See? I'm right!' Lalita was hysterical.

'All right! We'll go check it out, Lalita. Just calm down!' Andre said.

'Shut up, Andre! I know you're just jealous you didn't think of it first!'

'Me jealous of you? You must be joking, Lalita!'

'Whatever, Andre!' said Lalita.

Andre next said: 'It's a village full of evil-worshipping witches and demons! I say we first go and get the venators!'

'That's a bad idea. What if Immotshap's not actually down there!' said Inock. 'The venators don't joke around...'

'No! No! No! Believe me, he is down there!' said Lalita, forcefully. 'But of course, Inock's right; no venators just yet. It's a dangerous situation!'

'It's a whole village of evil powerful individuals against just us four!' argued Andre. 'We'll be killed for sure!'

Quietly, Villad said: 'I don't want to die...'

'Immotshap must be stopped, one way or another! Let's just get to that village!' said Inock, doggedly.

Andre tried to say: 'But we'll die if we don't-!'

'Who cares! If Immotshap and his evil cronies succeed, I can't imagine anybody will be safe!' argued Lalita. 'We either die today or a week from now; either way we must fight! No more discussion; let's hurry!'

And so Inock, Andre, Villad and Lalita left Inock's home, the ekinyo bird flying after them.

Andre didn't look pleased regarding their haphazard plan…

They headed to New Valley Village to hunt for Immotshap.

Inock knew one thing; if Immotshap was allowed to rise to power, the whole world would fall apart; the powerless masses would be subjugated and armies of dark witches and powerful evil demons would rule the world. And he certainly didn't want that!

Once in the valley village the foursome made straight for the long temple and entered. Again, there were people inside praying silently. Inock and his friends hurried to the back chamber where they pressed the trick brick and proceeded down the spiralling steps. Having mastered the illumination spell, Lalita created a light ball so they could see better.

The group heard voices when they got to the base of the steps. All four of them stopped immediately to listen.

Inock hoped the ekinyo bird was smart enough to stay silent for a while. It liked to screech and scream randomly.

'He's not teaching us anything, Anandre!' Inock recognised Barla's voice. It came from the room beyond the stairwell. 'And we are all that's left of the inner circle! He already killed two of us for not finding him sooner!'

'It is okay, Barla. It will take some time to get it out of him,' Inock recognised Anandre's voice. 'We simply have to appear loyal until he feels it's time to share the secrets to his immortality. I do however think I have a clue on what to do. Then we may eliminate the fool. The minds of the powerfuls in the village are sufficiently twisted, the mindless hordes will do anything we ask. The immortals will fall, one way or another! Just be patient.'

'Yes, but that's if he ever shares those secrets with us,' said Barla. 'I cannot wait any longer, Anandre! He is no good!'

'Quiet, Barla. He's coming!'

'Thank you for meeting with us, master,' Inock heard Barla say sweetly. He could just imagine her rearranging her stupid face to seem agreeable.

'It is good to see you, Barla.' Inock knew this to be Immotshap's voice; he remembered it from Barnarbo's visions. 'You have done very well with the village. I can't imagine better followers. They certainly are malleable; trusting without question.'

'Thank you, sir. You are worth it,' Barla said back.

'We need to start the takeover now, master,' Anandre spoke next.

'We must wait until we have more followers, Anandre,' Immotshap said, his voice stern. 'My plans to conquer were once thwarted. I cannot afford to be hasty.'

'But they are weak, master. They would all be easy, so simple to conquer! We can rule once more.'

'And what of the venators? They are a great force. Undeniable!' came Immotshap's voice again. 'They will not be so easy to defeat. I'm telling you confidants, we must wait!'

'I must contest, master! We've waited for you for far too long. The takeover must begin now, today even!' Barla argued. 'Look what those three did on Farewell Day. Mere children and they had the whole market terrified! I watched the whole thing. It'll be a doddle to rule everything. Mindless, stupid hordes!'

'Patience, young one! You think me incompetent? We—must—wait!' came Immotshap's voice so loud Inock trembled where he stood. 'Now that I am back, I have plans. Plans that must be followed precisely! You're certainly right, they are all mindless hordes to be ruled! Subjugation is my thinking.'

Lalita had heard enough.

'I think one of us should go and tell the venators where Immotshap is,' the girl said to Inock. Then, she turned to Villad: 'Villad, can you do it while me, Andre and Inock stay here and listen to their plans some more? Bring them straight here.'

'All right, I'll go,' Villad said with a nod. He tiptoed back up the steps.

Inock, Andre and Lalita listened on.

The ekinyo bird on the other hand seemed unsettled.

'It is a dense world we live in,' Anandre said next. 'It shouldn't be too troublesome to finally take the lead. We are many. A whole village-full and more.'

'You've done well, Anandre and Barla,' said Immotshap. 'I am most pleased with what you've accomplished. Indeed, it should not be too difficult. But I must stress to you both, we must be prudent in our approach.'

'If you are sure master, we'll wait,' Anandre said, sounding ever so humble, Inock thought.

Inock was pleased about one thing though; Immotshap's closest followers were duplicitous. They only cared about his immortality and nothing more. Their whole clan could fall if the right information was revealed to the right people.

Inock, Andre and Lalita were so engrossed in the discussions in the chamber beyond that they didn't see the witch that crept up behind them.

'*What are you children doing down here?*' the woman screeched, her voice ripe with suspicion. She had approached from the floors above.

The three friends froze with nothing to say. The witch walked past them and into the room beyond, then she looked back at them all and certain realisation showed on her face.

The woman went back into the chamber and called out: 'We've got some children spying in the stairs! What shall I do with them?'

'Get them before they tell of our plans! They cannot alert others to my whereabouts!' Inock heard Immotshap spit.

Inock surely needed no telling. Grabbing the ekinyo bird, he bolted it up the stairs, Andre and Lalita right behind him.

Inock led the others out of the temple and they kept running through the village streets. When he looked back, Inock spotted Barla, Anandre and the witch who caught them spying chasing them! The man and two women wore traditional robes of black.

Inock thought they might make it out of the village alive until Barla started calling out to every villager they passed: 'stop them! They wish to stop our master! They wish to stop our plans! Stop them!'

Many witches and demons they encountered joined the chase and before you could say, 'roaring gomorah,' a war broke out in New Valley Village.

The witches began aiming fireballs, lightning bolts, knives, stones and pointy icicles at the escaping three!

Inock, Lalita and Andre fought back by firing bolts and energy balls of their own, cancelling out many of the deadly projectiles.

'GET THEM! THEY WISH TO STOP OUR PLANS!' Barla yelled as she hurled a massive green fireball that just missed Inock's ear and crashed into a house setting it ablaze instantly.

'GET THEM!'
'STOP THEM!'
'GET THEM!'

Inock and his friends were hounded and chased by over thirty witches and demons, having way too many close calls with the array of projectiles launched at them. They ran placing energy shields behind them to stop fire, and Inock even used telekinesis to throw and smash many witches into walls and trees. And often he conjured a knife to throw. But the situation still seemed dire. Inock wondered if they took a wrong turn somewhere; they couldn't find the village exit fast enough.

But then after another turn into a wider street, Inock was never more pleased to see Villad, and the small boy was followed by over twenty venators and forty onis, of which, one was Radock the friendly venator. Clearly, the venators thought Immotshap to be a formidable enemy for that many of them to come, Inock thought.

At noticing the chase, the venators went into attack mode; many unhooked their venator whips.

'You are not welcome in this village, venators! Leave at once!' a male witch bellowed at the approaching horde of black men.

'you all must surrender!' a venator called back. 'you're harbouring an escaped prisoner!'

'surrender him!' said another venator, pointing angrily.

'leave, venators! You are not welcome here!' a squat witch shouted.

'then you leave us no choice but incarceration!' a venator shouted, careering at the powerfuls.

'we must take you all!' provided a different venator. 'we have every right!'

'this settlement is for powerfuls only!' a male demon in a long red coat blustered. '*not for your kind!*'

Many venators blew into their Onis flutes commanding the many onis to charge and attack.

It was a riot!

The venators and onis charged at the witches and demons. The mad scene looked like two rival armies at war; the venators and onis on one side and the witches and demons on the other.

The result was a vicious and violent affray!

All short of breath, Inock, Lalita and Andre ran to Villad while the venators, their onis and the powerfuls clashed.

'Brilliantly done, Villad!' said Lalita vociferously.

'You saved us!' cried Andre.

Witches and demons from all over the village joined the crazy fight. Onis lunged and sank their teeth into necks, some wrapped their long tails around witches and squeezed them until they collapsed; lethal projectiles were hurled at venators and onis alike; torrents of flames burned flesh; conjured

daggers were thrust into chests and backs; fireballs of various colours zoomed through the air; energy bolts tore into flesh; witches and demons turned into mini giants and pummelled bodies; deadly energy spears zapped bodies. And the venators certainly fought back, expertly snapping and lashing their black whips at anybody who wasn't a venator, draining them of all energy and magical power.

A broad range of projectiles were hurled and whizzed through the air; including ginormous blazing fireballs, some of which zoomed into space and some detonated the very ground, making everyone scream and dive.

New Valley Village turned into a riotous, deadly battlefield!

Inock, Andre and Lalita certainly did their part. Inock used many of the offensive powers he learned in the last year or so; he spun and threw witches using telekinesis; launched energy balls and fireballs; aimed crackling energy bolts that stunned many into collapsing, and even enlarged his body and thumped witches into the ground with his giant fists.

The ekinyo bird flew high above Inock, watching the fighting below.

Lalita appeared an expert at aiming sizzling energy balls and bluish energy bolts.

Andre transformed into a great number of creatures as he fought; one minute he was a stocky onis, and the next, a gomorah or a giant shadow bat screeching loudly, knocking unconscious many witches, or a really fat succubus; but the most fierce and indomitable beast he turned into was a mammoth yniqem that flew over the battle breathing jets of red fire on many enemies at a time; and countless witches aimed knives at him as he flew, but his yniqem hide was too

tough for them to do decent damage. Yniqem Andre even launched from his mouth, humongous red fireballs below, exploding the ground all around, making bodies fly like bullets!

The battle raged on for a lengthy period, with bodies and creatures zooming and flying all over, energy balls exploding, fireballs whizzing and smashing into houses and trees like thunder and setting everything ablaze.

Then Radock found Inock and thanked him for sending Villad to collect the venators.

'But where is Immotshap? I don't see him,' Radock said. 'Wait a second!'

The tall venator slashed his whip at a male witch who was sneaking up behind Inock. The witch yelped and fled.

'He's in a hidden chamber under the worshipping temple,' Inock said breathless; the fight was quite depleting.

'We'll have to get him after dealing with all these witches,' Radock said then re-joined the fight, lashing his venator's whip at the nearest witch.

Many people arrived into New Valley Village to watch the struggle. Inock guessed it was down to the bangs and explosions and screams that could probably be heard from Kasama Market and the surrounding villages.

The war surged and raged on for what seemed like hours to Inock.

In time, most of the witches and demons were defeated; some lay on the blood-soaked ground bound and gagged by onis, many fell unconscious, a good number fled and many others were restrained by venator whips.

But the witches and demons had indisputably done their fair share of damage; many venators and onis lay burnt, bloodied and defeated on the ground. Several were dead.

Looking around at the remaining rival powerfuls, Inock noticed Barla and Anandre were nowhere to be found.

As he shot a witch in the back with scorching bolts, Inock was surprised to see the male witch James run up to him, followed by the ever-beautiful Esmatilda and her sister Dentas.

'Inock! What's happening here?' James exclaimed, reaching Inock. 'We returned to Esma's and we heard all the terrible noise! The whole village is in an uproar.'

'We found Immotshap and then the dark witches attacked us!' Inock said, panting. 'We alerted the venators.'

'Well done, Inock!' said Esmatilda. She wore a white dress and white sandals. 'Immotshap must be stopped! That man gives the rest of us witches such a bad name!'

'Certainly,' said Dentas. She wore a black dress and matching sandals, her long hair tidy and straight.

'You found him? Where is he?' James asked.

'He's in a hidden place under the worshipping temple!'

'Can you take us there?' asked James. 'We must face the filth and stop him. Before the situation gets any more out of control!'

Inock agreed to take them. He led James, Esmatilda and Dentas away from the noisy fighting, creating a path by telekinetically flinging witches and onis out of their way, and as they ran, were joined by Andre and Lalita, the ekinyo bird following from the air.

As they went, Inock thought to inform the adults of something; he told them of Immotshap's true power source; the orb of power.

'And he told Maliki that it's his true power source, that if it were destroyed Immotshap would be mortal and just as powerful as the rest.'

'Excellent, Inock!' James exclaimed as he jogged. 'Fantastic news! This should make our task all the more easier.'

The group got to the temple and entered, the ekinyo bird following them in, then Inock led the way into the underground chambers. There, Inock deftly conjured a light ball and they searched until they heard voices coming from the glistening cathedral-like chamber beyond.

James put out an arm and halted everyone just outside the huge chamber.

'Let's wait and listen,' the man whispered.

'I really do insist we move you elsewhere, master,' Inock heard Barla's voice.

'No, child. I'll stay and fight. Let the venators come!'

'But we are losing the battle. The venators are fighting too well!' came Anandre's voice.

'They will lose. Let them come!' Immotshap said, and Inock could certainly hear the rage in his voice. The tyrant sounded violent! 'Perhaps it's time I made an appearance and finally stopped them!'

'We cannot let him do that, he will slaughter them all!' James said vehemently before marching into the chamber beyond.

The rest followed him in.

Chapter Twenty Two
Immotshap the Immortal

Immotshap, Barla and Anandre were stood in the middle of the chamber, a football-sized light ball high above them, giving light to the whole space, making the mosaic marble walls and floor glisten and glimmer.

'YOU HAVE TO STOP WITH YOUR PLANS!' James announced their entering, marching towards the diabolical trio, Inock and the others right behind him. 'YOU MUST GIVE UP TAKING OVER! SUBJUGATION IS A VERY TIRED MISSION!'

'James! It is good to see you again at last!' said Immotshap, arms outstretched as though inviting James in for a hug. He was dressed in black robes with dark sandals.

'Don't play games, Immotshap!' James said angrily, accusing finger jabbing. 'You have to stop! We all want you to stop! You give the immortals a bad name!'

'Get out of here, James!' seethed Barla. 'We gave you a chance. You cannot stop our plans!'

'Leave this place at once!' said Anandre, as furiously. 'You denied us! You're not welcome anymore!'

'Now, now, everyone. James is an immortal, one of us. He is always welcome into our fold,' said Immotshap arms still held out to James.

'If you won't listen, we'll stop you. And your deluded followers!' Esmatilda spoke up. She and Inock and the others all stood twenty feet from the witches.

'Of course they must be stopped!' said Dentas. 'The scum tried to recruit me. I refused so they chose to kill me! Like they killed james!'

Immotshap laughed a cold long laugh before booming, 'you intend to stop us? You three and those children and their pet bird?' His voice resounded in the long chamber, frightening Inock to bits. And indeed the ekinyo bird flew above everyone, watching the scene unfold.

'Leave the children out of this, Immotshap! There will be no more killings!' roared James. 'You get a choice; either give up; surrender to the authorities, or we drag you to them!'

'We will drag you there by your stupid silver hair!' snarled Lalita.

'HOW DARE YOU VERBALLY ATTACK THE LORD IN THAT MANNER!' screamed Barla. Without warning she conjured and launched a massive emerald fireball at James. James deftly conjured a wide energy shield before himself and the fireball collided with it and exploded with a deafening bang. The shield held.

'LEAVE ALREADY, JAMES! HAD YOUR CHANCE!' Anandre yelled before pointing, uttered a spell and unnatural winds came about, buffeting James's shield. Arm thrusting out, James maintained his energy barrier. The savage winds bombarding, the whole display gave off rushing sounds that pressed on Inock's eardrums.

'Concede these childish pursuits, immotshap!' James bellowed over the whooshing sounds. 'all of you must stop! Yield!'

'James, if you protest further, *I WILL KILL YOU!*' boomed Anandre. 'This time, permanently!'

'Wrong, anandre! All misguided in your attempts!' Dentas yelled. 'This world needs no leaders like you! Killers!'

'I will conquer! I will lead!' Immotshap shouted. 'Sheep to be tamed and led! Realise this! You cannot stop me!'

The immortal witch then thrust both arms to the heavens and not five seconds later, the entire chamber trembled; the floor quaked, splitting into huge slabs of marble making everyone dance about and the very walls shook. The ceiling cracked in places; rubble rained down on them all.

'Stop this! You aim to kill us all?' esmatilda cried, fighting to stay upright.

'that's the idea!' said barla, with a smirk.

'i will end your miserable existences!' bellowed immotshap.

Inock acted. He used telekinesis to hurl a huge slab of marble at Immotshap, but Barla swiftly deflected it with a vigorous wave of a hand.

Anandre had stopped with the winds, seeing as he could barely stand up straight.

Making vanish his energy barrier, James thrust out an arm, uttered a spell and a massive tunnel-sized jet of orange fire rushed at the three witches.

Barla was fast. She conjured a great transparent shield, stopping the torrents of flames. James kept up the flow for several seconds before he gave up. He lowered his arm.

Now the whole space felt like ninety degrees to Inock. He wished James hadn't just done that.

A huge section of the ceiling fell, crashing before Immotshap and the witch dived out of the way.

That's when the quaking ceased.

'Immotshap! Return to your prison!' james bellowed.

'take responsibility for what you did!' added inock.

'he invaded the venators!' supplied lalita. Then more viciously, 'ruling by force is never a good thing!'

'and you think me deluded! *You think i'd willingly return?*' immotshap yelled back, recovering. His robes were covered in dust. 'no surrender!'

Just then, Maliki and Adem ran into the battle-devastated chamber. They were at one end of the space. Inock, James, Esmatilda, Dentas, Andre and Lalita stood in between. Immotshap, Barla and Anandre were at the other end. Three groups spaced apart.

Adem and Maliki froze at the strange sight before them.

'What's happening?' asked Adem loudly. 'The whole place was shaking! Everyone thought it was the end!'

'Take care of those two, Inock,' said James, looking at Inock. 'We'll restrain Immotshap and his two followers.' Then he ran at Immotshap, hurling alarmingly big, green fireballs as he went, followed by Esmatilda and Dentas who did likewise.

As soon as the adults were engaged in battle, Adem looked to focus, arm stretched out and before you could say, 'exploding energy ball,' a thick earthy wall rose from the floor, creating a barrier between the children and the adults.

'No running for help to your friends!' Adem said with a wicked grin. 'I will make Immotshap proud!' Then he said six words and Inock was taken aback to see a wall of daggers materialise before the boy. With just one more word uttered the pointy knives flew at Inock, Andre and Lalita.

Lalita acted fastest. She conjured a bluish energy shield that stopped many of the daggers but some broke through. Inock had to quickly create a second barrier; he succeeded in stopping the rest. The knives clattered to the floor.

With telekinesis, Inock launched a stream of rubble at Adem and Maliki, wiping the glee off their faces. But Adem skilfully deflected the attack off to the side, sending the rocks smashing into a wall with a loud crash.

And there were even more bangs and yells coming from the other side of the wall Adem erected.

It was Andre's turn to attack; he morphed into an onis and with a frenzied dash and one great leap was above Maliki. Maliki had to dive out of the way to avoid onis Andre's full weight from crushing him. Andre then began lashing his two onis tails at Maliki, but the boy kept teleporting all over the place, guffawing, Andre chasing after him, growling fiercely.

Meanwhile, Inock transformed into a gomorah, took a mighty leap and punched Adem into a wall. The gomorah charged at Adem and with both hands crushed him very hard into the floor; he pinned him there, snarling in the boy's face, ropes of spittle dripping.

Lalita watched everything, waiting for her chance to strike.

Noticing Inock had Adem held down, Maliki yelled, 'GET AWAY FROM HIM!'

Maliki teleported over and hurled an energy ball at gomorah Inock, knocking him across the space and he crashed very painfully into a wall.

With a rapid recovery, gomorah Inock massaged his back where the energy ball hit. Without the hard animal back the

energy ball would have done serious damage! Looking at Maliki, Inock let off a loud enraged roar.

Adem willed a double-edged sword out of thin air, set the long blade on fire with a rapid incantation, then sprinted at gomorah Inock and strenuously slashed and hacked at him repeatedly. From his feral, murderous expression, Adem intended to kill Inock! The blue flames from the sword released acrid smoke; there was coughing.

Inock danced, dashed and dived again and again to evade the burning blade, but he had too many close calls.

Lalita saw her opening and attacked Maliki. The boy and girl threw many projectiles at one another, Lalita creating dagger after dagger to throw at the vanishing, cackling boy. They projected deadly energy bolts at each other, sometimes locking in struggles where one's blue electricity pushed against the other's! They tossed exploding energy balls too, Lalita getting frustrated many times since Maliki proved impossible to strike with his teleporting.

Andre in onis form lashed his tails at Maliki whenever the boy got close.

The chamber was loud with noises much like a grand battle of a major war, with deafening bangs and explosions, screaming and crying voices, and the unmistakable clashing of swords and daggers.

Inock willed his body to expand to something like quadruple its usual size and, taking a run at Adem, the space quaking from his giant footsteps, reaching the worshipped boy smashed him with his giant fists. Inock missed! And he was soon gasping when Adem grew to a size greater than his giant form by means of a rapid chant. The expanded powerfuls clashed; they wrestled and kicked and punched

each other. Inock tried very hard not to squash Lalita and Andre fighting around them.

Lalita finally struck Maliki with energy bolts, but the boy recovered too fast, making her grunt irritably. They resumed their attacks on each other.

With the clashing giants, Inock landed a good blow to Adem's stomach. Screeching like a mammoth pterodactyl, the young witch shrunk to his normal size in less than five seconds.

Adem looked incensed.

With complex hand motions, the young witch produced chains seemingly only of dark energies that rushed at giant Inock and bound him, snapping his arms and legs together!

Inock struggled with the shackles, trying to break them with his increased strength, but could not!

Adem laughed wildly.

The laughter angered Inock, so much so that he gathered all his strength, finally succeeding at breaking the magical chains. He aimed a hand and fired off enormous energy bolts.

Adem simply chanted and powerful gusts of wind came into being and reversed and redirected the bluish bolts!

Inock continued with the electric attack for as long as he could, but soon felt too drained. He stopped with the energy bolts.

Inock understood why Adem was worshipped; he was powerful!

Tired of being so big, Inock returned to his normal size. He knew he must somehow disable the annoying teen.

In a flash, Inock changed into a hulking onis and, racing towards him lashed his tails at Adem. The young witch

summoned his flaming sword lying on the ground and it flew into his hand. They attacked one another for a while.

Until Inock wrapped his two tails around Adem's feet and yanked him six feet into the air, suspending him there with his blazing sword hanging limply.

'I AM WORSHIPPED!' Adem cried attempting to cut off Inock's tails but couldn't reach. 'PUT ME DOWN RIGHT NOW! I AM ADORED!'

'NOT AGAIN!' called out Maliki at noticing.

Maliki fired an energy ball at onis Inock but Lalita was fast. She summoned and sent speeding her own blue energy ball at the one headed for Inock; the humongous balls clashed with a loud bang and a bright explosion of energies!

Onis Andre took advantage of Maliki's distractedness and charged at him, knocked him over like a bowling pin, wrapping his tails around him.

But Maliki teleported out of it with a hiss.

Just then, Radock the venator appeared into the chamber accompanied by three other venators, along with eight onis and Villad. The venators' eyebrows raised in surprise at the mad scene before them, not to mention the wild battle sounds coming from the adults on the other side of the earth wall.

Unaware of the venators, Maliki hurled an energy ball at Lalita who was cheering on onis Inock for restraining Adem.

Lalita never saw the energy ball coming; but Radock did. Speedily, the venator unhooked his venator whip, ran and jumped through the air and repeatedly lashed at the deadly energy ball reducing it to wisps that fast dissipated.

Lalita noticed what Maliki tried to do. Seething, she conjured and fired energy ball after energy ball, but Maliki just kept teleporting around the roaring blue balls, laughing

wildly, his voice rivalling the loud explosions and cries coming from the concealed adults.

And then Radock acted again. He took a great leap, landed behind Maliki and lashed his whip at him, wrapping it around the boy, and began doing what venators do with their whips around you. He sapped Maliki's energy, stopping him from using his powers any longer. Maliki couldn't teleport out of it.

Radock then blew into his Onis flute and an onis came over and restrained Maliki with its scaly tails.

The other venators clapped, but still had irate faces even as they did so.

Lalita whooped, punching fists in the air.

With his Onis flute, Radock commanded another onis to trot over and relieve Inock of the task of detaining Adem.

As soon as he was free of the task, Inock dashed to the earth wall that split the space in two, and staring at it with great focus used telekinesis to break a path through to the other side.

Inock, Andre, Lalita, Villad and the venators and remaining onis were greeted with quite a scene.

James, Esmatilda and Dentas were locked in an energy bolts power struggle with Immotshap, Barla and Anandre, their surrounds totally wrecked. There were burn marks all over and it appeared a bomb had gone off. There was a wide and deep hole in the floor, everyone avoiding it.

Inock and Lalita ran over to James's side and joined the power struggle, adding lethal blue bolts of their own.

Seeing so much power and magic clash violently between the two groups scared Inock!

'Barla, you look rather good for your age!' Lalita screamed as she maintained the fierce energy fire. 'You're ancient! I saw you in a vision from years and years ago!'

'SILENCE, CHILD!' Barla called back, her voice resounding in the room over the crackling of the energies whooshing and flying all around them. Beads of sweat trickled down her thin face. Her ponytail swished animatedly.

'Master, perhaps we're outnumbered,' Anandre said. 'They are many! They are good!'

'We are not! This is child's play!' Immotshap shouted, his thin face also sweaty. 'They will surrender!'

'We will not surrender, you filth! *You* must surrender!' James roared.

The struggle carried on for a time, each side trying to outdo and end the other.

Inock could feel immense power drain from him as he maintained the energy flow. It was more than he was used to; he could feel the scorching heat from the bolts clashing before him.

Then Anandre did something entirely unexpected; he broke his connection to the power struggle, dashed to Immotshap and yanked his orb of power from around his neck.

'I've finally done it! I got it!' Anandre cried, running from Immotshap. 'His secrets to immortality shall be mine!'

'Anandre! Well done!' yelled Barla then she too broke away from the power connection and ran to his side.

'Foolish! You betray me? You can never know the secret to my immortality!' immotshap roared, his voice very loud and reverberating. He was fighting alone now. Where the energy bolts connected was slowly shifting towards him.

Inock noticed his eyes bulged. Was it out of fear, or just exertion?

Then something even more unexpected happened next.

Inock's ekinyo bird, in its enlarged form, swooped down and grabbed the orb from Anandre's grasp in its beak. The magical bird then let off its unusual shrill shriek, shattering the jewel. Remainders of the orb sprinkled down from the bird's beak and to the damaged floor.

'LOOK WHAT YOU DID, YOU MISERABLE CRETINS! NEVER WERE WORTHY!' Immotshap screamed. He broke the power connection and replaced his bolts with an energy shield that blocked the attacks at him. 'I am far beyond your feeble attempts!'

Immotshap aimed a hand at Anandre, fired a beam of intense, white light at him that left a huge gaping hole in the man's chest; Anandre dropped to the floor with a thud; never to recover.

Barla made an attempt to run for it but Immotshap simply repeated the motion, but this time the brilliant beam hit and exploded her head, killing her instantly.

Inock, James, Esmatilda, Dentas and Lalita ceased fire.

Inock couldn't believe their luck; Immotshap was alone, and what's more, he was weakened and mortal. And when he looked at the others, Inock could see triumph on their sweat-covered faces; they might have been thinking the same thing.

'Now, everyone! He's mortal! Let's take the filth down!' cried James.

Everyone in the room including the onis, advanced on Immotshap; but the man merely scowled, raised his arms above his head as though lifting something very heavy and with a sound like a bomb going off, pointy earth spikes shot

out of the floor, trapping his foes in a forest of the things; they could barely move, the onis lashing their long tails at the enemy in vain.

Immotshap, with both his arms still raised to the skies, speedily chanted a spell and before Inock knew what was happening, thick black clouds formed below the high ceiling and it began to rain hail. The golf-ball-sized icy stones pummelled everyone in the space except their conjurer.

They all cried out in intense suffering.

It was severely frightening, painful for Inock.

Then, Esmatilda and Dentas seemed to share a look; they too raised their arms and after a fast, joint chant, a swirling vortex of orange fire formed above the black clouds, sucking them all up.

Cursing, Immotshap looked up distracted, and Inock took his chance. With telekinesis, Inock threw the witch into a wall; then as the once immortal witch was recovering from the massive wallop, thinking and acting swiftly, Inock used telekinesis once more and broke the earth spikes before one venator, freeing the man.

'Now! Get him with your whip!' Inock yelled. He pointed to Immotshap.

It took the venator a fraction of a second to understand; he dashed and lashed his whip at Immotshap, restraining him with it.

Immotshap crumpled to the floor within seconds; the whip did its job of draining his powers and energy.

With a quick spell, James reduced the earthy spikes to dust, freeing them all.

'It is finished! Immotshap is beaten!' James said to everyone.

They all looked battle-worn.

'You have our gratitude,' said the venator with his whip around Immotshap. 'You brought us to the escapee and helped defeat him. This witch's crimes can never be forgiven! He will be returned to his prison.'

'And don't forget Adem and Maliki, they freed him!' Lalita said to the venators. 'That's those two boys over there.' She pointed to Adem and Maliki where they lay subdued.

'Those two young men are in a lot of trouble. Why they would choose to free such a criminal is beyond me,' Radock said, walking to Maliki and Adem. He looked back at Inock. 'I've been speaking with the AVC. I knew Maliki wanted to free the prisoner Immotshap; I was onto him. Sadly, I didn't catch him in time. And fret not regarding Dentas. I'll put in a good word for the witch; she helped defeat Immotshap! She may live free; the venators will choose it.'

'They'll never choose it!' Maliki said bitterly from where he lay. 'Venators hate powerfuls and powerfuls hate venators! That is the way it is! That is the way it has always been! That is the way it will always be! I figured why not live it up … powerfuls are special! We deserve everything! We are gifted with magical power; you must know what that means! Why do you think I joined the witches…supposed to be my ticket to freedom…you idiots ruined it!'

'Be silent, young man. You are in more trouble than you realise!' Radock told Maliki seriously.

'I guess, instead he got a one-way ticket to prison, eh Inock?' said Andre, looking mirthful.

'Wow! That is a really good one for someone who thinks watching documentaries about water is fun!' said Lalita, cracking up.

'It is an improvement, buddy!' said Inock, laughing and playfully elbowing Andre in the arm.

Andre couldn't have looked prouder.

Maliki had on a sour face, staring daggers at Andre.

'Let us depart from this dark place,' said Radock.

Inock and everyone else, including the ekinyo bird now in its smaller state and perched on Inock's shoulder, all followed Radock out of the underground chambers, onis carrying Maliki, Adem and Immotshap in their long tails.

Outside, the village was recovering from the battle; venators and onis were everywhere, questioning the villagers and detaining some.

James, Esmatilda and Dentas separated from the group.

Radock, the other venators and the prisoners, all headed to the Kasama venator lookout, and Inock, Andre, Lalita and Villad walked back to the market with bright smiles on their faces; the dark and very sinistrous witch Immotshap was defeated.

Days later, at some point in mid-April on a very stormy day with fearsome thunder and lightning to boot, Inock, Andre and Lalita were in the Oracle's chamber, there to collect payment after a simple mission when Lalita said something unexpected.

'Oracle, did you know the secret to defeating Immotshap when you sent us to rescue that woman Dentas?' Lalita asked.

Sat at her table as usual, Mabiyah smiled before responding. As always, the room glowed turquoise.

'Indeed. I knew that particular secret. But Dentasa had to be freed none the less. It was after all your fault that she was arrested.'

Lalita looked like she wanted to argue but she did not.

'Okay, but did you know where Immotshap was all along? In the venator realm?' the girl asked and pushed her glasses into her face.

'No. I did not know where he was being kept, child,' the Oracle said, shaking her head. 'My abilities to see what may be and into other places have certain limitations. For example, I cannot see into other realms. That is why I simply couldn't locate Immotshap. But I had *seen* the misguided witch would return. And I knew things would unfold the way they should... Now, here is your payment for the job.'

A fat roll of ryza notes appeared before Inock and he very happily grabbed and pocketed it.

'Share it between you,' said Mabiyah.

'Thank you, Oracle,' said Andre.

'Inock, what have you learned of taking things that do not belong to you?' asked the Oracle.

'It's wrong and he shouldn't do it,' answered Andre.

'Well done, Andre,' said Mabiyah. 'Have you learned this?' She was looking at Inock.

'Yes, Oracle,' admitted Inock. 'I took the Demon's Amulet of Power from my father and then I lost it. But I gave it back. I know I did wrong.'

'And what about the things that people do?' asked the Oracle. 'You saw how I became immortal, how we achieved it. What are your thoughts regarding this?'

'That things aren't always so straightforward,' said Inock.

'Those people were ready to die,' said Andre. 'Strange...a tricky thing to choose, but I guess it's not really we three's business.'

'So I guess it was sort of okay what you five did,' contributed Inock. 'The ones on the crosses chose it...'

337

'Very good,' said Mabiyah. 'Though death is no laughing matter. It should not be taken lightly. So do not be deluded by what you witnessed.'

'And I suppose the reward was very worth it?' asked Lalita. 'It seems to be. You cannot die, Oracle! It's incredible!' Her eyes expanded; she looked positively manic.

'That is private, young one. Though I have lived a very long time,' said the Oracle. 'You three may now go.'

'Thank you, Oracle,' Andre said before he, Inock and Lalita exited the chamber.

Inock and Andre headed home to pack their suitcases. They would start university in just two weeks and were expected to move on campus in days. The boys had recently received their exams results and it turned out they both passed with flying colours, to Tehan's and Esttia's great pleasure. Inock got four A's, one for science and alchemy, a B for world history and three Cs. Andre performed very well too with six As; one for theoretical agriculture and hospitality, one for business studies and one for media studies, a B and one C.

The End

Longman Dictionaries

Express yourself with confidence!

Longman has led the way in ELT dictionaries since 1935. We constantly talk to students and teachers around the world to find out what they need from a learner's dictionary.

Why choose a Longman dictionary?

Easy to understand

Longman invented the Defining Vocabulary – 2000 of the most common words which are used to write the definitions in our dictionaries. So Longman definitions are always clear and easy to understand.

Real, natural English

All Longman dictionaries contain natural examples taken from real-life that help explain the meaning of a word and show you how to use it in context.

Avoid common mistakes

Longman dictionaries are written specially for learners, and we make sure that you get all the help you need to avoid common mistakes. We analyse typical learners' mistakes and include notes on how to avoid them.

Innovative CD-ROMs

Longman are leaders in dictionary CD-ROM innovation. Did you know that a dictionary CD-ROM includes features to help improve your pronunciation, help you practice for exams and improve your writing skills?

For details of all Longman dictionaries, and to choose the one that's right for you, visit our website:

www.longman.com/dictionaries

Man from the South and Other Stories
Roald Dahl

Roald Dahl is the master of the unexpected. Things are not always what they seem and nobody should be trusted. In this collection of his short stories we learn some strange lessons about the dangerous world we live in. But you will have to wait until the final pages of each story to discover the last, terrible twist!

Memoirs of a Geisha
Arthur Golden

Memoirs of a Geisha is one of the great stories of our time.

We follow Sayuri's life: her early years in a small fishing village and as a geisha in Gion. And throughout her struggle, we know of her secret love for the only man who ever showed her any kindness – a man who *seems* to be out of her reach.

The Moonstone
Wilkie Collins

The Moonstone is an ancient Indian diamond which brings disaster to everyone who owns it. Rachel Verinder's uncle gives her the diamond as a birthday present, but that same night it is stolen . . . *The Moonstone* is now seen as the first, and one of the best, English detective novels.

There are hundreds of Penguin Readers to choose from – world classics, film adaptations, modern-day crime and adventure, short stories, biographies, American classics, non-fiction, plays ...

For a complete list of all Penguin Readers titles, please contact your local Pearson Longman office or visit our website.

Captain Corelli's Mandolin
Louis de Bernières

Louis de Bernières is one of the best writers in English today.

This is a great love story set in the tragedy of war. It is 1941. The Italian officer, Captain Corelli, falls in love with Pelagia, a young Greek girl. But Pelagia's fiancé is fighting the Italian army ...

Captain Corelli's Mandolin is now a film, starring Nicholas Cage.

Brave New World
Aldous Huxley

Aldous Huxley's *Brave New World* is one of the great works of science fiction.

It is the year After Ford 632 in the New World. People are born and live by scientific methods. There is worldwide happiness and order. Then John comes from the Savage Reservation to the New World and with him he brings strong emotions – love, hate, anger, fear. Suddenly, danger threatens the New World.

The Chamber
John Grisham

The horror of death row is that you die a little each day. The waiting kills you.

Seventy-year-old Sam Cayhall is on Mississippi's death row. Sam hates lawyers but his date with the gas chamber is close, and time is running out. Then Adam Hall, a young lawyer arrives. Can he and his secret persuade Sam to accept his help?

There are hundreds of Penguin Readers to choose from – world classics, film adaptations, modern-day crime and adventure, short stories, biographies, American classics, non-fiction, plays ...

For a complete list of all Penguin Readers titles, please contact your local Pearson Longman office or visit our website.

www.penguinreaders.com

The Testament
John Grisham

Nate O'Riley is a powerful Washington lawyer. Returning to work after a long stay in hospital is difficult for Nate. Then he is sent on a journey that takes him from the tense courtrooms of Washington to the dangerous swamps of Brazil. It is a journey that will change his life forever... *Another great thriller from John Grisham, one of the world's most popular writers.*

Snow Falling on Cedars
David Guterson

It is 1954 and Kabuo Miyamoto is on trial for murder. He is a Japanese American living on the island of San Piedro, off the north-west coast of America. The Second World War has left an atmosphere of anger and suspicion in this small community. Will Kabuo receive a fair trial? And will the true cause of the victim's death be discovered?

Les Misérables
Victor Hugo

Jean Valjean is free at last after nineteen years in prison. Cold and hungry, he is rejected by everyone he meets. But Jean's life is changed forever when he discovers love. He spends the rest of his life helping people, like himself, who have been victims of poverty and social injustice – 'les misérables'.

There are hundreds of Penguin Readers to choose from – world classics, film adaptations, modern-day crime and adventure, short stories, biographies, American classics, non-fiction, plays ...

For a complete list of all Penguin Readers titles, please contact your local Pearson Longman office or visit our website.

www.penguinreaders.com

Great Expectations
Charles Dickens

Pip is a poor orphan whose life is changed for ever by two very different meetings – one with an escaped convict and the other with an eccentric old lady and the beautiful girl who lives with her. And who is the mysterious person who leaves him a fortune?

Oliver Twist
Charles Dickens

His mother is dead, so little Oliver Twist is brought up in the workhouse. Beaten and starved, he runs away to London, where he joins Fagin's gang of thieves. By chance he also finds good new friends – but can they protect him from people who rob and murder without mercy?

Crime and Punishment
Fyodor Dostoevsky

Raskolnikoff, a young student, has been forced to give up his university studies because of lack of money. He withdraws from society and, poor and lonely, he develops a plan to murder a greedy old moneylender. Surely the murder of one worthless old woman would be excused, even approved of, if it made possible a thousand good deeds? But this crime is just the beginning of the story. Afterwards he must go on a journey of self-discovery. He must try to understand his motives and explain them to others. Can he succeed?

There are hundreds of Penguin Readers to choose from – world classics, film adaptations, modern-day crime and adventure, short stories, biographies, American classics, non-fiction, plays ...

For a complete list of all Penguin Readers titles, please contact your local Pearson Longman office or visit our website.

www.penguinreaders.com

slap (v) to hit someone with the flat part of your hand

splint (n) a flat piece of wood or metal for keeping a broken bone in position while it mends

squeak (n/v) a very short high noise or cry

stale (adj) not fresh or pleasant

stove (n) a thing used for cooking, which works by burning fuel

stump (n) the short part of someone's leg, arm or finger that remains after the rest of it has been cut off

syringe (n) a medical instrument for giving injections, it consists of a hollow plastic tube and a needle

typescript (n) a document that has been typed

WORD LIST

album (n) a book that you keep photographs in

axe (n) a tool with a heavy metal blade on the end of a long handle, used to cut down trees or split pieces of wood

barbecue (n) a metal frame for cooking food on outdoors

barn (n) a large farm building for storing crops, or for keeping animals in

blister (n) a swelling on your skin, caused for example by a burn or continuous rubbing

blowlamp (n) a piece of equipment that produces a very hot flame, used especially for removing paint

blush (v) to become red in the face, usually because you are embarrassed

champagne (n) a French white wine with a lot of bubbles, drunk on special occasions

choke (v) to be unable to breathe properly because something is in your throat

contempt (n) a feeling that someone or something is not important and deserves no respect

dimly (adv) not clearly

dragon (n) a woman who behaves in an angry, unfriendly way

drift (v) to move or change slowly without effort

fascinating (adj) very interesting

foul (adj) very unpleasant

gasp (v) to make a sound by breathing in suddenly, especially because you are surprised or in pain

lawnmower (n) a machine for cutting an area of grass

mattress (n) the soft part of a bed that you lie on

misery (n) great unhappiness or suffering

punch (v) to hit someone or something hard with your fist

sarcastic (adj) saying things that are the opposite of what you mean, in order to make an unkind joke or to show that you are annoyed

sigh (v) to breathe out making a long sound, especially because you are bored, disappointed or tired